# A SCHOOL
## AS
# A LIVING ENTITY

# A SCHOOL AS A LIVING ENTITY

## The Growth and Development of a School as a Living Entity

**Implementation of a
Governance and Management Structure
Based on Living Systems and
Threefold Principles & Forming Impulses**

**by**

**Rea Taylor Gill**

AWSNA

Printed with support from the Waldorf Curriculum Fund


Published by:
The Association of Waldorf Schools
of North America
Publications Office
65–2 Fern Hill Road
Ghent, NY  12075

Title: *A School as a Living Entity*
Author: Rea Taylor Gill
Editor: David Mitchell
Copy Editor and Proofreader: Ann Erwin
Cover: AninA Formankova
© 2011 by AWSNA
ISBN # 978-1-936367-18-1

Printed by McNaughton & Gunn
Saline, MI 48176  USA

# Table of Contents

# Appendices

# Table of Figures

# Preface

by
Torin Finser

Within a few short years, we will celebrate the 100th anniversary of Waldorf education on this earth. As we prepare for 2019, it might serve the Waldorf movement to use the occasion to self-assess and reflect as well as celebrate. How can we characterize the past 100 years of Waldorf education in terms of phases, whether looking at decades or $33^1/_3$-year intervals? Where have our schools succeeded? Where have we come up short?

Already in 2011 we can sketch some tentative characterizations regarding the last two questions:

1. The curriculum in most of the 1000 Waldorf schools around the world is well established. In most instances, when I visit schools I find many of the common characteristics of the Waldorf curriculum are fully evident.

2. This is of course connected to the steady improvement in teacher education programs. Most schools I visit are fully committed to teacher education and professional development, despite the challenges of money and adequate time.

3. The publications available to Waldorf teachers and parents have increased significantly, although higher quality translations and foreign language editions are still limited.

4. At least in the schools in the United States with which I am most familiar, basic business and administrative practices have improved in recent years. In many cases volunteer boards have devoted countless hours to supporting schools financially.

5. Although it has been a struggle to prepare and support eurythmy teachers, for instance, one can also acknowledge that in most Waldorf schools, teachers as a whole are practicing "the art of education" in a way that appeals to the full spectrum of sensory experience.

6. Perhaps most important, I have visited many classrooms filled with eager, engaged students who are thriving, learning and working as a social unit.

This is just of the beginning of a list that might spur further additions in the years ahead. But now I would like to turn to the one area in which many would say the Waldorf movement has not yet met expectations: the ideals set forth by Rudolf Steiner in regard to threefolding of the social organism.

Many have spent years working to simply understand what was intended in books and lectures such as "The Threefold Social Order," "The Social Future," "World Economy" and so forth. And some have taken the indications further than others. Most worthy of mention in this brief paragraph are the efforts of Gary Lamb, Michael Spence, and the many colleagues who have participated in the growth of RSF Social Finance. Yet despite these efforts, it is hard to find a single school about which one can say, "Here is an example of the full implementation of these social ideals." One has a sense that the work in regard to "threefolding" remains incomplete, unfinished.

This is of course not a bad thing in itself, as the quest alone can spur people on to further understanding and the crucial change in consciousness that must precede any outer change. There are many also working outside the Waldorf movement, such as in biodynamic farms and Camphill Communities, who are striving toward the realization of Rudolf Steiner's social ideals.

But imagine my surprise and joy when I received a masters project submitted by Rea Gill as part of her degree completion at Antioch University! Here, in 200-some pages, was not just a theoretical rehashing of familiar concepts, but a step by step documentation of a real life implementation of the threefolding principle she led for 9 years at the Vancouver Waldorf School. Along the way Rea takes the reader through an overview of organizational dynamics, "kindred spirits," and a rigorous examination of the original intentions set forth by Rudolf Steiner.

What comes across most clearly in my reading of the text which now merits AWSNA publication is the sense of lived experience. The pages of this book have been forged on the anvil of real life, in a Waldorf school with real parents, teachers, budgets, challenges and success. Out of life experience and constant reflection and further deepening, Rea was able to develop a system of governance that was both living and clear, flexible and transparent. I had an opportunity to visit the school during both an early stage of implementation and a later stage of full development, and the excitement was palpable. It really happened!

Of course, nothing remains the same for long, and Rea herself has now moved on, recently taking up a lead role at the High Mowing School in Wilton, NH. She has entered another stage of her biography, and so has the Vancouver Waldorf School. A visitor to the school today may or may not recognize any of Rea's past work. That is the nature of all living systems, and who carries the work is as essential in administration as in the classroom. Yet now schools all over the world can learn from her experience, careful research and enthusiasm for the social challenge. This book can serve as an inspiration for others, not to copy, but to do the work. It is in the doing the work together that we realize our social ideals.

# Acknowledgements

I would like to give a special thank you to my teachers, Torin Finser and Christopher Schaefer, for the inspiration, support, tools and guidance they offered me over the years as I gained knowledge, capacities and skills that enabled me to persevere in undergoing the depth of inquiry and action research required to complete this book. A special thank you is due to Torin Finser for his invaluable mentorship as I conducted and documented my research and for encouraging me to pursue publication. Also thank you to David Mitchell at AWSNA Publications for his support and to those who support AWSNA Publications with donations. Thank you to Karen Humber for her steadfast confidence in me and my work and for her editing skills. My heartfelt appreciation goes to Bruce Wilkinson, who, with his unique skillset and extraordinary intelligence, provided invaluable dialogue, feedback, editing, technical support and artistic work. I want to acknowledge Silvia Formankova for her beautiful human development drawings.

In addition, I must thank the Vancouver Waldorf School and those amazing members of the faculty, staff, trustees and parent body—there are too many to mention but you know who you are—who worked alongside me as together we guided the school through a remarkable cultural transformation. Without the participation, contributions and support of my colleagues during the most intense periods of reorganization, growth and change, the transformations would not have been possible. In particular, I want to thank one of my closest colleagues, Walter Daroshin, for his unrelenting will to do the work, his invaluable wisdom, insights, and contributions; most of all I thank him for his friendship and for lending me a shoulder for the many tears I have shed over the years.

May our efforts bear fruit for the Vancouver Waldorf School, the Waldorf movement and other cultural-spiritual organizations who carry a positive social mission for the betterment of society.

A School as a Living Entity

## Chapter 1

# Introduction: Emerging Hypothesis

*We must be completely conscious that we have to accomplish
a great cultural deed in every sense of the word.*
— Rudolf Steiner

As modern human beings we have an opportunity—maybe even a responsibility—to find sustainable ways to exist in and be in relationship with our environment. This is just as true in the social realm as it is in relationship to our physical environment, and we need to invent, discover and utilize socially responsible forms. In fact, creating new effective forms of leadership and management that honor the relationships of the human beings and that also respect the living nature of an organization could possibly provide a model for social health in all organizations and in society in general.

As citizens of the 21st century it makes sense that we do what all scientists, including social scientists, are doing—engage in understanding the science of the time in which we live. We must shift our thinking and our understanding of how things work so that they are in alignment with how science, including social science, has evolved. Typically the way organizations have been and for the most part still are designed, managed and operated is founded on Newtonian physics, which is based on a materialistic natural scientific worldview that focuses on what can be seen, heard, touched, and/or measured by our five physical senses. The prevailing assumptions that have influenced organizational management over time are described by Margaret Wheatley (2006) in *Leadership and the New Science*:

> We manage by separating things into parts, we believe that influence occurs
> as a direct result of force exerted from one person to another, we engage
> in complex planning for a world that we keep expecting to be predictable,
> and we search continually for better methods of objectively measuring and
> perceiving the world. (p.7)

While the governance forms and structures of mainstream organizations for the most part still reflect the underlying assumptions of Newtonian physics and those accompanying images of how the world works, there is a growing awareness of a need to shift these assumptions. A new imagery that has developed out of quantum physics challenges the assumptions of a Newtonian worldview by focusing on the whole rather than on the parts and by recognizing the existence of systems that are interconnected networks possessing dynamic processes, relationships and unseen connections between that which Newtonian mechanics identifies as separate measurable entities. (Wheatley 2006) Out of this new science and an understanding of organizations as holistic systems or collections of interconnected, interdependent and interrelated networks and components, the mainstream corporate world is beginning to shift its approach to management, in particular by instituting collaborative methods that empower workers to participate in the operating and decision-making aspects of a business. There is growing awareness that a company will better develop and realize its potential if power and influence are not concentrated exclusively in leadership at the top of a pyramidal-structured hierarchy. The cultivation of knowledge and institutional learning horizontally across and through the organization will give access to the wisdom that exists in the organization as a whole, leading to greater effectiveness. This means that the company, as an entity, can effectively act and react in response to changes in its environment and in the world. The effect of this conscious awareness of the living nature of organizations is currently best demonstrated in a corporate environment where the principles and practices of a learning organization are utilized. The concept of learning organizations was coined and researched by Peter Senge (1994) and documented in detail in his book, *The Fifth Discipline: The Art & Practice of the Learning Organization.* Senge defines learning organizations as "organizations where people continually expand their capacity to create the results they truly desire, where new and expansive patterns of thinking are nurtured, where collective aspiration is set free, and where people are continually learning to learn together." (p.3) Senge highlights five fundamental disciplines that a learning organization, and the people who function within it, practice as the organization is constantly transforming and developing capacities in realizing its highest potential.[1]

The name 'learning organization' implies that there is a consciousness of working within and treating the organization as a living entity because only living things can learn. (de Geus 1997) Piaget defined the human being's capability to learn as "to change one's internal structure to remain in harmony with a changed environment." (de Geus 1997, p.20) An organization's capability to learn is also defined by the collective ability of the organization to adapt, grow and thrive in the face of change: "A successful company is one that can learn effectively." (de Geus 1997, p.20) In an article called "Reshaping the Way We View the World," Chalofsky says that shifting to a new paradigm is part of moving from the industrial era, where the machine was the focus, to a knowledge era where the focus is on the human mind. He says that learning is central to this new paradigm of thinking about organizations, and that it is "purposeful, occurs at the individual, group and organizational levels, and is for the mutual benefit of the individual and the organization." (p.54)

This new consciousness about the living nature of an organization and its ability to learn, grow, develop and change is allowing for the development of alternative and more effective approaches to a traditional authoritarian hierarchical management form.

However, despite this new consciousness and changes that result from applying the principles of fostering an organization as a learning organization, most mainstream corporations and businesses are still structured based on the assumptions underlying an owner/operator or stakeholder top-down leadership and governance model. It is possible that this ownership paradigm in businesses and corporations is actually blocking the development of new governance forms that would better support the principles of a learning organization. Christopher Schaefer, organizational consultant and co-author of *Vision in Action: Working with Soul and Spirit in Small Organizations* provides a provocative perspective. He points out that at one time in the history of humanity, it was considered moral, even necessary for one human being to own or be owned by another human being and that, of course, we now look back on this and are appalled that we ever thought this was acceptable. Schaefer suggests that in the future we will look back on the relationship that we currently have with organizations and we will be appalled that we thought we could own an organization.[2]

Arie de Geus (1997) had two main hypotheses on which he based his book, *The Living Company*: "The company is a living being, and the decisions for action made by this living being result from a learning process." (p.201) De Geus asserts throughout that learning is a capacity exclusive to living beings. Peter Senge was clearly inspired by the work of de Geus, and in the foreword to *The Living Company* supports de Geus' perspective by suggesting that "seeing a company as a living being implies that it creates its own processes, just as the human body manufactures its own cells, which in turn compose its own organs and bodily systems"; and that it "means that it [the company] is capable of regenerating itself, of continuity as an identifiable entity beyond its present members," and "that it can learn as an entity." (de Geus 1997, pp.ix–x)

This profound insight into our relationship to organizations and the possibility that organizations are living entities with unseen—considered by some as spiritual—forces connected to them, might be difficult to grasp with logical thought at this point in time, especially in relationship to owner-operated businesses where securing profit for the owner(s) is implicitly understood to be the purpose. Perhaps this is highlighting a flaw in our understanding of how our society should be structured. The accepted purpose of the economic sphere of activity in society to make money for the owner becomes redundant if materialism or profit is removed as its driving force. What then would be its purpose? Exploring the question of the relationship of materialism to the world economy and finance is beyond the scope of what can be explored here. However, it is actively taken up by others, including Christopher Houghton Budd (2003) of the Center of Associative Economics and author of *The Metamorphosis of Capitalism*, and Siegfried Finser, founder of RSF Social Finance, a foundation dedicated to bringing about positive change in the way the world works with money by providing investment and lending services to businesses and enterprises that are dedicated to improving society and the environment. Finser (2007) is the author of *Money Can Heal,* in which he writes about his life work with money and his experience of the spiritual forces that he believes exist in and behind different kinds of transactions. He highlights the positive effect that working consciously with money and these spiritual impulses can have on social life.

If the ownership paradigm in businesses and corporations is indeed blocking the development of new governance and leadership forms that would ultimately bring about the kinds of positive change to social life to which Budd and Finser have dedicated their life's work, then perhaps a profound change will not come from the corporate world. Rather, it might be in non-profit organizations, where there is no expectation to generate profit for the direct benefit of an owner, that new leadership and governance forms have a better chance to manifest. Is it possible that a template for creating change in how the economic and political spheres of society are managed can be created in the cultural realm where non-profits exist?

The Waldorf School movement, a revolutionary education movement in the cultural sphere of society, has the potential to set new profound standards of operating that could be a model for a unique living systems approach to governance, and ultimately could have a transformative effect on all social life. The revolutionary quality inherent in the philosophical underpinnings of Waldorf education contains insights into how to create the governing organizational forms that will serve the manifestation of a truly living learning organization. Rudolf Steiner (1996), founder of the Waldorf School movement, said this in his address to teachers at the opening of the first Waldorf school in 1919: "We must be completely conscious that we have to accomplish a great cultural deed in every sense of the word." (p.31)

What are the new governance forms and structures that will make it possible to operate an organization as a living learning entity, such that it can be an example for other communities, organizations and ultimately for society as a whole? This is a question that has not yet been fully explored in the Waldorf movement despite having been suggested in the early nineteenth century by the founder of Waldorf education, Rudolf Steiner. Steiner's philosophical body of work called anthroposophy, translated as the wisdom of man, provides indications for new social forms for a threefold ordering at the macro level of society. While Steiner provided a vision for how society could be ordered in a threefold way, these new forms are easiest to understand by studying the principles that are at work both in society and in the human being, but particularly and specifically how they manifest in the three living human systems.[3]

Guido Preparata, Associate Professor of Political Economy at the University of Washington, in a 2006 article wrote that there is a radical more humane alternative approach to the current day materialistic approach to economics. Preparata drew a parallel between the threefold human organism and the threefold nature of the social organism. He believes that approaching the design of a social structure from this understanding of the functions and relationships of the three systems of the human organism is valid and necessary when designing a more humane economy for the betterment of society as a whole:

By way of analogy: just as the human organism comprises three tightly interrelated but functionally independent "systems" (the metabolic system of digestion, the "head" system of brain and nerves, and the circulatory system of blood and lungs), society, likewise, may be construed as a composite body consisting of three conjoined spheres of activity (a triarticulation of economics, politics, and spiritual dissipation). (p.627)

Economics is society's stomach, in that it procures the necessary sustenance for the perpetuation of the great social hive; laws and rights manage the dynamics of interrelationship; and the spiritual sphere sustains the power of the ego: the innovative "I."... The source of social evil, Steiner believed, comes from the trespassing of one particular sphere on the purview of the others. It is as if society becomes transmogrified by developing in excess one particular system at the expense of the other two, so much so that the over swollen organ comes, by tumorous obstinacy, to colonize and assimilate the other vital centers, and thus creates imbalances leading to a variety of more or less virulent reactions and maladies. (p.627)

Preparata concludes that Steiner provided a remedy for what is needed to bring health to society and an ailing societal economic-metabolic system:

The only foreseeable remedy, said Steiner, can come from a more intense involvement of the workforce in the doings of the spiritual sphere, and from a heightened protection by the rights-state ... set out therefrom [sic] to codify laws and diffuse initiate knowledge. ... The "right thing" will be found only through all three independent branches of the body social, conjointly, in working together for a social end. (Steiner 1923, p.114) (Preparata 2006, pp.632–634)

As Preparata points out, the impulses or principles that are at work, and the need for an interconnected yet independent working, are the same whether looking at a social structure or a living physical structure.

The challenge is that, unlike in the case of the physical structure of a living being that possesses living systems that we can actually see, in a social structure we cannot see the systems. However, studying physical living systems with our human senses, while utilizing our capacities for thinking and feeling and developing sensitivity for what underlies the physical, can give us insights into social systems that we are not able to see or touch. The indications for the new social forms given by Rudolf Steiner have been further developed by many others and extended and applied to the understanding of social organisms as threefold entities. Much can be learned from the work of these others. Studying and penetrating the concepts in order to gain understanding also provides the opportunity for developing our own capacities to understand what we cannot see.[4]

Unlike many mainstream organizations, businesses and corporations where the form and operating structure are still based on a clear hierarchy of owner/stakeholder-driven leadership and management, Anthroposophical organizations like Waldorf schools, have had the benefit of Steiner's guiding principles for new organizational forms for the past nine decades. In Waldorf schools worldwide there is ongoing striving to manifest these forms into effective leadership, management, and governance structures with clearly defined and articulated roles, responsibilities and accountabilities for those working in them.

In the same way that an educational system can only provide an education that serves the healthy development of a growing child if the system is designed with a deep and meaningful understanding of human development, so too is it true with organizations. Before we can participate in the design of new effective social systems and organizational forms and structures that serve the well-being of the organization, we must first understand them as evolving life-forms. (de Geus 1997) (Senge et al.2004) (Senge 1994) (Wheatly 2006) In order to positively impact social systems we must understand the phases and stages of organizational development as well as the needs of organizations as developing, growing entities. (Schaefer & Voors 1996) Approaching organizational development from this paradigm will assist us in manifesting effective governance, leadership and management forms and structures, and in cultivating and nurturing healthy organizations and organizational life.

The intention in what follows is to describe what has been learned and discovered about how an organization's development can be guided and can thrive over time when it is treated as a living, growing, developing entity, utilizing new living forms inspired by the principles and indications of Rudolf Steiner. Beginning with viewing an organization as a life-form, as well as one that is a reflection or expression of the threefold human being, a framework can be provided for how an organization comes into being and matures and how it develops the living systems that enable it to maintain health and ultimately stay connected to and serve its purpose for existing. It is also possible, when an organization grows and develops as it should, that it would then be able to not only serve its purpose but serve a higher social mission of modeling a way to bring global and universal well-being to the rest of society. If we are to see a positive change in current social structures with a resulting healthy cultural-spiritual, political (legal-financial) and social-economic life on earth for humanity, perhaps the remedy is that organizations must be treated not only as theoretical living systems but as actual living social entities with very specific and unique developmental needs.

While mainstream corporate organizational development thinkers are making progress with a new consciousness based on a quantum physics scientific paradigm, and on the premise that organizations contain the characteristics of living learning entities, the actual forms and structures are still amorphous within the prevailing traditional hierarchical top-down management models. On the other hand, the cutting edge living systems forms and structures that Waldorf schools strive to apply to governance and management often lack the new understanding that has emerged in the mainstream corporate world developed from advances in science, in particular quantum physics and its relationship to social consciousness. What follows is the culmination of a combination of qualitative research, practical application of the interpretation of that research, and implementation of living systems at the Vancouver Waldorf School in Vancouver, Canada. The results of this work will unite the understanding of a threefold ordering of organizations rooted in Steiner's threefold spiritual philosophy of life with the new living systems paradigm rooted in quantum physics, in order to create organizational forms and structures that result in a modern vision of effective organizational development that is co-evolutionary. In other words, the hypothesis is that the result will not only be the manifestation of an innovative, more effective, resilient organizational form and structure that enables the organization to fulfill its mission, but it will also have the kind of positive evolutionary effect on the rest of society that is highlighted by Margaret Wheatley's work (2006).

Drawing on the theories developed by contemporary mainstream thinkers like de Geus, Senge, and Wheatley, who have done groundbreaking research on social organisms as dynamic living entities, Chapter 2 will establish how the foundational threefold principles identified by Steiner as fundamental in the human being and in society, when intentionally nurtured and cultivated, are also important and essential forming principles in these dynamic living entities we call organizations.

Chapter 3 will provide a basic understanding of how an embryo develops and differentiates into three distinct yet interdependent life-giving systems. Understanding the differentiation, development and function of these systems in the human organism is essential to create a foundation for understanding the development and differentiation of organizational systems, in this case in a Waldorf school. This will help in understanding a social organism as a living social entity and as such, as a reflection or expression of the threefolded human being from this systems perspective. Facilitating the differentiation and development of the life-giving operational systems of an organization will be most successful if it is approached with an understanding of how organizational systems are formed and how they function and are maintained. Chapter 3 will also describe the phases of development that a school as a social organization goes through and will highlight the correlation with the differentiation of the human embryo and fetus. Insights gained from this knowledge guide the intentional threefold differentiation and development of an organization.

Finally, Chapter 4 will document the process of intentionally facilitating a threefold differentiation of the Vancouver Waldorf School using as a foundation the assertion that an organization is a living entity with developmental needs that must be met by the people working in service to the organization. This is accomplished by intentionally working with and modeling the forms and structure while applying the principles that underpin the development and function of the three human systems. These are the same principles inherent in the greater societal structure.

Chapter 5 will document the outcome of the threefold differentiation, as well as conclusions reached and possible next steps that can be taken to further the research.

*Chapter 2*

## Organizations—Dead or Alive?

*Like whirlpools, living forms depend on a constant flow of matter through them,*
*like flames they transform the materials on which they feed to maintain their activities*
*and to grow; but unlike whirlpools or flames,*
*living structures also develop, reproduce, and evolve.*

*– Fritjof Capra*


The introduction of quantum theory in the 20th century, and a subsequent recognition of the interconnectedness of all things, has resulted in a major shift in scientific thinking. However, despite this growing appreciation for the importance of living systems and the basic concepts associated with them, in particular the relationships between the parts that make up a whole reflected in networks of interconnected parts, Newtonian thinking *still* generally permeates our approach to understanding how the world works, in particular in relationship to organizations and the relationships within them. Newtonian science sees and attempts to understand everything through the lenses of mechanics and predictability and uses logical linear analysis of the joining and disassembly of the parts in order to understand the whole. (Wheatley 2006) It is only recently that we are starting to see this mechanistic approach to humanity's relationship with itself, to others and to life, begin to weaken and be replaced by living systems thinking. Senge (1994) describes this as a shift to "a discipline for seeing wholes" and "a framework for seeing interrelationships rather than things" (p.68) or unrelated parts. This living systems thinking enables us to differentiate between things that are dead and things that are alive. Dead or inanimate things are without self-will or life-force and are "impacted by events but do not decide to make things happen" (de Geus 1997, p.85) in contrast to living things, which respond to changes and events in the environment. This differentiation between inanimate objects and living things can help us see organizations as open systems affected by and responsive to the environment in which they exist. This further suggests that the parts of an organization that make up the whole are interrelated and interconnected in such a way that they behave dynamically in the same way that the parts and elements of living systems behave in relationship to each other.

Fritjof Capra (1996), PhD, physicist and systems theorist, has conducted research for over thirty years that has provided a new scientific understanding of living systems, in particular social systems as living systems. He points out the following:

Since the early days of biology, scientists and philosophers have noticed that living forms … combine the stability of structure with the fluidity of change. Like whirlpools, they depend on a constant flow of matter through them, like flames they transform the materials on which they feed to maintain their activities and to grow; but unlike whirlpools or flames, living structures also develop, reproduce, and evolve. (p.177)

Organizations are not easily identified as living entities as such because they do not possess physical tangible systems that explicitly tell us they are alive. In the book, *Presence*, Senge et al. (2004) bring awareness to the connection between consciousness, change, growth and wholeness and the current state of organizational development. Senge et al. suggest that organizations, corporations and institutions are life-forms, even part of a new species, that have the ability to re-shape the world in an increasingly impactful way because of the new global economy. The current changes taking place globally are the "consequences of a life-form that like any life-form has the potential to grow, learn, and evolve. But until that potential is activated, industrial age institutions will continue to expand blindly, unaware of their part in a larger whole or of the consequences of their growth, like cells that have lost their social identity and reverted to growth for its own sake." (p.8)

The idea that organizations are alive but governed by our habitual machine-age thinking that values control, predictability, standardization, productivity and efficiency (Senge et al. 2004) is important to consider if we, as a human species, are going to take responsibility for the effects the operation and existence of our organizations have on the well-being of social structures in the broader cultural, political and economic spheres. It is essential that we understand the impact that organizations have on society and take responsibility for the consequences, acknowledging that organizations are composed of living systems that self-organize and self-renew (Senge et al. 2004) and consequently impact—either negatively or positively—the world in which they exist: "Global structure emerges from local activity rules, a characteristic of complex systems." (Lewin 1992, p.47) By taking up the challenge and responsibility to create organizations that exist in service to an organizational vocation, which in turn is in service to a better world, we can become co-creators of a better future. We can become empowered to realize positive change and growth in the greater society.

However, in the same way that a deep and meaningful understanding of human and child development must underpin an educational system if it is to positively serve the healthy development of a growing child, in order to manifest positive impact on the development of social systems, we must adopt the premise that an organization is also a life-form, and we must understand how an organization as a life-form grows and develops. We must learn how this life-form comes into being, grows and matures so that we can be the stewards who serve the development of the living systems that enable it to maintain health and ultimately stay connected to and serve its mission and higher purpose. There is a paradigm shift needed about how we think of organizations, social structures and leadership. In order to make a positive change in the current social structures, we need to see organizations as actual living entities that are part of, affected by, and that affect the greater universal whole. What will it take for us to understand this greater whole and the role that we play at an organizational level?

Senge tells a story which highlights how the functioning of the parts affects the whole. It is a story about a project that set out to develop a new car. An analysis of the organizational systems showed clearly that decisions and actions taken by teams in isolation led consistently to problems for other teams. (Senge et al. 2004) The absence of collaboration, inter-organizational cooperation and associative working as a means of connecting the parts to a whole ultimately undermined the entire project.

At an organizational level it can be difficult to understand how this concept of a living network of interconnected systems applies or could be applied. As human beings we can see and easily understand that a human, animal or even a plant is a living being and around that being and its dynamic systems is an unseen life-force that sustains and maintains its network of systems, keeping it alive. Human beings as living beings do not function by virtue of a top-down hierarchical system, with one system or individual element dictating how and when everything else functions. Rather, human beings function as living beings by virtue of a dynamic natural hierarchy[5] and a network of independent interconnected systems that sustain life. It requires a paradigm shift in thinking to see that the same can be and is true about organizations. This paradigm shift is not yet apparent in the forms utilized in mainstream governance and management structures.

Edgar Schein, Sloan Fellows Professor of Management Emeritus, MIT Sloan School of Management, is a prominent current day theorist on the topic of corporate culture and open systems in relationship to organizations. In a recent article in the *Ivey Business Journal*, Schein describes the current-day challenges of a leader working in a typical modern organization—with a traditional hierarchical (top-down leadership) structure—in organizational environments that are growing increasingly complex. Schein (2009) says a new form of leadership is required. However, he does not describe a new structural form of leadership. He describes instead a new approach to leadership, the essence of which focuses on the ability and desire for leaders and subordinates to accept, offer and give help; however, he also admits that this approach will be problematic for leaders:

> The leader of the future will have to both seek and give help. The problem is that both giving and receiving help are activities that are, to a considerable degree, countercultural for leaders. (¶16)

> In normal encounters between superiors and subordinates, fairness or economic equity is achieved when the subordinate shows the proper deference and the superior shows the proper demeanor. (¶21)

The point is that offering, asking for and/or receiving help are disruptions of the normal flow of the social order and must therefore be handled with care. ... The pitfalls of helping are inherent in any relationship, especially in a relationship governed by a [traditional top-down leadership] hierarchy. The higher-ranking person ordinarily finds it difficult to ask for help from a subordinate, not for personality reasons but because the social order defines it as "abnormal," that is for the higher up to need help from the subordinate. It might be considered a loss of face for the boss to go to the employee for help, so it is unlikely to be done even when necessary. (¶17)

What Schein describes here is the essential problem with a hierarchical top-down leadership/social structure that relies on the ability of a leader to compensate for a structure that does not recognize the inherent living nature of an organization. In reality, it is *neither* the leader *nor* the subordinate that needs to learn to change the way they relate to one another in order to compensate for the mechanical top-down hierarchical structure, but rather it is the *structure* that needs to change in order to enable collaborative, cooperative, associative relationships within an organic living systems governance structure with a natural network-based hierarchy. In other words, what is needed is a structure with a hierarchy that shifts the authority depending on the specific expertise and particular function needed in a given context.

Capra (1996) describes two kinds of opposing tendencies that exist in social structures: *self-assertive* and *integrative*. Self-assertive tendencies include rational, analytical, reductionist and linear thinking, with expansive, competitive, quantitative, domineering values. Capra says that "power, in the sense of domination over others, is [an] excessive self-assertion" tendency and "that the social structure in which it is exerted most effectively is the [top-down] hierarchy." (p.10) The description of self-assertive tendencies contains many of the same descriptive adjectives used when talking about a Newtonian approach to understanding how the world and organizations work. It is no wonder that leaders working in such a top-down hierarchically structured environment may struggle with this form of leadership in the way that Schein describes. On the other hand, the other tendency, which Capra describes as integrative in nature, includes intuitive, holistic, and non-linear thinking, with values that are conservative, cooperative, qualitative, and collaborative. These are all tendencies that are present in the network structure, which is likely to have some form of natural hierarchical leadership form or decision-making protocol, as opposed to a traditional top-down hierarchical leadership structure. This new paradigm, with its natural hierarchy, is based on "power as influence of others"[6] (p.10) versus power over others and is informed by the same frame of reference and thinking required when attempting to understand the world and social organisms through a quantum physics approach.

A complete paradigm shift in the mainstream corporate environment from one that thinks about organizational structure as top-down hierarchy to one that sees it as a dynamic network structure, a paradigm of thought that would result in new forms—new governance, operating and management forms—which would eliminate the need for leaders to compensate for excessive self-assertive tendencies. This kind of paradigm shift, and the resulting new governance structure, and operating and management forms, has clearly not yet happened at a global level in the mainstream corporate world.

When looking at organizations using this new living systems network paradigm, one can see that there is something more to an organization than is obvious. There exists a life-giving unseen structure that underpins a network of interconnected parts, which is organized, dynamic, systematic and essential to maintaining organizational life. We must accept the possibility that an organization is more than a social construct within which a group of people attempt to realize goals and objectives. There is this unseen life-force connected to the organization that supports, sustains it and keeps it alive. This is an element that is not ordinarily thought of as part of an organization. Schein is correct in his assessment that a new form of leadership is needed; however, it will take more than compensatory behavior on the part of leaders to manifest that new form. The new form needs to be structural, consist of a natural hierarchy of interconnected networks, and embrace the concept of organizations as living entities possessing a connecting life-giving element.

Rudolf Steiner's entire body of work, including thirty books and thousands of lectures, describes and defines this unseen element as spiritual in nature. He explores and describes the spiritual nature of the human being and the world in which we live, the evolution of humanity and the world, and the practice of personal development and inner work in the light of this spiritual nature. Throughout his material Steiner identifies, describes and explores the threefold nature of the human being, of society and of social life.[7] In his book, *Theosophy*, Steiner (1971) describes the human being as possessing a spirit, a soul life and a physical body. He talks about how, when these three aspects are functioning as an integrated whole, they enable the 'I' or ego-being of the individual to be present. It is this ego-being that enables the human being to be dynamically engaged in life and to engage in self-observation and to think about thinking. In 1922, Steiner delivered several lectures to doctors, published under the title *Fundamentals of Anthroposophical Medicine*, which describe the human being and the three physical systems through this lens of the spiritual nature of humanity. The human being is described as possessing interconnected systems, including a nerve-sense system, a rhythmic system (the circulatory and respiratory systems), and a metabolic-limb system. When healthy, all three systems work independently yet in concert with one another to maintain the form of the human body and thereby provide the vessel for the human spirit and soul to exist. This enables the threefold activities of thinking, experiencing a range of feelings, and acting (or doing) to take place.

In a 1922 lecture entitled "The Organization of the Waldorf School," Steiner spoke about wholeness and organization in its relationship to a social organization, specifically in reference to the first Waldorf school:

When we speak of organization today, we commonly imply that something is to be organised, to be arranged. But in speaking of the organization of the Waldorf school I do not and cannot mean it in this sense, for really one can only organize something which has a mechanical nature. One can organize the arrangements in a factory where the parts are bound into a whole by the ideas which one has put into it. The whole exists and one must accept it as an organism. It must be studied. One must learn to know its arrangements as an organism, as an organization. (GA 305, Lecture 7 ¶1)

We know that in 1922 Steiner was already thinking from the perspective of a living systems (network) paradigm in relationship to organizations, and what he was suggesting was a new organizational and leadership form.

The question arises as to whether it reasonable to see an organization as a living entity containing the elements of a living being. Is it advisable to use abstract scientific metaphors of living systems to understand and support the argument that organizations are something more than mechanistic social constructs? Wheatley (2006) suggests not only is it advisable, it is necessary to recognize that "organizations are living systems, possessing the same capacity to adapt and grow that is common to all life" (p.15) and that using science as metaphor is simply a way for us to begin to understand a reality that is never possible to completely know and understand.

The first step in making a paradigm shift in our approach to organizational development is to set aside the old paradigm that comes out of the science of 17th century physics or Newtonian mechanics. In the Newtonian mechanistic paradigm everything in the physical world is determined and understood by reducing the whole into its composite parts, with the parts interacting through applied forces. (Jantsch, 1992) Things are defined in terms of the laws of mechanics and cause and effect and are theoretically predictable, measurable and controllable. There is no room for creativity in the Newtonian world. (Wheatley 2006) There is no dynamic quality and therefore no reason to attempt to understand the nature of the relationship between the parts that create the whole, and no attempt to understand the whole. The principles that drive the Newtonian approach are the same principles, thinking and consciousness that have determined the design, forms, leadership structure and function of many of our organizations. Without creativity, spontaneity, relationship dynamics and chaos, there is nothing alive, nothing human, in the Newtonian scientific approach.

Wheatley (2006) identifies one of the main differences between Newtonian thinking and the new quantum physics science as a "focus on holism rather than parts. Systems are understood as whole systems, and attention is given to relationships within those networks." (p.10) She refers to an ancient Sufi teaching that describes how in understanding one you might think you understand *two* because *one* and *one* are *two*. But in order to truly understand *two* you must understand the *and*; therefore to really understand *two* we must come to know the very *nature* of the *dynamics* that exist *between the parts* rather than simply understand the parts as isolated participants in the relationship. (Wheatley, 2006)

The principle of holism is the foundation of this new science. This simple yet paradoxically elusive principle is also what stands behind Steiner's threefold philosophy of life. Holism is a foundational principle that can be understood by observing life itself. Paradoxically, paradigm shifts themselves are an activity defined by the new science. We hear talk of quantum leaps in thinking, which is a paradoxical experience; in other words, we are using a new way of thinking to achieve a new way of thinking.

When considering organizational development and the management of organizations from the perspective of this new holistic living systems paradigm, in designing operational forms and structure, it is important to recognize that

> … [O]rganizations are never changed by imposing a model developed elsewhere. So little transfers to, or inspires, those trying to work at change in their own organizations. In every organization we need to look internally, to see one another as the critical resources on this voyage of discovery. We need to learn how to engage the creativity that exists everywhere in our organizations. (Wheatly, 2006, pp.8–9)

However, it is a central assertion of this research that, while organizations are living entities that are responsive, changing, growing and learning, the organizational living forms and structure cannot be amorphous, ever-emerging, ever changing forms. There is an archetype that underlies the forms and structure. All organizations function as social organisms created by human beings. An organization can be seen as a reflection or projection of the human being. Understanding the development, differentiation and functioning of the interconnected and interdependent human systems can provide insight into how an organization develops and functions as a living entity. Utilizing this insight when designing organizational forms would not involve imposing a theoretical pre-conceived model of governance onto the organization. Rather, utilizing the implicit wisdom of the human form or archetype, consisting of three independent interconnected systems, would result in facilitating the unfolding of a governance structure that combines the new consciousness regarding the living nature of organizations and the principles of quantum physics, while acknowledging that this living nature is a reflection, extension and/or projection of the threefold human form. This is achieved by acknowledging that the threefold principles present in human life are also present in organizational life. It must be an inside-out organic process of facilitating the growth and development of three independent but interrelated living systems that are already inherent in the organization as an underlying archetype. It does not involve imposing a predetermined model onto the organization, but rather, acknowledging that there already is a form there, possessing unshakable life-giving forming principles unique to social structures, just as there is an archetypal form present in the human being.

Rudolf Steiner presents pictures of the threefold human being with its three physical systems and of society with a threefold social structure containing three spiritual impulses, which are also present in the three physical systems. The different levels, layers and the working of the three impulses are portrayed in the following chart:

| Realms of Society | Cultural / Spiritual | Political (Legal-Financial) | Economic |
|---|---|---|---|
| Impulse | Freedom | Equality/Rights | Cooperation/ Brotherhood |
| Central Activity | Enhance the freedom & creativity of the individual | Administer to the law, legal norms & societal mores | Provide goods/services & generate capital that serve human needs |
| Human Being | Spirit | Soul | Body |
| Human Systems | Nervous-Sense System (Nerves + Senses) | Rhythmic System (Respiratory + Circulatory) | Metabolic-Limb System |
| Human Activity | Thinking head | Feeling heart | Willing hands |

**Figure 1:**   *Threefold Social Order – Threefold Human Being*

Steiner originally attempted in the early 1920s to introduce his ideas about the importance of manifesting a new social structure that would address challenges facing individuals and the world as a whole at that time. These ideas are the source of his inspiration in the writing of his book entitled *Towards Social Renewal: Basic Issues of the Social Question*.[8] In an introduction to a later collection of lectures entitled *Faculty Meetings with Rudolf Steiner* (1998) spanning the period from 1919 to 1924 and documenting the first Waldorf school faculty meetings, Betty Staley provides insight into the historical context in which Steiner first attempted to bring his ideas for a new threefold social order:

> With the end of World War I, the situation in Europe was unstable. Germany had collapsed and revolution had begun. In Russia the Revolution and the civil war that followed were tearing the country apart as power was redistributed. The call was out to workers everywhere to join forces to overthrow the bourgeois system and embrace Marxism. ... The situation in Germany worsened as the country suffered defeat and monumental inflation; people began to look for a scapegoat for a lost war, millions of unemployed and widespread disorganization. Anything could happen.
>
> This was the environment into which Steiner introduced his ideas on social threefolding, with the hope that it would bring about a new social order. He had already written his "Call to the German People and the Civilized World" in February 1919. It was circulated by means of flyers and

newspapers in Germany, Austria, and Switzerland. His book *Towards Social Renewal* was published in April that year. The Union for the Threefolding of the Social Organism was begun, which generated a great deal of enthusiasm among some European statesmen. ... Steiner lectured to many large audiences on the subject. At the same time, though there was extensive interest, his ideas threatened the established power of entrepreneurs, trade unions, and state officials, and it evoked much opposition. The time was not yet right for a new kind of ... social order that respected the rights and beliefs of each individual. (pp.xiv–xv)

Steiner (1977) suggested in lectures and outlined in detail in his book, *Towards Social Renewal*, that there are unshakable laws and principles underlying human social life that need to be acknowledged and worked with consciously in order to successfully create a social structure that will provide an antidote to the ailments of humanity. He was convinced that this threefold ordering at a societal level would bring needed change to human social life.

Steiner's work in the social realm is succinctly outlined in an article called *Nine Propositions in Search of the Threefold Social Order* by Christopher Schaefer (n.d.), which is included in full in Appendix F of this book. In summary, Schaefer suggests that Steiner provided us with guidelines in the form of formative and foundational principles and social laws to assist humanity in its search for new healthy social forms. While Steiner was not successful in his attempt to introduce the Threefold Social Order at a societal level, he responded to a request from Emil Molt, director of a factory, to establish an education that would enable children to develop the required physical, social-emotional, and intellectual capacities that would ensure the future social well-being of humanity and society. His hopes for the future were placed in the establishment of an education system that was to become the Waldorf school movement.

Schaefer goes on to say the following:

Central to the ideas of a threefold social order are the dignity of the human being and a new relationship of culture to the economy and the political sphere. The day of the centralized state, with its power over the other branches of public life, was to end. A new relationship was needed that would anchor cultural life in individual freedom; so that free initiatives could arise, economic life would be based on associations of producers and consumers, who would in freedom be able to support human community; and political life would recognize fundamental human rights under the law. Steiner saw that if major changes in this direction were not taken, violent solutions would be sought to doom the old system, as was already happening in Russia. Under the threefold social order the spiritual-cultural domain of education would be freed from state control; the power of the state in education would be limited and placed in the hands of teachers' associations. Parents would choose the schools they wanted for their children. When the impulse for threefolding society could not be realized, the Waldorf school kept alive the seed that had been planted there. (Steiner, 1998, p.xv)

Steiner's and Molt's original intention for Waldorf education clearly involved a social mission and an educational task in the light of Steiner's specific spiritual philosophy. In a lecture published in *The Spirit of the Waldorf School*, Steiner (1995) said the following:

> Our intention is to take a first step along the path we would want the cultural life of the Threefold Social Organism to take. In establishing the Waldorf School, Mr. Molt has, to a large extent, felt motivated to do something to further the development of inner spirituality. He hopes to do something that will point the way for the present and future social tasks of the Threefold Social Organism. (p.7)

In an essay written for a newspaper dedicated to promoting the threefold social order, Steiner (1985) referred again to the social mission of the Waldorf School: "The aims Emil Molt is trying to realize through the Waldorf School are connected with quite definite views on the social tasks of the present day and the near future. The spirit in which the school should be conducted must proceed from these views." (¶1)

Steiner's intention was for Waldorf schools to be a force for social change and ultimately a model for society. In his work on the evolution of the universe, Jantsch said, "The evolution of the universe is the history of an unfolding of a differentiated order of complexity. … Unfolding implies the interweaving of processes which lead simultaneously to phenomena of structuration at different hierarchical levels." (p.75) Jantsch is referring to what Steiner knew: Introducing a change in the evolution of education would have a co-evolutionary effect at the macro level of society. Steiner reflected this in how he set up the curriculum, the structure and the management of the school. Waldorf schools have the potential to fulfill this social mission and to be examples for the rest of society of how organizations can operate effectively as living, emergent learning organizations and also accomplish their primary (educational) task most effectively. To accomplish this, the leadership, management and operation of a Waldorf school must be inspired by the very same principles that are embedded in the Waldorf curriculum, in the threefold human being and in Steiner's expression of a threefold society. Steiner (1995) was emphatic about this at the founding of the first Waldorf school: "Obviously, the Waldorf School can be successful only if it is completely inspired by the Spirit that aspires toward the threefold nature of the social organism. …What we strive for here is a transformation of the present social configuration." (pp.7–9)

An important step towards implementing an organizational structure and forms that are inspired by these principles is to acquire a basic understanding of how living systems differentiate into independent, but interconnected systems that work as a whole to support the organism as needed.

## *Chapter 3*

# Human Systems and the Correlation with Organizational Systems

*It is intended that human thinking and feeling learn to sense
the vital potentialities in contemplating the natural organism and then
to be capable of applying this sensibility to the social organism.*
— Rudolf Steiner

In a lecture published in 1919 in the book Basic Issues of the Social Question in his attempt to describe the threefold social structure and its underlying unseen forming forces, Steiner insists that an attempt at "transplant[ing] some observation of the human being to the social organism" (Chap. 2, ¶8) is not being made. Steiner was being cautious in making direct correlations between human living systems and social systems because he wanted to be clear that he was not suggesting that social organizations are actually physical, biological beings. He referenced the work of social scientists of that time, e.g., Schäffle, who wrote a book about the structure of the social organism, wherein Schäffle infers that there is a direct equivalence between the organization of a 'physical living being' and an 'organizational being' such as human society. (Steiner 1919) Steiner also referenced Meray who described biological facts about living organisms and equated them exactly to a human societal organism as if it possessed physical (not social) cells, tissues, bones and organs. (Steiner 1919) Levine (1995) describes why social scientists would take this approach:

> … [I]t is metaphorical to say that human society is a biological organism. A number of social scientists have employed this metaphor to model certain ways of studying society, to generate insights about social phenomena, and to legitimize certain social values. … [A] train of distinguished scholars has struggled to secure a science of society modeled on the precise practices of the natural sciences. High among their intentions has been a wish to strip the language used by social analysts of its poetic baggage, to sanitize its rhetoric and cleanse it of its ambiguities, so that the communication of true knowledge could be reliable as with mathematical symbols or their verbal equivalents. (¶3)

Steiner was pointing out that it is important not to misunderstand the intention in correlating social organisms with biological organisms. He suggests that one must study and observe the nature of biological organisms, and that through this observation and study of life, one can develop capacities for sensing the working of spiritual impulses in these *biological* organisms that sustain them as organized living entities. Already in 1884, long before Steiner introduced the suggestion that there are unseen spiritual impulses that work in and behind everything in the world of human beings, poet John Ruskin was quoted in *Nature: A Weekly Illustrated Journal*: "Newton explained to you or at least was supposed to have explained why an apple fell, ... but he never thought of explaining the exactly correlative but infinitely more difficult question [of] how the apple got up there." (Ley p.353) Steiner was suggesting that capacities developed by observing and studying the apple, allowing one to begin to sense that which "put the apple in the tree," can be used to understand *social* organisms and the correlating systems and aspects that also have the same spiritual impulses (or unseen forces) working in them in a social-organizational context.

It would be a mistake to think that the social scientists were in fact, trying to directly apply the scientific facts as if social organisms were actually biological organisms. This is of course not sensible or possible, and it is not what is being suggested here nor is it what Steiner (1919) was suggesting when he made correlations between the threefold human being and the threefold social order as a living entity. Instead, what is being suggested here is exactly what Steiner suggested in the very same paragraph as he cautioned against inappropriately projecting observations about the physical world onto the non-physical social world: "Quite the contrary, it is intended that human thinking and feeling learn to sense the vital potentialities in contemplating the natural organism and then to be capable of applying this sensibility to the social organism." (Chap. 2, ¶8)

As he does in so many other places in his body of work on the threefold human being, society, and social life, Steiner is saying that we must use our human thinking and feeling and develop capacities or extraordinary sense organs of perception, which we can use to sense or 'see' the spiritual that stands behind the physical and use those capacities to translate our understanding of what is at work in what we can see, touch and feel with our ordinary senses to that which we cannot analyze directly with these senses. This is the only way that we can begin to understand that which we cannot see, touch, feel, hear or smell, and, as Wheatley said, metaphor is one way to begin to understand something that is invisible to our physical senses. It is the first step in developing the capacities to sense the unseen which stands behind the not visible social organism, which is already something that is not possible to understand with our ordinary senses.

How do we define an organization through a living systems lens? Steiner (1919) goes on to say in the same lecture that if a "social organism is to function in a healthy way, it must methodically cultivate three constituent members." (Chap. 2, ¶10) The three systems that keep a human being alive and thriving can be seen (and sensed, as Steiner suggests) as archetypal or spiritual forms, and when "the vital potentialities" are understood as such, the knowledge can then be transferred to understanding social organisms and how an archetype works in them.

It is interesting to note that in paragraph 2 of the same chapter in *Basic Issues of the Social Question*, Steiner (1919) points to the need to compare the social organization to the human organization in order to form mental pictures that will guide us in restoring health to social organisms:

> In order to clearly characterize certain driving forces by means of a comprehensive, universal observation of the social organism, I would like to start with a comparison. It should be borne in mind, however, that nothing more than a comparison is intended. Human understanding can be assisted by such a comparison to form mental pictures about the social organism's restoration to health. To consider the most complicated of all natural organisms, the human organism, from the point of view presented here, it is necessary to direct one's attention to the fact that the total essence of this human organism exhibits three complementary systems, each of which functions with a certain autonomy. These three complementary systems can be characterized as follows. The system consisting of the nerve and sense faculties functions as one area in the natural human organism. It could also be designated, after the most important member of the organism in which the nerve and sense faculties are to a certain extent centralized, the head organism.
>
> A clear understanding of the human organization will result in recognizing as the second member, what [I] would like to call the rhythmic system. It consists of respiration, blood circulation and everything which expresses itself in the rhythmic processes of the human organism.
>
> The third system is to be recognized in everything which, in the form of organs and functions, is connected with metabolism as such. These three systems contain everything which, when properly coordinated, maintains the entire functioning of the human organism in a healthy manner. (Chap. 2, ¶2)

Understanding how an undifferentiated single whole fertilized zygote cell develops first into an embryo and then a fetus with three clearly differentiated functioning independent yet interdependent life-giving systems can shed light on and provide tremendous insight into the corresponding development of living organizational systems, specifically in a cultural-spiritual organization like a Waldorf school.

One of the underlying fundamental concepts is that organizations are dynamic living social organisms, not simply with amorphous nebulous ever-changing living social systems, but rather are social organisms created by human beings and therefore are reflections or projections of the same archetypes that exist in the living human being. Beginning with this foundational idea, living organizational social systems can be intentionally modeled on mental pictures formed out of a study of the development of the physical living systems in a developing human being. In this way, such a correlation (not a direct equation) can be drawn between the development of human systems and the development of organizational systems.

## Differentiation of the Human Being

The National Institute of Child & Human Development with its collection of 10,000 human embryos, including the Carnegie Collection of Human Development consisting of 650 serial microscopic cross-sections of human embryos, provides images and descriptions of how a fertilized egg differentiates from a single cell into a human baby. Invaluable information on embryology and fetal development has been made available not only to the medical and scientific communities but also to the general public via a website hosted by The National Institute of Child & Human Development and The Carnegie Collection of Human Development (2006), called *The Visible Embryo*.[9] Unless otherwise indicated all references to the developing embryo and fetus in the following sections were acquired from this body of work. This site is connected to scientific, medical and more than 600 educational facilities. This work provides a major resource for understanding how the three human systems organically differentiate into three separate systems that interface and ultimately work in concert with one another as a functioning complex whole organism.

Very early on, at just thirteen days post ovulation, when it is only 0.2 mm in size, the embryo already has three foundational layers. These layers, called the endoderm, mesoderm and ectoderm, form the beginnings of the three human systems:

> [The] ectoderm is the top cell layer of the embryonic disc and will later form the baby's skin, hair, lenses of the eyes, lining of the internal and external ear, nose, sinuses, mouth, anus, tooth enamel, pituitary and mammary glands, and all parts of the nervous system. [The] mesoderm [is the] middle cell layer of the embryonic disc and [is the] precursor to the muscles, bones, lymphatic tissue, spleen, blood cells, heart, lungs, [circulatory], reproductive and excretory systems. [The] endoderm [is the] inner cell layer of the embryonic disc from which will form the lining of the lungs, the tongue, tonsils, urethra and associated glands, bladder and digestive [system].
> (National Institute of Child & Human, 2006, Stage 6, ¶5–7)

At seventeen to nineteen days post-ovulation, while it is blood cells that first start to form around the embryo (0–1.5 mm) in the placenta and its yolk sac, the first system to become visible and identifiable as an independent system in the embryo proper is the nervous system, and one of the first organs to develop is the precursor organ to the embryo's nervous system.

Twenty-three to twenty-five days post ovulation, when the embryo is 2.5–3.0 mm in size, marks the first appearance of a rudimentary S-shaped rhythmically beating heart, with fluids pulsing through the embryo. At this stage, the central nervous system is still clearly the first and most developed system, with the circulatory system beginning to form. Between twenty-three and thirty-eight days post-ovulation, the circulatory and blood-flow and respiratory systems, including the heart and lungs, develop rapidly, with critical heart development complete by fifty-six days post-ovulation.

While there is some liver cell development at these early stages, it is not until the beginning of the second trimester, ten weeks post-ovulation, when the digestive system can begin to be identified as an independent functioning system. When the intestines have fully migrated from the umbilical cord into the fetus itself, the "digestive tract muscles are functional," "nutrient-extracting villi line the folded intestines," "the liver starts to secrete bile stored in the gall bladder," and "the pancreas [is] complete" and "produce[s] insulin." (National Institute of Child & Human Development, 2006, ¶4)

By studying this rapid development of the three human systems, it can be observed that the nervous system, which includes the brain, is the first to establish itself. The circulatory-respiratory system or rhythmic system is second, and finally the digestive or metabolic-limb system last. The development of living organizational systems in a cultural organization like a Waldorf school can and should be correlated to this development of these three human systems.

## The Human Nerve-Sense System and the Pedagogical Sphere of Activity in a Waldorf School

### Human nerve-sense system development.

The brain and the nervous system ensure there is adequate and appropriate internal communication to keep the human systems healthy. In his book *An Introduction to Nervous Systems*, Ralph Greenspan (2007) provides a simple description of the function of the human brain, the central organ in the human nervous system:

> So why do we need a brain [nerve-sense system]? It is the only way that we, or any other creature that moves through the world, can deal with the constantly changing panorama of sights, sounds, smells, tastes, and touches, not to mention gravity, and (for some animals), electrical and magnetic fields. Brains [and the nerve-sense system] allow us to perceive the world, respond to it, move through it, and act on it. The amount of brain we have, measured as the number of nerve cells (neurons), determines how much of a repertoire for perception, response, movement, and behavior we have at our disposal, quite a lot for a human … 100 million neurons. (p.1)

Steve Parker (2007), author of *The Human Body Book*, points out that the brain is also the seat of human consciousness and creativity and that it not only controls motor movement and receives outside sensory information, but it also has an additional function of receiving and interpreting information from inside the body so that it can monitor and maintain the other body systems. The brain and the nerve and sensory systems are centrally important to the human being—it is this collective system that enables the monitoring and maintenance of a person's physical systems, and also allows the human individuality to take in, react and respond to the world, and ultimately to make intentional choices about how to live life and fulfill a chosen destiny path.

### Organizational 'nerve-sense system' development.

Just as the nervous system is the first system to become independent and recognizable as a unique system in the developing embryo, the pedagogical realm in a developing Waldorf school when it begins as an initiative with a class of children is the first realm to become visible in an organized form. A parallel can be drawn between a faculty of teachers and staff, and their pedagogical management group and committees that develop, and the nerve-sense system of the developing human being. The pedagogical body and the entire pedagogical sphere of activity can be identified as the organizational nerve-sense system. Just as the human nerve-sense system enables monitoring and maintenance of the individual human being's systems and functions, so too do the people—the teachers and staff who serve the pedagogical sphere of a Waldorf school—fulfill this function for the school as an organization. As part of their work in the classroom and in the school, these teachers and staff must also ensure that the school's systems are appropriately formed, structured and maintained so that they adequately serve the teaching and the development of the curriculum and programs, and ultimately the education of the children. The manner in which the school grows and develops must also serve the vision or the organizational destiny of the school as a Waldorf school and as an educational institution. This pedagogical body is the body that ensures that the focus of the organization as an entity is on education, specifically on delivering the Waldorf curriculum, and on the teacher-child and child-parent relationships. (Cohen 2006)

In a Waldorf school, as an independent school not governed by state or government, the driving impulse can and must be the same impulse that underpins all cultural-spiritual activities, initiatives and organizations in the cultural-spiritual sphere of the greater society. At the founding of the first Waldorf school, Rudolf Steiner and Emil Molt, the director of the cigarette factory where the school was established for the workers' children, were clear that the school as an organization firmly positioned in the realm of cultural-life, must be permeated with the central principle of the cultural realm, i.e., 'freedom.' It must not be driven by a society-based economic or political agenda. Steiner and Molt ensured that the name of the school, The Free Waldorf School, reflected the fact that it was a non-government school and independent from the state. (Steiner 1995)

Humanity's ethics, morals and values are developed in the cultural sphere of society; therefore, the curriculum of the Waldorf school was developed in a way that supported the social mission of the education, such that the students would develop capacities that would achieve this cultural-social mission, i.e., social skills, social sensitivity, and social understanding. (Lamb 2004)

*[handwritten margin note: Goal of Waldorf ed.]*

And finally, the self-administration of the school arose out of the reality of the classroom, out of the unique curriculum, which Steiner declared had "three essential points as the goal of this new method of education: enlivened science, enlivened religion, and enlivened art."[10] (Molt 1991, p.144) The economic or political sphere of society was not going to inform or influence the form of the administration that would then dictate what happened in the classroom (Lamb 2004). Here was the requirement in the establishment of the first Waldorf school, insisted on by Steiner, which in turn ensured that the co-evolutionary and transformative effect of Waldorf education became a possibility.

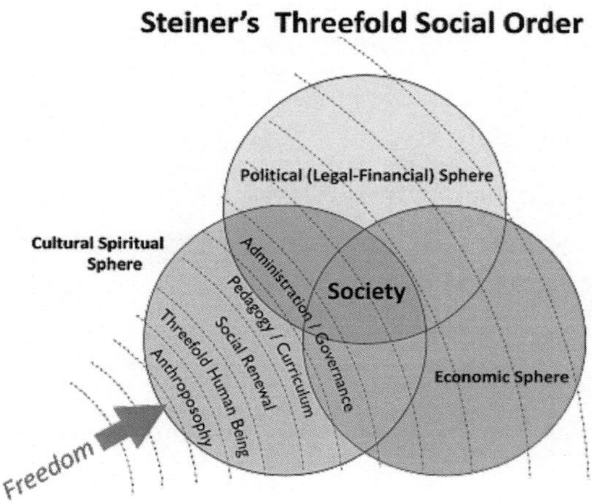

*[handwritten margin note: econo/ political can't control what happens in classroom]*

Steiner's Threefold Social Order

**Figure 2** *Co-evolutionary transformative effect of Waldorf education on the macro-sphere of society* [11]

This vision of self-administration that was to ensure the school was free of societal economic and political agendas was to be safeguarded by establishing a role for the teachers and the curriculum in determining how the school operated as an educational organization. Steiner selected the teachers for the school and then also involved them in the process of making decisions about the operation of the school as an educational entity. This faculty of teachers engaged in meetings focused on pedagogy, child development and child study and on sharing and reviewing what was happening in the classroom. The children, the classroom, the curriculum and the pedagogy became the central focus of and reason for the school's existence. This was what informed how the school was organized.

What was emerging was the first Waldorf school's first living system—the organizational 'nerve-sense system,' which can be compared to the first system that emerges in the differentiation of a human embryo. The first Waldorf school was self-administered, and in four years' time had started to differentiate into what could be seen as the early stages of development into a threefold structure. What emerged was an extended full faculty circle that included all faculty members, and then there was also a sub-group of teachers consisting of class teachers and senior specialty teachers only (a college or council of teachers or pedagogical carrying group). (Steiner 1998) Rudolf Steiner himself was the director of this realm of activity, not in a position of power but rather based on the "free will and confidence of the teachers." (Steiner 1998, p.xxiii) His role was in service to the children, teachers, curriculum and pedagogy, and so in that sense he was in fact a Pedagogical Administrator in service to the beginnings of the organizational 'nerve-sense system,' or the spiritual realm of the school. The school was already beginning to differentiate, develop and threefold itself, with a full faculty body, a pedagogical carrying group consisting of a smaller group of teachers, with faculty committees or task groups to follow, and with Steiner as Pedagogical Administrator.

## The Human Rhythmic System and the Governance (Legal-Financial) Sphere of Activity in a Waldorf School

### Human rhythmic system development.

The heart, lungs and circulatory or cardiovascular system and the respiratory system together can be seen as one system called the rhythmic system. It consists of the aspects of the physical human being that work rhythmically in conjunction with each other to ensure that the blood and nutrients that are deposited or collected and the oxygen taken in by lungs for the cells are circulated continually in a regulatory manner. The lungs deliver oxygen from the air to the blood, which is carried by the arteries, all part of a circulatory network that extends to every crevice and cranny of the body. The lungs also remove the unneeded byproduct carbon dioxide from the blood in the veins on its way back from the cells through the network of the circulatory system. This rhythmic circulation of blood through the heart and lungs is regulated by the heart and is steady and unrelenting. These aspects of the rhythmic system work together to ensure that oxygen and nutrients are delivered to and waste is collected from the cells of the entire body. Hormones are distributed; heat is delivered for temperature control, and contributions to fighting infection and the healing processes are made. (Parker 2007)

The heart, one of two main organs of the rhythmic system, is not only associated with the regulation of blood flow and the delivery of nutrients and removal of waste, but it is also associated with the feeling and emotional life, which provides a place for virtues such as love and courage to exist. (Parker 2007) It is the heart that speaks to us when interpreting the spirit of the law within the letter of the law, as well as when translating social mores and societal ethics into guidelines for behavior. The seat of consciousness might exist in the brain, but the source of conscience is the heart and the feeling life, which is centered in the human rhythmic system.

### Organizational 'rhythmic system' development.

As in the human embryo the organizational rhythmic system is the second system to differentiate into an identifiable system. The organizational nerve-sense system, which would include the Pedagogical Administrator and/or Faculty Chairperson—if they exist or as they evolve—the realm of the faculty and pedagogy, and any and all pedagogical committees and groups, comes first with the children and the establishment of the school as an official entity.

Next to appear is the organizational 'rhythmic system,' which includes the School Administrator or Director, the Non-Profit Society[12] and its membership,[13] the appointed Board of Trustees, and any and all committees, groups and staff connected to financial, legal, governance/structural and business management. This system provides specific middle-realm functions as well as a mediating, harmonizing, coordinating and weaving function in relationship to the bigger organizational picture. The middle organizational 'rhythmic function' provides the following:

- the protection and care, and administering to the management of all human and financial resources

- the monitoring and implementation of good governance and operational structures (always informed by the pedagogical realm[14])

- the oversight of legalities relating to the laws of the land and the mores and ethics of the organization (again informed and defined by the pedagogical realm based on the education, the curriculum and the classroom)

- the development and implementation of the Long Range Plan and monitoring of Community & Resource Development activities and pedagogical activities to ensure interconnectedness and a working together in such a way that assures a connection to the purpose, mission and values, thereby achieving its organizational goals, aims and objectives

- observation of all official communication, including publications, promotion and official letters to ensure consistency with the school's mission

It has already been highlighted how, as part of the threefold differentiation of the first Waldorf School's organizational structure, visible boundaries between systems emerged. Rudolf Steiner himself was the director in a role in service to the children, the curriculum and the pedagogy, with a full faculty body, and an internal Collegium of teachers working together to be the vessel for the pedagogical impulse. Here was the organizational 'nerve-sense' system in this the spiritual realm of the school. Also, during the first four-year period, a Board of Directors was established, and there are indications that Karl Stockmeyer who, along with Steiner and Molt as founding members in the first school, acted as the School

Administrator, with a bookkeeper to do the accounting. (Steiner 1998) This was the beginning of the differentiation and formation of an independent organizational 'rhythmic system.' And finally, Emil Molt was the patron who provided the economic support, both personally and through the factory, and this was an essential source of funds for the school's operation. This was the beginning of the first Waldorf School's organizational 'metabolic system.'

## The Human Metabolic System and the Community & Resource Development Sphere of Activity in a Waldorf School

### *Human metabolic system development.*

The nerve-sense system is the first system to become visible in the human embryo at just twenty-five days post ovulation; this is followed by the rhythmic system (circulatory plus respiratory) as the second system to become visible at fifty-six days post ovulation. The last of the three human systems to become visible as an independent and distinct system is the metabolic-limb system. The intestines migrate from their initial location in the umbilical cord to inside the fetus itself. The upper and lower limbs form first and then distinct fingers and toes that are no longer webbed. With the beginning of spontaneous movement by ten weeks post-ovulation in the second trimester of pregnancy, the metabolic-limb system has begun to establish itself in the human body proper.

The metabolic system is responsible for the liberation of energy from the ingested food, which is utilized for the formation and use of muscles, cells, tissues and organs.

> [The metabolic system] has a complex range of functions. It chops and chews food, stores and then digests it, eliminates waste products, and passes the nutrients to the major gland, the liver, which makes optimal use of the various digestive products. (Parker 2007, p.15)

"The liver is the main organ of the metabolic system and is the body's major nutrient processor." (Parker,2007, p.173) Torin Finser (2007), in his book *Organizational Integrity: How to Apply the Wisdom of the Body to Develop Healthy Organizations*, describes the root meaning of the word *liver*. He says in German *leber* means "to live," the French *foie* (as in *foie gras* or "fattened duck liver") is "derived from the fig tree or tree of life," and "in Russian the liver is called *pyetchen*, which comes from *pyetch*, the stove, which is a central element of the Russian house." The human liver functions much as the body's stove as it "regulates the ebb and flow of [life-giving] energy." (p.65) The metabolic-limb system is also the seat of the human will. This system ultimately consists of the limbs and many organs working in association with each other, which will continue to form and develop in the second and third trimesters.

### Organizational 'metabolic system' development.

As in the human being, where the metabolic system is the last independent system to become visible, the organizational 'metabolic system' is the last functioning system to form in a cultural organization such as a Waldorf school. The organizational 'nerve-sense system' has by this stage manifested at one pole as the Pedagogical Realm, and the 'rhythmic system' has formed in the middle as the Legal-Financial/Governance Realm. The organizational 'metabolic system' at the other pole, can be referred to as the Community & Resource Development Realm and would include all development staff, management groups and committees that coordinate and do the diverse work of this sphere of activity, including parent volunteers, parent association and council, and alumni, donors and friends who support the school with their contributions of finances, time and/or goodwill.

By the end of the first four years of its early development, the first Waldorf school, the Free Waldorf School, had a well-defined, identifiable and functioning Pedagogical Realm (organizational 'nerve-sense system'), which included Rudolf Steiner as the Director of pedagogy or the Pedagogical Administrator, the Full Faculty Circle, and a pedagogical management Collegium, all working to provide Waldorf education for the children, while ensuring that the school adhered to its founding principles. The school's organizational 'rhythmic system' was also beginning to establish itself with a Board of Trustees, with Stockmeyer as the School Administrator, and a bookkeeper in a finance department.

The Free Waldorf School's 'metabolic system' was just barely beginning to become visible with the presence of a first layer of donors and the gift of tuition paid by non-factory families, as well as the pioneering contribution and participation of Emil Molt as the founding patron. There were also dedicated attempts to access other sources of gift funding. One of Steiner's founding principles was that no child would be turned away because of an inability to pay (Steiner 1998). This resulted in ongoing attempts during those early years to establish sources of revenue that would assure economic and financial security for the school's future. These attempts can be seen as the forming impulse of the metabolic system at work in the initiative. The attempts included the following points, which are summarized from a description in Lamb's *Social Mission of Waldorf Education* (2007).

1. Seed money and on-going subsidization from the Waldorf Astoria Cigarette Factory

2. Tuition paid for children from non-factory employees' families (factory workers' children attended tuition free and were subsidized by the owners of the factory)

3. Donations and support from patron, Emil Molt

4. Patron sponsorships of children whose families could not afford to pay tuition

5. Contributions from individual donors including wealthy parents, local supporters, and people associated with the Anthroposophical movement

6. Establishment of a Waldorf School Association responsible for raising funds for the school and for outreach initiatives that would raise awareness about the education and the existence of the school

7. Founding of a holding company called The Coming Day, which was an association of businesses and educational and research organizations, whose mission was to model for society how the economic realm could contribute substantial revenue to cultural organizations, including educational ones like the Waldorf School

8. Establishment of businesses that would generate revenue for cultural organizations like the Waldorf School from the sale of new products and inventions

9. Establishment of a World School Association that would raise funds for Waldorf schools worldwide

There were varying levels of success in these attempts to establish a functioning organizational 'metabolic system' for the school, for example the World School Association was never realized. (Molt 1991) However, what this list of initiatives illustrates is that in the very first Waldorf School there was a concerted effort and focus on establishing a system that would provide the resources necessary for it to thrive.

In Waldorf schools today, at least on the North American continent, this organizational 'metabolic system' comes about initially when parents bring their children to the school with their gift of tuition revenue and the offer of a contribution of their volunteer time and support. The parents form this first layer of donors in the initial manifestation of the economic-brotherhood impulse of the Waldorf school as a cultural organization. This organizational 'metabolic system' will hopefully continue to grow and develop as the school matures. Ultimately, it would manifest in a system that would fully embrace and engage this important and essential first layer of donors, the parents and guardians of the children. The resulting ultimate organizational 'metabolic system' would provide adequate support and resources, both financial and human, in the form of community development, outreach, enrollment and tuition, donations, bequeaths, land, buildings and resources, volunteerism, and support to enable the pedagogical realm to deliver the education and keep the school, the curriculum, and the pedagogy alive, developing, improving and thriving.

## Translating the Threefold Form and Function to a Waldorf School

At the first meeting Emil Molt had with Rudolf Steiner where they discussed the idea of a school for the children of the Waldorf Astoria Cigarette Factory workers, they focused on the need for social renewal and talked about education as its vehicle. (Molt 1991) Hence, Waldorf education was founded based on the need for an educational system that would provide children with physical, social-emotional, and intellectual capacities while embracing a social mission for social renewal as its intention.

Steiner determined that the structure and administrative life of a school must arise out of what happens in the classroom and not out of a political or economic agenda. It must embrace the following principles (personal communication, October 20, 2005[15]):

1. The name must reflect the reality that the school is independent and a non-government school retaining freedom to develop its own curriculum.

2. The self-administration must arise out of the reality of the classroom and the curriculum, not the other way around. In other words, the administration does not determine what happens in the classroom because this could inappropriately introduce the influence of the economic or political impulses of society.

3. No child either male or female should be turned away for financial reasons.

4. Ethics, morals, and values are developed in the cultural sphere of society and therefore the curriculum of the Waldorf School is to be developed in a way that supports the social mission of the education so that students develop the capacities of social skills, social sensitivity, and social understanding.

5. The children are to be educated out of an understanding that a child possesses physical, emotional and spiritual aspects.

As a society, most particularly in North America, we have an "excessively partial view of reality" (personal communication, October 20, 2005[16]); with life viewed from a predominantly materialistic economic perspective. We have a propensity to materialism and tend to be driven by the 'economic engine.' This defines the forms—our social forms are related to our worldview. The implicit intention in the mainstream education system is to enable its students to be successful in the economic sphere. The curriculum of the educational institutions is most often informed by this implicit intention and the administration defined by the government or political sphere, which enables the manifestation of this intention.

Society is a holistic, threefold organism and similar to the case of the human being, if one part is removed or out of balance, it cripples the rest. Education lives in the cultural/spiritual sphere of activity and the form of that activity must be informed by a cultural/spiritual philosophy, and must *not* be driven by the economic or political engines. Lamb says that in education, developing the sensitivity for the threefold nature of society is as important as mathematics and that it is the cultural/spiritual life and activity that counterbalance the destructive nature of the economic life. (personal communication, October 20, 2005[17])

It is important for Waldorf schools to remember their social mission. The education must manifest an administrative structure that is developed directly out of the curriculum or pedagogy, which in turn is developed out of an understanding of the need for social renewal. This in turn is based on the holistic/spiritual view of the human being which comes from the understanding of the human being as a threefold being.

There are many levels or layers to consider when looking at the human being as a threefolded being, existing in a living threefolded social structure. At a physical level, one can see the human being possesses three main physical aspects: the trunk-limbs, the chest cavity with the heart-lungs, and the head, which in a healthy developing human being collectively manifest as the physical human form or vessel containing components that function in concert and collaboration with each other throughout the life of the person. The human being can also be seen as possessing a physical body, an emotional soul life, and a spiritual essence (individual ego being). These aspects enable the human being to be active and engaged in life in willing (or doing), feeling and thinking. Finally, the human being can be considered as a differentiated collection of three interconnected, independent, yet interdependent systems—metabolic-limb, rhythmic, and nerve-sense—that provide the dynamic processes by which the whole human being can exist as a physical, living, breathing organism.

At the beginning of this chapter the process is described by which a human embryo and fetus develops and differentiates into a recognizable functioning human organism with three distinct, yet interdependent, functioning systems. These systems, listed now in the order in which they develop, include (1) a brain and a nerve and sensory system, (2) heart and lungs centrally located in the circulatory-respiratory (or rhythmic) system, and (3) arms, legs, trunk and digestive organs related to the metabolic-limb system. The relationship between the development of these human systems and the development of systems in an organization, specifically a Waldorf school, has also begun to be described. The school as an organization, beginning as an idea and in a sense with fertilization taking place as a result of a pioneering initiative acting on the idea, ideally proceeds to grow and develop into a threefold organization with three distinct systems that enable it to exist. If consciously guided and nurtured, the systems differentiate appropriately in service to the organizational vision, mission and values, and as such the organization remains dynamic, responsive and alive.

In the case of a human being, once fertilization and implantation takes place, hidden or unseen forces facilitate the differentiation of the life-giving systems as described and illustrated by the work of The National Institute of Child & Human Development and The Carnegie Collection of Human Development. Looking at a social organization as a living entity, we see people working together to provide a conduit for these same forces, thereby facilitating the differentiation and development of the life-giving operational systems of the organization.

This differentiation process, and the positive health and maintenance of these systems, would have a greater chance at success and healthy development if there is a conscious and clear understanding of how these organizational systems are formed, how they function and are maintained. Understanding the phases of development through which an organization like a Waldorf school progresses over time can provide a beginning framework and context for the conscious and clear understanding of how organizational systems form and can be formed.

We can begin by examining the characteristics, elements and aspects of growth that are present as an organization develops over time and how that could correlate to the overall phases of development of the human embryo and fetus. Christopher Schaefer, PhD, organizational consultant, and faculty member, founder and Director of the Waldorf School Administration and Community Development Program at Sunbridge College, describes the phases of growth of an organization as displaying characteristic qualities that he has found are present in a diverse selection of organizations that have started and grown over time. (Schaefer and Voors 1996) These phases of development are *pioneering* or initiative, *differentiation* or diversification, and *integrative* or associative and mature.

## Phases of Organizational Development

### *Pioneering or initiative phase of development.*

Schaefer describes the early or pioneering phase of development as containing the following qualities and characteristics:

> It is generally of small to medium size, … has a shallow, flexible structure
> with a limited hierarchy, with … key decision-makers … often involved
> in the full scope of organizational activities. … [I]t is person oriented,
> rather than function-oriented [with] leadership … [that is] personal and
> direct. … Decision-making is intuitive … decided more by hunch or by feel
> [rather] than through a long process of rational analysis … [which means]
> that the pioneer organization is able to respond rapidly to changes in the
> environment. … The pioneering organization has a family atmosphere
> about it. Everyone contributes as they are able, and … the staff has a strong
> sense of loyalty to the founding group and to the initiative. Motivation and
> commitment … are high [and] the goals of the organization are implicit
> —carried in the minds and personalities of the carrying group. This phase
> of an organization's life is exciting, somewhat insecure, and very creative.
> (Schaefer et al., 1996, pp.31–32)

Schaefer (et al. 1996) also says that "developing an initiative is a process of providing the body, or sheaths, for a new identity to emerge." (p.32) He suggests that this phase of development is when this identity becomes visible to a certain extent, and this emerging identity will be determined by the purpose and objectives of the initiative. The beginning of the initiative can be likened to the beginnings of a human life, when the egg is fertilized and the creation of a new being is initiated. In a human being, in what can be compared with the end of this pioneering phase of development of an initiative, the physical foundations for the development of all three human systems are in place by the end of the first trimester of pregnancy (fifty-six to sixty days post-ovulation). It is also at the end of the first trimester that the nerve-sense system is the most developed. In an organization in the pioneering phase, it is the Pedagogical Realm and the organizational 'nerve-sense system,' which is most clearly formed.

The pioneering phase of an initiative's development, when the identity of the initiative is beginning to emerge, can be compared to the first trimester of embryo development, when the zygote has gone from being just a collection of cells at two to three days post ovulation, to being a human fetus with an identifiable human face by the end of the first trimester.

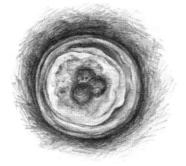

Zygote 2–3 days post-ovulation:
Unrecognizable collection of cells

Embryo 56–60 days post-ovulation:
Emerging identity

**Figure 3:** *From a collection of cells to an identifiable human form and face* [18]

### Differentiation or diversification phase of development.

Schaefer (et al. 1996) describes the environment when an organization has grown in size and is preparing to enter the differentiation or diversification phase of its development.

As the organization expands there are likely a substantial number of new people who join the initiative who are not necessarily connected to the pioneering group and the implicit vision, values, purpose and goals, and experiences and history that the pioneers shared. (Lievegoed 1991) The intuitive informal centralized decision-making style needs to be replaced with more "complex structures of decision-making" in order for the organization "to cope with increased size and complexity." (Lievegoed 1991, p.33) The vision and direction, which was shared implicitly by the pioneers, now needs to be made explicit so that everyone is working in service to identified organizational goals and not to individual desires or interpretations of those goals. There is a need to ensure that everyone understands the structure and how to work within and in service to it.

The differentiation phase is about diversification and what Schaefer calls "functional specialization" (et al. 1996, p.39) which means to have explicitly assigned and defined roles, responsibilities, and accountabilities, through mandates, job descriptions and policy formation, and defined procedures and protocols for various work assignments and activities. There need to exist clearly defined processes for reviewing and evaluating what works and what needs to change. This phase of development is also referred to as the Administrative phase and, just as in the developing fetus with the nerve-sense system most advanced and the rhythmic system now starting to be more clearly articulated, so too is the organizational 'rhythmic system' becoming more defined. In this Administrative phase of development, the focus is on the role and functions of the middle realm—the Governance (Legal-Financial) and structural aspects of the organization. It is during this time in a Waldorf school that the Board of Trustees (or Board of Directors) is formed or at least begins to take on more responsibility, especially in relationship to budget and financial matters. Often, it is during this phase of development that an Administrator or School Director is hired, and a Finance Department established with a Finance Manager or Bursar and Bookkeeper. These employees are hired as part of "functional specialization" (Schaefer et al. p.39) but also as an essential part of the development of the organizational 'rhythmic system,' with the Administrator or Director working in service to the whole middle realm or 'rhythmic system.' The Finance Department forms a sub-system—the organizational 'respiratory system'—of this middle realm. The Finance Department staff work in service to this sub-system of the greater organizational 'rhythmic system,' and are ultimately accountable to the Administrator or School Director.

During this phase of development, the organization needs to find the ways to bring about conscious functional differentiation and specialization without forfeiting individual creativity and participation. (Schaefer et al. 1996) If the differentiation phase is successful, the following[19] will be achieved:

1. Increased size

2. Clearer policies and procedures

3. Differentiated structures and mandates

4. A higher level of professionalism

5. More functional rather than personal leadership

6. More rational, analytical decision-making

7. Greater clarity of work activities

However, the risk of the differentiation and diversification process is that individuals can experience explicitly defined form and structure, with accompanying policies and procedures, as having a deadening effect on creativity and as a threat to individual freedom. This can be alienating, creating a sense of disconnection, lack of motivation and/or resistance to the differentiation process. Ways need to be found to ensure that interconnectedness is retained, that the organization as a whole is the primary consideration, with a focus on human relationships, collaboration, associative working, and the recognition and development of individual capacities. This is the time in the organization's development where the practices of a learning organization defined by Senge (1994) need to be applied.[20]

The characterization and gesture of this phase of organizational development is defined by its name: differentiation and diversification. The same two words could be applied to the second trimester of fetal development

Embryo 56–60 days post-ovulation: Emerging identity

Fetus at 22 weeks near the end of 2nd trimester: Defined and refined features and functions

**Figure 4:** *Embryo at 50–60 Days and Fetus at 22 Weeks* [21]

### Integrative or associative and mature phase of development.

The changes and growth that occur during the first two phases of development are easier to define and observe than in this third phase because the earlier changes are major, visible and quantifiable.[22] During the pioneering phase the initial physical and identity-related elements come together to form the vessel in which the initiative can begin to come to life. The focus is on creating the very basic physical foundations for operating a school. During the differentiation or administrative phase of development the focus is on form, structure, policy, administration and ensuring that the school operates effectively. In the third integrative phase of development, the changes are subtle and the focus is related to process, responsiveness, human needs and capacities, and rhythms. The nature of the development in this third phase is qualitative; it is about consolidation, simplification, flow of information, communication, and flexibility.

Schaefer (et al. 1996) proposes that the subtle qualities of the integration phase "suggest a type of awareness, a way of looking at and understanding organizations and people from a less analytical, but deeper, more whole and conscious perspective." (p.53) He says that there is a dedication to the improvement and refining of the quality of the service, that leadership, decision-making and "the creation of structure and work processes … take human needs" and "capacities [more] into account," and it becomes a "process organization in which structures reflect the requirements of central work processes rather than administrative control mechanisms." (p.53) The results are self-directed teams and process-oriented "horizontal thinking" (p.53), with a clearly empowered leadership structure with individuals who have and accept the responsibility and authority for guiding the organization.[23]

The other interesting observation that Schaefer (et al. 1996) makes—one that draws another parallel between the development of the organizational 'metabolic system' and the human metabolic system—is that it is during this phase of the organization's development that the organization begins to create what he calls "the organs for an association." (p.53) It is about establishing intentional channels of communication with the stakeholders, friends and broader community in which the organization is operating. This is really about establishing a strong community in and around the organization. The form and structure, along with the processes, events, activities and relationship-building that become part of the organizational structure, become the manifestation of the functioning organizational 'metabolic system.' It is significant that Schaefer uses both the term 'association' and 'organs' in relationship to this aspect of this phase of development. It correlates with the gesture of the metabolic system, where the association of human organs serves the needs of the human being and the parallel system of the economic sphere of the greater society, which is one of brotherhood, fraternity, and associative or cooperative working in producing goods and services to meet the needs of society.

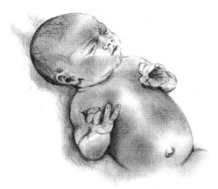

Full term baby: Fully developed, integrated functioning systems

**Figure 5:** *Full Term Baby* [24]

The changes that happen in this third phase of development, while subtle and not very visible, are no less important or profound and can be compared with the subtleties of the third trimester of the developing fetus. The systems and organs practice and become ready to function in conjunction with each other, independently from the mother and the womb; the fetus utilizes its muscles and limbs, practices breathing, develops its own immune system, swallows amniotic fluid and eliminates urine, and fat is formed providing energy and insulation. The eyelashes, fingernails and toenails form, the eyes open and the pupils begin to detect and respond to light. (Gasser, 1975) These are all subtleties of this phase of development as the human being prepares for independent existence. The development in an organization in the integrative phase of development is also about subtleties and fine-tuning, and preparing for self-sustaining existence.

The threefold development of the human systems is one that can be closely and accurately studied thanks to advances in science in the field of embryology and fetal development, and in technology that allows us to record three- and four-dimensional images of the developing embryo and fetus. Utilizing an understanding and insights gained through studying this development of the three physical human systems which *are* visible can provide indications for how threefold social systems which are *not* visible develop. These insights and indications provided a foundation for the development of the vision for the threefold social system implemented at the Vancouver Waldorf School during a period between 2001 and 2009.

* subtleties, fine-tuning, self-sustaining existence

- retirement plans
- program size to match income /enrollment
- long-range planning
- examining effective /best practices in administration
- Communication: how & how well
- process (governance, concerns, etc.)
- evaluations: are we doing our best work — * how are we holding each other accountable

*Chapter 4*

# Action Research:  Implementation of a Threefold Structure

*These three archetypal social organs are demands of all social or community life.*
*Their separate working and the realization of this will be increasingly critical*
*as we move into the future. In every community, organization, or institution,*
*something of each of these three organs must be present and actively nurtured*
*in some form, if the community is to be healthy. If any one is missing, or is not properly*
*formed, then there will sooner or later be ill health in that community.*
*Any one such organ can function in a healthy way only when the other two*
*are also there in the community. The three can work separately only*
*when they form a threefold unity.*

– Michael Spence

## Review of Hypothesis, Research, Development Methods and Methodology

The main assertions and hypotheses of this research project are that organizations possess characteristics of dynamic living organisms and when treated as such can thrive and ultimately have a positive evolutionary effect on the rest of society. Furthermore, organizations are not just amorphous living organisms, but rather, are reflections or expressions of the threefold human being with systems that mirror the same three dynamic systems that give life to the human form. They are social organisms created by and in service to human beings.

One such living social organism at a macro level is society itself, which possesses three forming impulses that give life to the three social systems or spheres of activity—the cultural, political (legal-financial), and economic spheres. Understanding the development and differentiation of the three human physical systems and getting a sense of the nature of the forming forces that guide the development of these systems, along with how these unseen forming forces also are at work in the differentiating organization and in the threefold society, can help people effectively serve and provide stewardship for the emerging organization. The result can be the manifestation of new forms and structures that will serve the individual organization and also be co-evolutionary for society. In other words, it will not only result in a more effective resilient organization that achieves its mission, but it could also have a positive evolutionary effect on the ordering of the rest of social life. Just like the paradoxical idea that we can use our thinking to create a paradigm shift in our thinking, so too can we use an understanding of our threefold existence and a threefold society to create a threefold organization that could lead to a transformation of the rest of society.

The question arises: What precisely are the new governance forms and structures that will make it possible to effectively operate an organization as a living learning entity, such that it can be an example for other communities, organizations and ultimately have a transformative effect on society as a whole? Pursuing this question is the focus of the action research undertaken at the Vancouver Waldorf School and is described in what follows. The research that formed the foundation, upon which the practical implementation of new governance and operating forms at the Vancouver Waldorf School is based, was inspired by, and focused primarily on the work of several people:

1. Arie de Geus (1997), in his body of work entitled *The Living Company*, describes a company as a living being that "manufactures its own cells, which in turn compose its own organs and bodily systems … and … that … [learns] as an entity." (de Geus 1997, pp.ix–x) De Geus supports his profound hypothesis with many years of experience and advice from his hands-on work in the corporate field.

2. Peter Senge (1994), inspired by de Geus and the notion of organizations as living learning entities, developed and describes a methodology that creates and maintains an effective living organization within the owner-operator corporate context in the form of what he coined "The Learning Organization."

3. Margaret Wheatley (2006) describes a new paradigm for thinking about organizations from a quantum physics or new science perspective (as opposed to the Newtonian mechanistic perspective). Her work helps us to shift our consciousness when thinking about organizations to focus on the whole rather than on the parts, and on the existence of systems that are interconnected networks. These networks possess dynamic processes, relationships and unseen connections between what Newtonian mechanics identifies as "separate measurable entities" (pp.10–11, 33). Out of this new science and an understanding of organizations as holistic systems or collections of interconnected, interdependent and interrelated networks and components, the mainstream corporate world is beginning to shift its approach to management, particularly by empowering workers to participate in the operating and decision-making aspects of a business. There is now awareness that a company will better grow and realize its potential if power is not concentrated exclusively in the leadership at the top of a pyramid-structured hierarchy. Generating knowledge and institutional learning horizontally across and through the organization gives access to the wisdom of the organization as a whole, leading to greater effectiveness.

4. Rudolf Steiner, with his broad philosophical, spiritual scientific observations of the universe, the earth, society, humanity and the individual human being and life—in particular his ideas on a threefold social order, the threefold human being, and the interconnectedness of humanity in the world in the form of a social organism—is the predecessor of all of the above contemporary thinkers. Steiner's primary contribution to this research is the indications he

provided for threefold forms for a living social organism that, through its manifestation and as an example, could ultimately have the kind of positive evolutionary effect on the future of humanity that he, Wheatley and Senge each describe in their own ways.

While these four have provided large bodies of research and documentation in the realms of a new social science and new governance forms for organizations, which provided a foundation for the qualitative and action-based research documented here, there are many others who could be referenced as well who have done profound research and have provided important insights.

Erich Jantsch (1992), astrophysicist and author of *The Self-Organizing Universe, Scientific and Human Implications of the Emerging Paradigm of Evolution*,[25] developed a paradigm that understands life as more than a series of adaptations for survival of the fittest. He set out to support that not only does life evolve, but the environment in which life takes place also evolves and that there is a co-evolutionary aspect and a connection and dynamic element that exists between the two.

> The emergent paradigm of self-organization permits the elaboration of a
> vision based on the interconnectedness of natural dynamics at all levels of
> evolving micro and macro systems. From such an interconnectedness of the
> human world with overall evolution springs a new sense of meaning. (p.xiii)

He asks the question: "How is evolution to continue in the human world?" (p.251) and he provides the following opinion: "I believe that sociocultural man in "co-evolution with himself basically has the possibility of creating the conditions for his further evolution—much as life on earth, since its first appearance 4000 million years ago, has always created the conditions for its own evolution toward higher complexity." (p.251)

Christopher Schaefer also believes in the possibility of positively affecting the environment in which human life exists and evolves. He says, "If we can consciously work with principles of threefoldness in our lives and institutions, and if we are able to see and articulate these formative principles at work in society, then we will be able to promote social healing in the world."[26] Gary Lamb (2004) described how the cultural/spiritual life and activity in that realm of society have the capacity—and by implication, the responsibility—to counterbalance the destructive nature of the economic life. These hypotheses can be extended further to suggest that the realm of culture and spiritual life in society, the place where ethics, morals and values are developed, where individual creativity is expressed, and where education, religion and spirituality, medicine and the arts live, must work to transform the other two spheres of activity. The social mission of Waldorf education is to contribute to this co-evolutionary goal.

It is hoped that the practical research documented in the following chapters will make a contribution towards this lofty goal through a very specific approach to articulating and working with formative threefold principles. The attempt is made to illustrate the value in understanding the forces that result in the formation of the three human systems, and also to translate and correlate this understanding to a social organization by demonstrating the intentional creation of a living threefold operating structure. An intentional choice was made to do this specifically in a Waldorf school with the belief and hope that it would in even a small way further the manifestation of the new social order that Steiner envisioned when he responded to Emil Molt's request to start a school.

In her introduction to a publication entitled *Faculty Meetings with Rudolf Steiner*, Betty Staley said:

> Since the first Waldorf school was founded in Stuttgart, Germany, in 1919, the Waldorf educational movement has grown to include more than seven hundred schools in over fifty countries. Waldorf schools exist in rural areas, cities, suburbs, small towns, a kibbutz, and inner city neighborhoods. In addition, Waldorf education has inspired initiatives in state schools, in refugee camps, in day-care centers, homeless shelters, and in juvenile prisons. In 1994, the UNESCO (United Nations Educational, Scientific, and Cultural Organization) honored Waldorf education with a special exhibition for its contributions to the world. The establishment of the Independent Waldorf School may one day be regarded as one of the most significant initiatives of the twentieth century.

> The establishment of the [Free] Waldorf [S]chool not only answered an educational need of our times but was a deed of spiritual proportions. Rudolf Steiner spoke at the founding of the school:

> It is our duty to be aware of the importance of our task. This we shall achieve when we realize that this school is to become the bearer of quite a special impulse. And so, first of all, we must direct our thoughts toward the consciousness that something special is to be borne into the world through this education. Such a realization will come about when we no longer view this act of founding the school as an ordinary, everyday event but as a festive act in the ordering of the world. (Steiner 1998, xiii)

Many people in Waldorf schools and other Anthroposophical organizations have been engaged for years in the study to understand and work with the principles of 'threefoldness' or 'threefolding' as it is called and as indicated by Steiner. However, because of the many different ways and interpretations of how these principles are at work at a social-organizational level, the insights, benefits and results can seem amorphous at best and confusing at worst. The principles of threefoldness work at many different levels and it can become perplexing to those working with these principles in a school or other organization. In fact, threefolding and the interconnected nature of it, means that each impulse is present at each level and in every layer, and in every fold of each and every level and layer. This results in a threefolding of each one of the folds, and then a threefolding of each one of those folds, with each threefolded whole a part of a greater threefold whole, and each part threefolding again into a threefold whole down to the micro-level, and so on. What happens is a never-ending story of threefolding upon threefolding within threefolding, all of which is constantly in a process of unfolding. This makes it extremely challenging to define the boundaries of any one of the given folds at any given point in time. The following table illustrates the nature of threefolding upon threefolding within threefolding.

| Exists | | | |
|---|---|---|---|
| in Society as | Cultural/Spiritual Sphere | Political (Legal Financial) Sphere | Economic Sphere |
| in the Human Being as | Spirit | Soul | Body |
| in the Human Body as | Head | Heart | Hands |
| in Human Systems as | Nerve-Sense | Rhythmic (Respiratory/Circulatory) | Metabolic-Limb |
| in Human Activity as | Thinking | Feeling | Willing |
| in a School Community as | Teachers | Non-Profit Society Members | Parent Body, Friends, Donors |
| in School Departments as | Pedagogical | Governance (Legal-Financial) | Community & Resource Development |
| in School Carrying Groups as | Pedagogical Carrying Group or a College of Teachers | Board of Directors or Trustees | Community & Resource Development Group or Committee |
| in Management Staff as | Pedagogical Administrator | School Administrator | Development Administrator (Director) |
| as an Impulse as | Freedom | Equality/Rights | Cooperation/Brotherhood |
| as an essential activity to | Enhance the freedom and creativity of the individual | Administer the law and the legal norms; monitor financial health; distribute finances equitably; oversee societal structure | Provide goods/services and human resources and generate capital that serve needs |
| in a Waldorf school to | Administer to the pedagogical life | Administer to good governance and legal-financial business | Administer to the community and resource development activities |

**Figure 6:** *Threefold Principles at Work in Life*

It is important when talking about one of the folds to understand that it is always in relationship to the other two folds of that same layer or level. When attempting to manifest a threefolded operating structure, it is essential to remember the following:

the social organism … is arranged according to its functions in the same way as the natural organism of man. The human organism deals with thinking through the head, not through the lung, and breathing not through the head or nervous system. Health is there wherever the nerve-sense system and the rhythmical system of blood and breathing coexist independently and work together in a living way." (Karutz 1998, p.17)

When applying this principle to the implementation of an organizational operating structure, any reference to threefolding is at an organizational *systems* level. Any reference to other aspects, levels, or layers is always done as a frame of reference and only to clarify what is being described at a *systems* level. The impulse at work in one of the three aspects at a systems level might correspond to a similar aspect at a society level or at a human systems level. However, the level or layer is specific to the level or layer that is the subject of consideration at the time. The process of implementing the threefold living structure that follows is intended to be considered always from this operational systems perspective and any reference to the principles working in other ways, in relationship to other levels or layers, or to physical or *biological* systems as opposed to *social* systems, is added only to provide a context for the *principles* and *impulses* that are common throughout and across all levels and layers. Cross-referencing in this way also illustrates the degree of interconnectedness of and between these systems, layers, impulses and principles.

The following tables provide a picture of what has been described—taking the threefolding from a starting point of a threefold society, then to a threefold human being, and finally to the organization as a whole, with three independent, but interdependent systems. The tables are grouped to make it easier to see the principles, impulses and unseen forces at work in society as a social order, and the correlation with the three human systems and organizational systems, specifically in a cultural organization, e.g., a Waldorf school.

| *Realms of Society* | *Cultural / Spiritual* | *Political (Legal-Financial)* | *Economic* |
|---|---|---|---|
| **Impulse** | Freedom | Equality/Rights | Cooperation/ Brotherhood |
| **Central Activity** | Enhance the freedom & creativity of the individual | Administer to the law, legal norms & societal mores | Provide goods/services & generate capital that serves human needs |

**Figure 7:** *Threefold Social Order*

| *Human Being* | *Spirit* | *Soul* | *Body* |
|---|---|---|---|
| **Human Systems** | Nervous-Sense System (Nerve + Senses) | Rhythmic System (Respiratory + Circulatory) | Metabolic-Limb System |
| **Human Activity** | Thinking head | Feeling heart | Willing hands |

**Figure 8:** *Threefold Human Being*

| School Bodies or Spheres of Activity | Faculty | Non-profit Society | Parents, Friends, Donors |
|---|---|---|---|
| Central Activity | Oversight of the Pedagogical & Organizational Vision | Oversight of Effective Governance, Legalities & Finances | Oversight of Community & Resource Development |
| Carrying Groups | Pedagogical Carrying Group (aka College of Teachers) | Board of Trustees | Development Carrying Group or Committee |
| Pedagogical Threefold Differentiation | Full Faculty Collegium | Pedagogical Carrying Group (aka: College of Teachers) | Pedagogical Committees |
| Pedagogical Committees | Programs & Curriculum Development | Pedagogical Human Resources Committee | Pedagogical Practical Needs |

**Figure 9:** *Threefold Organizational Structure*[27]

## Implementation of a Threefold Governance Structure at the Vancouver Waldorf School

I came to the Vancouver Waldorf School with a clear vision for a threefold governance and operating structure. However, as Wheatley (2006) states, "Organizations are never changed by imposing a model developed elsewhere." (p.8) It is important to note that the vision introduced to the School, which I had developed in the years preceding my employment at the School, was not a preconceived fully formed model that was intended to be imposed on the organization. It was not a *model* but rather a *vision*[28] informed by and developed out of intense and deep study of Rudolf Steiner's principles and indications for a threefold social order and the threefold human being from a living systems perspective, through the lens of an organization as a living learning developing entity. The vision, and the principles and life-giving impulses that permeated the vision, had to then be applied as in Wheatley's (2006) assertion: "In every organization we need to look internally, to see one another as the critical resources on [a] voyage of discovery" and "to engage the creativity that exists everywhere in our organizations." (pp.8–9) In other words, it is essential for the successful implementation of living systems in an organization that it be an engaging, collaborative organic process that utilizes the inherent wisdom of the people whose task it is to create the vessel in which the organization can exist and thrive. Steiner (1996) said this in his own way in his opening address to the teachers of the first Waldorf school, addressing how the school should be organized and operated:

> Therefore we will organize the school not bureaucratically, but collegially, and will administer it in a republican way. In a true teachers' republic we will not have the comfort of receiving directions from the School Board.[29] Rather, we must bring to our work what gives each of us the possibility and the full responsibility for what we have to do. Each one of us must be completely responsible. (p.30)

Tom Donahoe (1993) worked on public school reform through the Telesis Foundation. Out of this work, he wrote a journal article for *Phi Delta Kappan* on how schools as organizations must "confront [the] critical question: How does a school generate and sustain the characteristics of effectiveness?" (¶2) He suggests that schools must "break" not simply "bend" (¶4) the traditional administrative structure and change how they are organized in order to actually shift the culture and formally restructure and rearrange so that they operate with an interactive culture and a supporting infrastructure that would ultimately improve student learning. He says the following:

> The kind of culture and supporting structure schools now need reduces …
> top-down bureaucratic direction. In the Telesis Foundation schools, the team
> leaders and project coordinators do not in any sense supervise units or teams
> of teachers. Rather, they are elected volunteers from among the staff whose
> role—in addition to teaching, counseling, or administering—is to facilitate
> the upward (and lateral) movement of influence through the organization.
> Schools require a very special nexus of culture, time, and structure, in
> which a certain kind of culture assumes the function that authority plays
> in traditional organizations, classic bureaucracies. A diagram of the formal
> organization of a school restructured in this manner might show overlapping
> circles representing spheres of influence, rather than boxes representing
> areas of responsibility and levels of authority. (¶29)

Operating a school in this way, collaboratively and collegially, engaging the teachers and staff in the decisions about how to administer to the school, means that changes, growth or development will involve processes that require time and resources to manage.

The following pictures illustrate the development of the threefold vision (not model[30]) for a threefolded organization, with the kind of overlapping spheres of influence representing the kind of radical new approach to a school structure and a different culture referenced by Donahoe and that Steiner also knew was essential if educational organizations were to accomplish their cultural-educational goals. The pictures also illustrate the correlation between the threefold vision, the threefold social organization and the threefold human being. An

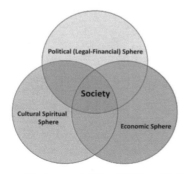

**Figure 10:** *Steiner's Threefold Social Order*

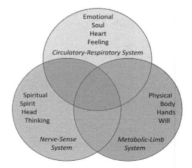

**Figure 11:** *Threefold Human Being*

**Threefold Organizational Structure for a Waldorf School**

**Figure 12:** *Threefold Organizational Structure*

**Threefold Organizational Structure Threefolded**

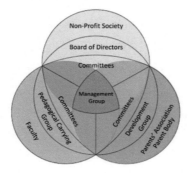

**Figure 13:** *Threefold Organizational Structure Threefolded*

illustration of the threefold social order is shown first, followed by an illustration of the many layers and aspects of the threefold human being. Finally, there is an illustration showing the threefold organizational structure, and one illustrating the structure threefolded, all with the three overlapping spheres as a consistent repeating element.

It was impossible to begin at the beginning to implement a threefold operating structure at the Vancouver Waldorf School because the School was already 33 years old when I arrived. It was also impossible for any transformation to be instant; this was a school that had been in operation for many years and we could not start at the beginning organically developing, facilitating and implementing a threefold structure through the normal pioneering, differentiation or administrative, and integrative phases of development. Rather, much had first to be unraveled and understood in relationship to how it had developed in the preceding decades.

A starting point for beginning the transformation of the governance and operating systems had to be found, and a collaborative, organic inside-out process that was relative and responsive to the existing reality was initiated. The facilitation of the implementation of a living threefold structure requires not only that the form be defined but that the dynamic[31] change to reflect the threefold form. At the Vancouver Waldorf School, this took place over an extended period of time, in stages or phases. Of course, the development of the structure was not a linear process and the stages or phases overlapped in time and space; also, it will become evident—reflected in Chapter 5—that over the course of implementing the threefold vision at the Vancouver Waldorf School, both the form *and* the dynamic did not change adequately to allow for a complete transformation. I have documented the process in stages, which hopefully will make it easier to understand. It should also make it possible to repeat and improve on the process of implementing a threefold living systems operational structure in another context.

## Step I    Beginning the Re-Differentiation Process

It appeared to me as though over the years, the School had swung back and forth between a Board of Trustees-run school and a College (Faculty) of Teachers-run school. There was an entrenched mentality of 'us-versus-them' between Board of Trustees and College of Teachers, College of Teachers and Faculty, Faculty and Administration, parents and College of Teachers and Faculty; between departments—Early Childhood Faculty and Grade School Faculty, and Grade School Faculty and High School Faculty; and between individuals.

When my employment started, the School was operating under a mandate system model introduced three years prior to provide a way to restructure the School's administration and governance. Out of the recognition of a desire to change, a whole community process had led to a decision to dissolve the existing structure and try something different. The College of Teachers, which at that point was carrying the primary responsibility for managing the School, was dissolved. With the help of a consultant, a mandate system was designed, implemented and imposed on the existing organization in an almost instant restructuring of the School's governance and operating structure.

The model, in short, consisted of approximately twenty committees and/or groups, all of which were mandated and accountable to the Board of Trustees and were required to report regularly to a central Hub Coordinating Committee.[32] While the Hub Coordinating Committee had no authority to make decisions, its mandate was to ensure through regular and direct communication that the work of the School's committees was completed. This was described as providing a coordinating function.[33] The Hub was responsible for reporting regularly to the Board of Trustees and to the Faculty at the Full Faculty meetings. The Hub agendas were set in consultation with the Faculty, and the Hub was responsible for facilitating the Full Faculty Meeting.

Existing committees and groups, including the College of Teachers, were dissolved, or in some cases redesigned. In the case of the Board of Trustees, faculty participation and representation were secured with changes to the Society Bylaws, mandates were written, committees struck, and the new operating structure was in place. The agreement was that this system would remain in place for a minimum of three years, after which time a review would be conducted to determine what was working, what needed to be changed, and what should remain in place as the School's operating structure beyond the three years.

When I was hired as Administrator, the three years had just passed and it was time to conduct the review. In my new role I assumed the responsibility for guiding the process of designing the review. A mandate for a Mandate System Review Committee[34] was created and approved by the Board of Trustees. The Committee was formed based on the selection criteria detailed in the mandate, and in April the Committee began its work. The deadline for completion of the review with recommendations was the end of May; and while the Committee found that it could not complete the review because of the overwhelming response and amount of information that was offered by the community, it did make recommendations for immediate changes to the operating structure that would address the most urgent issues and concerns, as well as allow the review to continue.

I saw this review as the entry point that I needed to introduce to the existing mandate system an intentional threefold structure, beginning with forming the Mandate System Review Committee using a threefold process, i.e., by defining the skills, knowledge and attitudes that were necessary to have represented on the committee so that it could successfully complete its task. Utilizing a committee to conduct the review was the initial act of beginning the process of deciding how to transform the mandate system in order to reflect a threefold structure. With it we were already beginning to use some of the fundamental disciplines that Senge (1994) identified as present in a learning organization,[35] in particular, utilizing the experience and wisdom of the people already working and participating in the organization.

The recommendations that came out of this Committee,[36] in conjunction with my being hired on as the Administrator, marked the beginning of a transformative process of unfolding, exposing and developing a complex living threefold operating structure for the Vancouver Waldorf School. My employment was a serendipitous event that proved to be a catalyst and led to the implementation of a threefold structure. But this was only possible because the school was at a point of development that made it ripe for this transformation. Also, I had already extensively studied the threefold principles in relationship to the social realm and had developed a vision of what this could look like in a living organizational structure and governance context. I was ready to work with this vision at a practical level at a time when the Vancouver Waldorf School cleaned the slate, introducing a mandate system that provided a foundation for the introduction of a threefold structure. Working in the middle realm, in relationship to financial/legal and specifically governance in the cultural realm was clearly my vocation in life. I had abandoned my first career as a police woman [in the political (legal-financial) realm of society] and instead pursued with passion and drive, a career in the realm of organizational development, specifically in the realm of Waldorf school administration in the cultural sphere of society.

In spite of, or perhaps in addition to, this seemingly coincidental convergence of organizational and individual destinies, it is the role of a School Administrator or Director, along with the Non-Profit Society, the Board of Trustees, its committees, and the Legal-Financial Department staff, to function collectively as the organizational 'rhythmic system.' They work collaboratively in service to the organization, with a mediating, harmonizing and coordinating function between the two poles represented in the organization by the other two systems. The raison d'être of this middle realm in a Waldorf school is to "enable the faculty and pedagogical staff to maximize their attention toward students and pedagogy, while ensuring continuous improvement to the School's financial and physical health." (personal communication, March 3, 2010[37])

In review, the organizational 'nerve-sense system' is correlated with the human nerve-sense system. As stated in Chapter 2, a parallel can be drawn between the organizational 'nerve-sense system'—i.e., faculty of teachers and pedagogical staff, and the pedagogical management group and committees that develop as a school grows—to the nerve-sense system of the developing human being. The pedagogical body and the entire pedagogical sphere of activity can be identified as the organizational 'nerve-sense system.' Just as the human nerve-sense system enables the monitoring and maintenance of the individual human being's systems and also allows the human individuality to take in, react and respond to the world, and ultimately to make intentional choices about how to live life and fulfill a chosen destiny path, so too do the people—i.e., the teachers and staff who work in and serve the pedagogical sphere of a Waldorf school—fulfill this function for the school as an organization.

This supports the idea that the organizational 'nerve-sense system,' which includes the teachers, pedagogical staff, Faculty Chairperson and/or Pedagogical Administrator, pedagogical management group (or Pedagogical Carrying Group or College or Council of Teachers), pedagogical committees and all pedagogically-related activity, provides a thoughtful dynamic[38] as it fulfills its function of developing and delivering the curriculum and ensuring that the school's systems are formed, structured and maintained in service to the teaching and development of the curriculum and programs and that the school's growth and development serves the organizational destiny and vision of the school.

At the other pole, the human metabolic system takes in raw materials and processes and absorbs the nutrients or releases them into the blood and circulatory system (Parker 2007) where they become available for the use of the living organism. The organizational 'metabolic system,' which includes all Community & Resource Development staff, groups, and committees, the community of parents, friends, and donors, and all of the activities related to community and resource development,[39] is at the other pole of the organizational structure fulfilling the role of fostering relationships in the interest of providing resources, both human and financial, that are needed by the school and that make the education possible. This organizational *metabolic system,* located at the opposite pole of the organizational structure to the *nerve-sense system,* has movement, initiative, and generation and transformation of substance or resources as its central dynamic.

The middle system or the organizational '*rhythmic system*,' which correlates to the human circulatory and respiratory systems, provides an interface and a mediating, coordinating, harmonizing gesture between the poles, and consists of the School Administrator, Finance Department staff, the Non-Profit Society[40] members, its Board of Trustees and committees. Huseman et al. (1996) describe the relationship of these systems in the human structure:

> If merely these two opposing systems [the nerve-sense system and the metabolic system] were present, they would be engaged in a ceaseless battle that would negate both their functions, just as cold and heat combine to form a lukewarm mixture, or positive and negative electricity destroy one another in a short circuit. This danger is removed by the formation of a third system, which functions as a mediator between the other two. It is this mediation that guides the tension between the opposites to further development. This phenomenon is aptly described by Goethe's concept of "enhancement of polarity." Pursuing the above train of thought, we shall have to seek this system spatially in the middle region of the body. (p.4)

Huseman et al. (1982) also point out that, "in considering the nature of the rhythmic system [in the human being], we are concerned here primarily with the pure activity of the organs, with their dynamic, that they are placed between two poles and mediate between them." (p.4) This imagination of the three organizational systems and the dynamic between them is important when designing and implementing a threefold organizational structure. It was at the foundation of my thinking at that initial review point when recommendations were made for the implementation of a threefold structure at the Vancouver Waldorf School. The initiating recommendation from the Mandate System Review Committee that brought about the reformation and differentiation of the pedagogical realm and marked the beginnings of the formation of a new effective and well-defined organizational 'nerve-sense system' was the following:

> Based on the principles that the review committee has been working with, the committee could suggest for the long term, that the School establish three umbrella groups, one in each sphere—pedagogical, financial/legal/ governance, community & resource development (economic)—to guide, steer, and coordinate the activities and nurture the impulse of each sphere. Umbrella groups would be responsible for identifying the need for mandate groups, will define each mandate, and select committee members. They will ensure that each committee has adequate and clear policies and procedures and that these are part of the mandate document. They will receive minutes and reports, monitor and ponder these, and evaluate the effectiveness and/ or need for the committees at regular pre-determined intervals. These groups would take input, suggestions, and feedback from the larger body

associated with its specific sphere and consult with the other spheres when appropriate. They will delegate task groups or individuals that will take up other pedagogical, financial/legal/governance, or community & resource development tasks as needed. The immediate need however is to establish a Pedagogical umbrella group that would carry the pedagogical area in the above manner and take the pressure off the Principal. The feedback indicates that this is a step that requires immediate implementation.[41]

*Figure 14* is an illustration of human systems from Huseman et al., *The Anthroposophical Approach to Medicine: Volume 1. Figure 15* illustrates how the same principles work to create the same living dynamic in an organization.

## Dynamic Human Systems

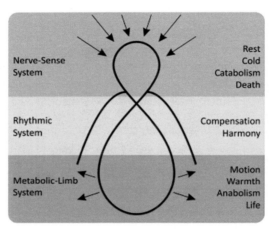

**Figure 14:** *Dynamic Human Systems*[42]

## Mediating Impulse Between Poles

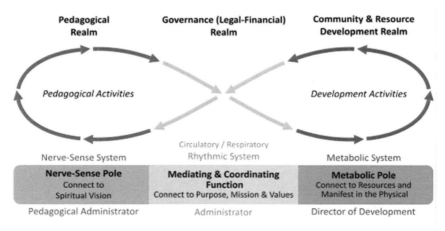

**Figure 15:** *Dynamic Organizational Systems*

This recommendation came from the recognition that despite the fact that the School was already decades old, the boundaries between realms or organizational systems were not clearly defined. In fact, in the existing structure the Board of Trustees mandated and managed all committees, including pedagogical ones. When the body responsible for the legal, structural and fiscal wellbeing of the organization also takes responsibility and authority for overseeing and managing the pedagogical vision and activities of the School, it constitutes an impingement of one impulse on another. More appropriately the faculty and the entire pedagogical realm should form and be the system that oversees the work in the pedagogical sphere.

Huseman et al. (1982) suggest that impingement or discontinuity between systems in the human being result in disease. Karutz (2001) also speaks to this in relationship to social organisms:

> The triad of systems in the social organism corresponds with the three great ideals of the French Revolution:
>
> - Freedom corresponds with the sphere of spiritual creativity, the spiritual life.
>
> - Equality corresponds with the sphere of law, the state, politics.
>
> - Fraternity corresponds with the economic life.
>
> Each ideal brings its own sphere of influence to the life but will weaken, perhaps fatally, if carried over into the other two spheres. For example:
>
> - If freedom dominates the legal sphere, then all rules are undermined, bringing insecurity and chaos.
>
> - If freedom prevails in the economic sphere, it will lead to irresponsible exploitation of man and nature, to annihilation, pollution and destruction.
>
> - If equality in spiritual life becomes the most important aim, it will lead to the paralysis of spiritual, creative forces. The result is stagnation and decay.
>
> - If equality enters economic life, then the productive forces will be suffocated by the bureaucracy of a planned economy.
>
> - If fraternity dominates the spiritual life, this will also lead to paralysis of individual forces and quickly to formation of closed circles and lodges, to separation into brother and non-brother.
>
> - Fraternity in the sphere of law can easily develop into lobbying, favoritism, corruption and thwarting of true justice. (pp.28–29)

When there is impingement or discontinuity between one sphere or system and another in a social organization, the result is 'dis-ease'[43] as described above by Karutz. In the review process report, disease was evidenced in the form of a lack of pedagogical vision driving the work of the committees, inadequate input loops resulting in uninformed decisions at a committee level, lack of trust in the group processes, inadequate expression of pedagogical ideals, and ongoing lack of student retention and adequate enrollment. Impingement by the Board of Trustees from the Legal-Financial sphere on the Pedagogical sphere had resulted in stagnation and decay in the pedagogical environment in the School.[44]

The recommendation to establish a Pedagogical Carrying Group to take over from the Board of Trustees' management of the pedagogical realm of activity was the first step in re-differentiating the School's systems based on the principles of threefolding. This was an essential first step, as it is in human embryo development where the first system to become identifiable as an independent system is the nerve-sense system. So too in a school social organization, where the systems are a reflection of the human being and an expression of the corresponding threefold social order, the first system to appear and be firmly established should be the organizational 'nerve-sense system' in the realm where pedagogical activity takes place.

### Social structure and the relationship with organizing impulses

In 1962 Michael Spence (1999) was part of a pioneering group that started Emerson College in England, an adult educational institution inspired by the work of Rudolf Steiner. He also worked as the College bursar and in other capacities for twenty-seven years. In a book called *Freeing the Human Spirit* he shares his observations, as well as subsequent insights gained, while working with the principles of the threefold social order during and after his time at the College. He concludes:

> These three archetypal social organs are demands of all social or community
> life. Their separate working … and the realization of this will be increasingly
> critical as we move into the future. In every community, organization, or
> institution, something of each of these three organs must be present and
> actively nurtured in some form if the community is to be healthy. If one
> is missing, or is not properly formed, then there will sooner or later be ill
> health in that community. Any one such organ can function in a healthy
> way only when the other two are also there in the community. The three can
> work separately only when they form a threefold unity. This is true for all
> communities and organizations, irrespective of in which sphere of social life
> their work lies. (p.121)

I have now begun to demonstrate how this forming of a threefold unity of three independent systems and specifically how the implementation of an explicit threefold structure was beginning to unfold at the Vancouver Waldorf School. I have also begun to define how social organizational systems reflect or are an expression of the threefolded human systems. To set the context for the continuation of the story of the unfolding of this process at the School, I want to first provide some imaginations, which I call *The Plumbing Imaginations*. These pictures are presented to further clarify the relationship between a cultural-spiritual organization and the greater cultural spiritual sphere of society, and how the specific underlying impulses or unseen forming forces that are unique to each sphere work in and through these structures and systems.

First I will review Venn diagrams that illustrate the relationship between the threefold human being and a threefold society:

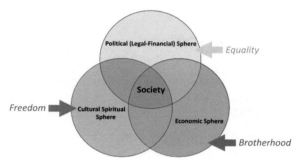

**Figure 16:** *Threefold Social Order*

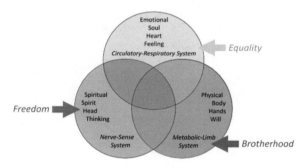

**Figure 17:** *Threefold Human Being*

These diagrams provide a picture of the relationship between the level or layer of the threefold social order and the human being as a member of that social order. They also illustrate that the forming forces behind the various aspects of the human being are the same as the impulses behind the corresponding spheres of society.

The following diagram provides a picture of a Waldorf school organization. When looking at this diagram it is important to remember that this entire threefold organization is wholly extrapolated from the Waldorf education field of the Education Branch of the cultural sphere of society. So it is in fact, a micro threefold picture taken when focused in on the macro cultural sphere of society and then again on the meso sphere of education:

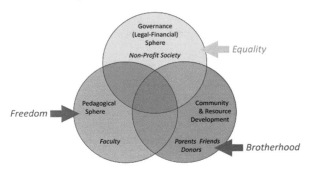

**Figure 18:** *Threefold Waldorf School*

### The impulse of freedom and the pedagogical structure of a Waldorf school.

The next diagram, the first of three Plumbing Imaginations, further illustrates these relationships between the threefold social order and the social organization of a threefold Waldorf school:

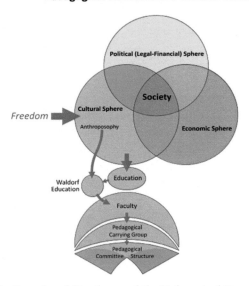

**Figure 19:** *The Impulse of Freedom and the Pedagogical Structure of a Waldorf School*

Note that the impulse for the cultural sphere of society is freedom. Education is a branch within the cultural sphere of society, and Waldorf education is a sub-category within education. The impulse for the greater cultural sphere, for education, for Waldorf education, and for the Waldorf schools is the same—*freedom*. The organization and operation of the entire school is and should rightly be driven by the impulse of freedom.

In two separate sources Steiner makes reference to the nature of the cultural-spiritual sphere of society and how important it is that it retains autonomous status with regard to its function in relationship to the other two spheres. He also highlights that education, as a sub-branch or sub-category within the cultural-spiritual sphere of society, must also maintain autonomy in its administration:

> The nature which spiritual life has assumed requires that it constitute a fully autonomous member of the social organism. The administration of education, from which all culture develops, must be turned over to the educators. Economic and political considerations should be entirely excluded from this administration. Each teacher should arrange his or her time so that [s]he can also be an administrator in his[/her] field. [S]he should be just as much at home attending to administrative matters as [s]he is in the classroom. No-one should make decisions who is not directly engaged in the educational process. ... What is experienced in the teaching process would then flow naturally into the administration. By its very nature such a system would engender competence and objectivity. (Steiner 1977, p.12)

> [T]he movement for the threefold social order strives for the complete disassociation of the educational system from government and industry. The place and function of educators within society should depend solely upon the authority of those engaged in this activity. The administration of the educational institutions, the organization of courses of instruction and their goals should be entirely in the hands of persons who themselves are *simultaneously* either teaching or otherwise productively engaged in cultural life. In each case, such persons would divide their time between actual teaching (or some other form of cultural productivity) and the administrative control of the educational system. It will be evident to anyone who can bring himself to an unbiased examination of cultural life that the peculiar vitality and energy of soul required for organizing and directing educational institutions will be called forth only in someone actively engaged in teaching or in some sort of cultural creativity. (Steiner 1985, p.75)

These references are the source of the notion that Waldorf schools—in fact educational institutions of all kinds (Cohen 2006)—must be faculty-run, or more accurately, *self-administered*. This same principle can and should be applied to the pedagogical sphere in a Waldorf school. The organizational 'nerve-sense system,' i.e., the pedagogical sphere, is the spiritual organ of a cultural-spiritual entity, for example the Vancouver Waldorf School, which is in turn part of the cultural realm of education, which is a branch of the greater cultural-spiritual sphere of society. The pedagogical sphere of a Waldorf school as the organizational spiritual organ must retain autonomy in the administration of the pedagogical business and activities of the school, just as Steiner describes that autonomy must exist in the greater cultural-spiritual sphere of society.

This can be confusing as we attempt to understand the layering and overlapping of threefolding and the working of the impulses and principles, at micro (pedagogical sphere in a Waldorf school), meso (threefolded Waldorf school) and macro levels (threefolded Society).

### The impulse of equality and the governance (legal-financial) structure of a Waldorf school

The following Plumbing Imagination provides an imagination for how the organizational 'rhythmic system' for a Waldorf school differentiates out of the cultural branch of education, Waldorf education to be specific, in the cultural sphere of society, and therefore is imbued with the impulse of that sphere, i.e., *freedom*. It also shows, however, how the impulse of equality that enters through the political (legal-financial) sphere of society overlaps and mixes with the impulse of freedom to work in the legal-financial/governance realm of the school's structure.

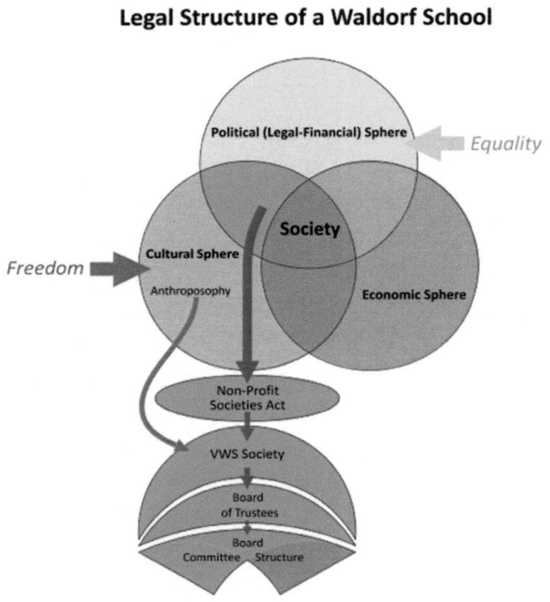

**Legal Structure of a Waldorf School**

**Figure 20:** *The Impulse of Equality and the Governance (Legal-Financial) Structure of a Waldorf School*

The impulse of *equality* for the legal structure or the organizational 'rhythmic system' of a Waldorf school comes from the place where the cultural sphere overlaps with the political (legal-financial) sphere of society. It is still imbued with the primary impulse of *freedom* and is in no way driven by or comes directly from the political (legal-financial) sphere of society. There is an overlap in the cultural sphere, and it is from that place of overlap that the school's rhythmic system gets its life-giving impulse.

*The impulse of brotherhood and the community & resource development-structure of a Waldorf school*

The following Plumbing Imagination illustrates the same principle except in relationship to the community and resource development realm of a Waldorf school. In this case, the impulse of *freedom*, as the primary impulse for every sub-sphere within a Waldorf school, mixes with the impulse of *brotherhood*. The overlap takes place between the economic sphere and the cultural sphere and that is what informs the gesture of that aspect of the school's structure.

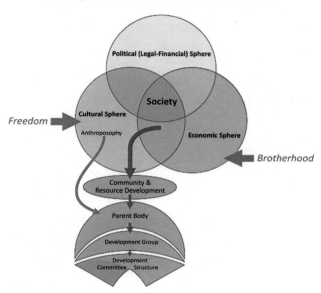

**Development Structure of a Waldorf School**

**Figure 21:** *The Impulse of Brotherhood and the Development Structure of a Waldorf School*

## Step II    Revisiting Vision, Values, Mission, Goals, Aims and Objectives

In a human being when there is an absence of or inadequate interface from the rhythmic system in the middle, between the systems at the two poles, and there is a resulting impingement of one system on another, or discontinuity between one system and another, the result is disease. In the case of impingement it can be either a hot disease such as an inflammatory condition like arthritis, or in the case of discontinuity, it can be a cold disease like sclerosis. (Huseman et al. 1982)

It is my observation and experience that organizations as living entities also show signs of 'dis-ease' when there is impingement or discontinuity between one system and another. Looking for the places of impingement in the working of one sphere on another, or where the work of one sphere was disconnected from one or both of the other two, became my modus operandi as the School was guided by the vision to manifest a living threefold organizational structure. In other words, I watched for places where either the primary driving impulse for specific work in an area was not the correct one or where there was no appropriate interconnection between one impulse and the other two. This showed up as work, activity or an initiative that was unproductive, ineffective and self-serving at best or disconnected or compartmentalized and destructive at worst, rather than functioning in service to the whole.

However, the healthy re-differentiation and creation of threefolded operating systems was not the only important focus in beginning the transformation of the School's governance and operating structure. Huseman et al. (1982) describe how a doctor, when considering the well-being of a human being, has to consider the dynamic of the three working systems in the context of the person's developmental age:

> It is necessary for the doctor to discover not only which tendency is predominant in an organism, but also how this tendency is related to the person's age, that is, to time. Man has not only a spatial form (*Raumgestalt*), but also a temporal form (*Zeitgestalt*). The action of the forces in the threefold man, as described above [in the picture of the dynamic relationship of the three human systems[45]], as well as that of the supersensible members of man's being, changes in the course of man's development. (pp.10–11)

An organization, like a human being, not only develops or manifests a dynamic threefold form in space,[46] but also develops that form over time,[47] so developmental phases become important when implementing the threefold structure. Understanding these phases could prevent attempts to force the manifestation of a form too early, or vice versa, i.e., waiting too long for a needed form.

As a decades-old organization with at that time a faculty and staff of over forty people, six buildings located on two campuses housing Early Childhood, Grade School and High School programs, with enrollment of approximately 250 children and a $1.7 million budget, it could be expected that the School was at the very least firmly in the differentiation phase or the integrative phase of development. However, it was difficult to readily discern where this School was in its overall development. It seemed that the School had been making repeated efforts to differentiate and to define a clearly articulated operating and administrative structure, but the results of these efforts were not immediately or clearly apparent. I suspect that this had been a recurring theme for many years with the School experiencing an extended transitional period between the pioneering and differentiation phases.

Schaefer (1996) calls the transitional phase the "crisis of the pioneering phase of development." (p.34) In this transitional phase the organization will experience "a loss of confidence in leadership," "a [lack of clarity] about goals and directions that at an earlier time were embodied in the [initiative] group," and a "need for a definition of responsibilities and decision-making authority." (pp.33–34) Schaefer (1996) highlights the challenge of entering the phase of differentiation: "to move from the personal, intuitive, improvising mode of a smaller pioneer organization to a more objective, clear and functional way of meeting a larger organization's [needs and] objectives." (p.35)

It appeared to me that the School was stuck in this transitional phase and had been for some time.[48] Therefore it was perpetually in crisis mode, stuck in what can be defined as the crisis of the pioneering phase, trying unsuccessfully to move through and transition into the next phase of development. The next phase would have resulted in confidence in leadership, an explicit shared direction, responsibilities clearly assigned and decision-making authority explicitly defined.

One way to begin moving through the transition is to ensure that there is a collective awareness and acceptance of guiding principles and values, mission or direction, as well as organizational goals, aims, objectives, and policies, procedures and protocols that explicitly define how individuals can contribute to manifesting the vision and achieving the mission (Broholm 1990). In the pioneering phase of development, when the initiative is small, everyone meets everyone on a regular basis and is involved in every decision, it is appropriate that the vision, values, mission and goals are implicit. (Schaefer et al. 1996) This is no longer appropriate for a larger, older organization. The risk is that the implicit guiding standards and intentions become subject to individual interpretation, and the work of individuals can stray from an intention that is the result of a truly shared vision of that which would serve the greater good to one that is misguided or self-serving.

This was the impetus for the other initial and essential recommendation made by the Mandate System Review Committee: Conduct a whole community re-envisioning process.[49] This would result in an explicit vision and statement of values, a mission statement or statement of purpose and direction, with goals, aims and objectives that would guide the emergence of the Vancouver Waldorf School's organizational identity, defining and diversifying the structure and functions, and thereby moving it through the crisis of the pioneering phase of development, through an eye of the needle, and placing it squarely into the differentiation or administrative phase of development. Here the focus could be on the differentiation process rather than always returning to the intuitive and spontaneous pioneering approach to operating, which could no longer serve or meet the needs of the larger more complex organization.

The School did have a preexisting vision statement, and it was printed in various places, but it was only a vision statement with no clearly articulated mission or goals and objectives. As far as I could determine, it had become a platitude with no real effect on the way the people conducted themselves. (Broholm 1990)

Both initial proposals from the Mandate System Review Committee were approved by the Board of Trustees. The faculty was given the green light to begin to define a Pedagogical Carrying Group to take over management of the pedagogical life of the School. I was given approval and the finances to plan a re-envisioning Community Forum event. The Community Forum Envisioning Conference took place over a day and half and was attended by fifty people, including teachers, administrative staff, parents and supporters of the Vancouver Waldorf School.[50] A committee was formed and tasked with collating the input generated at the conference. They were to develop a Vision, Values, and Mission Statement with clearly articulated Goals, Aims, and Objectives, with regular input and reporting to all stakeholders, for presentation to and final approval by the Faculty and Board of Trustees. This was completed and approved—the full statements are included in the appendices[51,52]—with one exception. The Committee did not develop a comprehensive action or long-range plan because it was apparent that there were too many gaps in the administrative and organizational structure to provide the human and financial resources needed to implement such a plan. In particular, the pedagogical realm had not yet been clearly defined. The Pedagogical Carrying Group had not yet been created and the committee structure was still the old mandate system with pedagogical committees mandated by the Board of Trustees. Despite the enthusiasm and excitement and the meaningful and clearly articulated statements that were generated out of the conference, there was still foundational work to be done before a fully developed plan could be created.

## Step III    Re-Differentiation of the Pedagogical Realm: Establishing the Organizational 'Nerve-Sense System'

There are three distinct parts or stages to the differentiation of the pedagogical realm in a Waldorf school. To understand this, it is helpful to try to look at the pedagogical realm as a whole or an entity separate from the other two realms or systems. This does not happen in reality of course because the three systems are inextricably connected, overlapped and intertwined. But for the purposes of explaining this concept, let us for now consider the pedagogical realm as a standalone entity, looking from the whole to the parts. The following diagram (p75) provides an imagination of how the pedagogical realm as a whole differentiates into three distinct yet interconnected parts.

The first step in re-differentiating the pedagogical realm and establishing the organizational 'nerve-sense system' at the Vancouver Waldorf School was to delineate the role and responsibilities of the Full Faculty Circle from the role and responsibilities of the Pedagogical (management) Carrying Group. Once these two groups were clearly differentiated, defined and functioning, the next step was to define the pedagogical committee system.

It was obvious to everyone that the Full Faculty already existed as a group because it met on a weekly basis. However, the purpose of meeting was amorphous with a mixture of study, artistic activity, oral reporting and business brought by the various school groups,

## Pedagogical Realm Threefolded

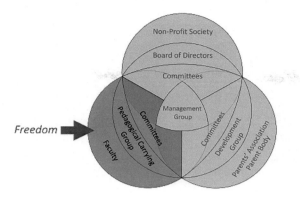

**Figure 22:** *Pedagogical Realm Threefolded*

committees, and departments. The agenda was formed by the Hub and the Faculty Chair. While there had earlier been a smaller group called the College of Teachers that carried school business, it had not been formed from the constituent group of the Full Faculty Circle utilizing a conscious and explicit differentiation process, with its own unique and clearly defined purpose, along with an equally clear purpose for the Full Faculty Circle.

The actual process of differentiating the pedagogical management group out of the body of the Full Faculty Circle, using the threefold vision, involved engaging the Full Faculty Circle in developing and approving an operating constitution for a carrying or management group—called the Pedagogical Carrying Group or PCG—to be responsible for the School's business in the pedagogical realm of activity. The Full Faculty Circle appointed a small task group to create a draft constitution. This task group created and presented many versions for input before the final constitution was approved. This constitution has evolved over time to accommodate changes in the pedagogical committee structure and other departments in the School with which the PCG interfaces, and also to reflect the refinement of processes, responsibilities, roles and authority of the PCG, the Full Faculty Circle, and the committees.[53] The Full Faculty Circle also approved a PCG membership selection criteria and protocol, which also has evolved over time.[54] The constitution and membership selection process is intended to be reviewed and amended by the Full Faculty Circle on a regular basis.

The inaugural members were officially appointed by the Full Faculty Circle, and the PCG began to meet to do the work of managing the business of the pedagogical realm of the School. Business was no longer conducted at Full Faculty meetings except if there were broad or critical issues that required input and participation of the Full Faculty Circle. The PCG and the committees now mandated by and reporting to the PCG, assumed responsibility for all pedagogical business. The pedagogical realm was supported administratively with a part-time Pedagogical Administrator[55] in addition to and with a different role than the Full Faculty Chair.[56] Once the PCG was established, it assumed responsibility for the hiring, evaluation and termination of the Pedagogical Administrator. The role of the Pedagogical Administrator was redefined to administer to the needs of the PCG and pedagogical business, support faculty in the classroom, and liaise with the Ministry of Education for curricular and program-related issues.[57] As of June 2010, the PCG membership included the chairs of the main pedagogical committees, the Full Faculty Chair, a full-time Pedagogical Administrator, the Administrator, the Director of Development, and representation from the three faculties in the School— Early Childhood, Grade School, and High School. The PCG is responsible for mandating and appointing faculty members to committees—all faculty members on a three-quarters time equivalency and above are required to serve on a committee.

The task-related responsibilities of the Full Faculty circle are:
- appoint the members of the PCG,
- review and renew the PCG constitution,
- appoint faculty members to the three faculty-appointed Board of Trustees positions,
- appoint faculty members to the Faculty Support Fund Committee, and
- nominate and select the Full Faculty Chair.

Also, over and above the specific *tasks and responsibilities* of the Full Faculty Circle is the *raison d'être* of the Full Faculty Circle, which is to maintain a connection to the spiritual impulse of the School and Waldorf education through study, artistic activity, sharing of classroom and other inspirational pedagogical experiences, biography work, and conversations or dialogue around critical or significant issues that could affect the School's ability to manifest or adhere to the School's vision. Initially, the Full Faculty Circle met once a week and the faculty departments—Early Childhood, Grade School, and High School—also met once a week to deal with specific departmental business. The committees met weekly immediately after the Full Faculty meeting, and the PCG met weekly following the committee meetings.[58] As part of its inaugural work, the PCG immediately began to review and renew the educational programs, engaged a team of outside evaluators to conduct a whole school evaluation of every teacher in every program, and initiated the final step in the differentiation of the pedagogical realm by dissolving and restructuring the pedagogical committee structure.

The pedagogical committees that were in place under the old mandate system before the restructuring began, included Hiring, Professional Development and Mentoring, Pedagogy, Health and Safety, Workload, Evaluation, Festivals, and Issues Management. Each of these committees was responsible and accountable to the Board of Trustees, with reporting requirements through the central Hub Coordinating Committee. However, the Hub Coordinating Committee had no decision-making power and no authority to take any action other than to collate and generate reports and make recommendations to the Faculty and Board of Trustees. On the other hand the PCG's newly designed pedagogical committee system was based on threefold principles. The PCG had full authority, as vested in it by its Full Faculty constituent group, with regard to all pedagogical business and committees—the PCG is the regulatory, mediating and coordinating body in the *pedagogical* realm. The PCG established three large committees:

- **Human Resources Committee**, which has three sub-categories, including:

  - hiring and termination,

  - mentoring and professional development, and

  - evaluation

- **Programs and Curriculum Development Committee**,

- **Practical Needs Committee**.[59]

These committees then sub-divided into task groups (sometimes with only one person responsible for a given task) and took up the work in the three categories. Regular reports and policy and program recommendations were brought to the PCG by the Chair of each committee, and in turn, new tasks and assignments flowed from the PCG back through the Chair to the committee. The implementation of this committee structure completed the most important and significant aspect of the differentiation process of the pedagogical realm of the Vancouver Waldorf School.[60] Ongoing refinement, review, and policy, procedure and protocol development must now continue, the most important of which is to ensure that there are adequate and effective input loops and information flow from the group responsible for managing and doing all pedagogically related work, to the Board of Trustees—essential if the Board of Trustees is to be effective in its function in the middle.

The following diagrams are imaginations or pictures to help connect the practical differentiation and the creation of the organizational 'nerve-sense system' with the conceptual principles of threefolding, and the notion of threefolding upon threefolding upon threefolding. At this point, as the differentiation at a meso-level of the school structure—the pedagogical realm—becomes visible as part of a threefold structure, with threefold impulses and gestures, it can be helpful to compare it to the macro-level of the greater school organization, and to the corresponding picture of society. This can help with understanding how the different impulses and gestures are at work and can also provide an understanding of why it can become confusing and why, for example, the PCG could think that it is supposed to be carrying the regulatory mediating and coordinating function for the whole school[61] rather than exclusively for the Pedagogical Realm.

*Figure 23* illustrates the specific dynamic of the Pedagogical Realm as a separate or, rather, as a unique dynamic which actually exists within the greater dynamic of the whole. *Figure 24* is an illustration of the dynamic of the whole organization within which the dynamic of the Pedagogical Realm exists.

Dynamic of the Pedagogical Realm
PCG
Full Faculty Circle
Pedagogical Committees
Pedagogical Administrator
Mediating / Coordinating
Pedagogical 'Nerve-Sense' Function
Pedagogical 'Rhythmic' Function
Pedagogical 'Metabolic' Function
Connect to and Nurture Spiritual Vision
Oversee, Approve, Administer to Pedagogical Policy
Limbs or Will of the Pedagogical Realm

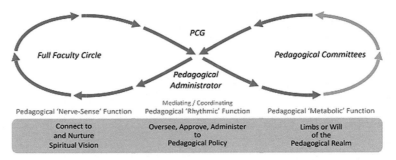

**Figure 23:** *Dynamic of the Pedagogical Realm compared to the Dynamic of the Whole*

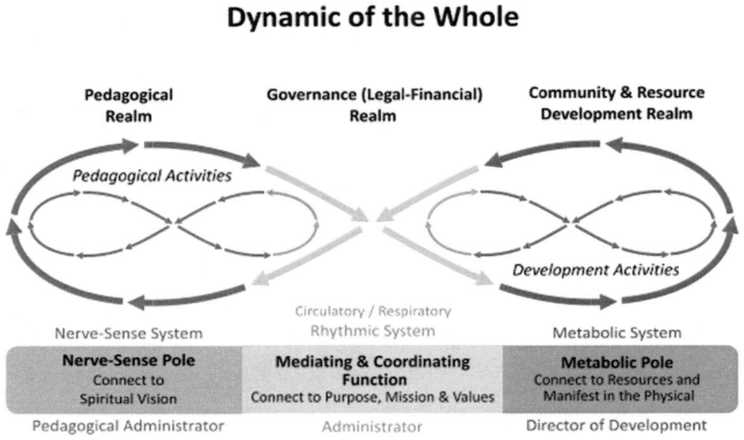

Dynamic of the Whole
Pedagogical Realm
Governance (Legal-Financial) Realm
Community & Resource Development Realm
Pedagogical Activities
Development Activities
Circulatory / Respiratory
Nerve-Sense System
Rhythmic System
Metabolic System
Nerve-Sense Pole
Connect to Spiritual Vision
Mediating & Coordinating Function
Connect to Purpose, Mission & Values
Metabolic Pole
Connect to Resources and Manifest in the Physical
Pedagogical Administrator
Administrator
Director of Development

**Figure 24:** *Dynamic of the Whole*

The following diagram illustrates how at the micro-level of committee structure there is a threefolding that can evolve as it did in the pedagogical committee structure:

Pedagogical Committee Structure Threefolded
Human Resources Committee
PCG
Programs & Curriculum Development Committee
Practical Needs Committee

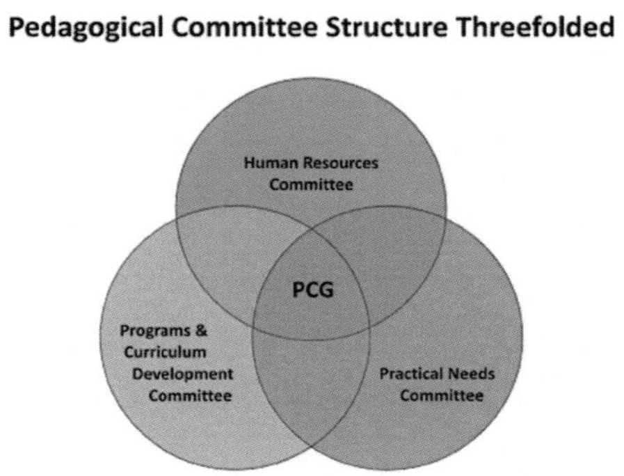

**Figure 25:** *Pedagogical Committee Structure Threefolded*

Finally, the following diagram illustrates how a committee can even threefold further into three distinct aspects with impulses that correspond to the basic threefold principles:

**Human Resources Committee Structure Threefolded**

**Figure 26:** *Human Resources Committee Structure Threefolded*

## Step IV    Re-Differentiation of the Governance (Legal-Financial) Realm: Establishing the Organizational 'Rhythmic System'

The next logical step in the reorganization and the re-differentiation of the Vancouver Waldorf School systems would be to have gone through a similar process in the legal-financial and governance sphere of activity as was detailed above in the pedagogical sphere. Unfortunately, this process did not happen at this point. Some restructuring, re-differentiation and redefinition did take place in this realm, as will be described below in the sub-section entitled *Consolidating, Redefining and Expanding Legal-Financial Functions*; however, it was incomplete and chronologically not consistent with the development of the correlating human rhythmic system. I believe this was a misstep in the intentional facilitation of the Vancouver Waldorf School's development and it had consequences, which will be explained in Step VI below. What actually did happen next is explained now in the following Step V.

## Step V    Reorganization of Administration

The introduction of the Board of Trustees-managed mandate system was a process of consolidation and re-differentiation, a kind of regrouping that ultimately paved the way for the implementation of the threefold structure that was soon to follow. In a similar way the consolidation of Administration was necessary and intended to pave the way for a re-differentiation using the threefold vision and principles.

Consolidating and restructuring Administration presented the most difficult challenges to date because it involved the dissolution of entrenched committees and administrative positions staffed by long-time employees and volunteers who were attached to their work and had become identified by their work by virtue of a phenomena I will call the "cult of personality,"[62] a term coined and described by Walter Daroshin in a report to the Board of Trustees. Daroshin said that underpaid staff or, conversely, under-resourced work can lead existing staff and volunteers to work and contribute beyond what can reasonably be expected in a specific position or context. While this creates the possibility for a tremendous amount of work to get done by a small number of people, it can also result in work being done out of a sense of obligation or guilt. The undefined workload can start to define the person rather than the work being explicitly defined by the position. The tendency for people to sacrifice their own needs in the interests of the needs of the organization in this way is a manifestation of the Basic Sociological Law formulated by Steiner and reiterated by Schaefer (n.d.[63]):

> At the beginning of culture, humanity strives to create social arrangements in which the interests of the individual are sacrificed for the interest of the whole. Later developments lead to a gradual freeing of the individual from the interests of the community and to an unfolding of individual needs and capacities. (p.4)

Schaefer indicates, based on his experience working with organizations, that this social law holds true. In fact, in the pioneering phase of development, in order to become established the organization requires the energy of individuals and sacrifice of individual interests, and it is not until the later phases of development that the organization is more able to respond to the needs of individual members. The cult of personality phenomenon, coined for use in this context by Daroshin, is a result of an organization's remaining too long in the pioneering phase of development and ultimately not healthy because the needs of the individual rather than the needs of the organization are defining the work and because the individual is being defined by the work, which can lead to working out of obligation rather than giving freely.

In a more mature organization the needs of individuals are considered and met by intentional differentiation and diversification. These are both elements of the administrative or differentiation phase of development and lead to a clear ordering and an explicit definition of workloads, job descriptions, and committee mandates. This means that employees and volunteers engage in "extraordinary activity out of free will"[64] and the cult of personality is replaced, as Daroshin points out, by "institutional memory,"[65] which is an appropriate approach for an administrative phase of development.

It became apparent that changes were needed to the form, structure and positions of the administrative unit in order to improve the quality of support provided by the administrative staff and to further develop and unfold the threefold organizational structure. There was a history of tension between Administrative staff and Faculty. With the threefolding living systems vision and the inherent principles now clearly placed at the foundation driving the School's growth and development, it was important to bring the form, structure and positions of the Administrative unit into alignment with this vision. This process involved consolidation, redifferentiation, definition, and expansion. The remnant non-pedagogical committees still in place from the Board of Trustees-mandated mandate system were dissolved along with four administrative positions. This included dissolving the Building, Finance, Fundraising, and Issues Management Committees, along with the positions of Enrollment Coordinator, Registrar, Finance Manager and Accounting Assistant. Other positions that had become a catch-all for work that did not naturally belong anywhere else were reconfigured.

The administrative staff members in Waldorf schools, as in most organizations, are often viewed as a collective separate entity that possesses management, supervisory or decision-making policy-setting authority. In fact, in the Waldorf school movement a commonly adopted threefold governance model places Administration in the structure as one of the three folds or realms next to the pedagogical realm and the legal-financial-governance realm. This structure leads to development of tension between the Administration and the Faculty. Contrary to this approach, in the threefold living systems vision of governance for a Waldorf school, the members of the administrative staff exist to administer to the organization in service to the educational and social mission of Waldorf education and do NOT function or hold a place as one of the governing bodies in the structure. Rather, each position is established and defined based on the impulse that the position serves. In addition, the administrators and managers must be or become transformational servant leaders. A study on transformational servant leaders that was the result of a servant leadership research roundtable says the following:

> Transformational leaders and servant leaders are visionaries, generate high levels of trust, serve as role models, show consideration for others, delegate responsibilities, empower followers, teach, communicate, listen, and influence followers. ... Transformational leadership "occurs when leaders broaden and elevate the interests of [staff and] employees, when they generate awareness and acceptance of the purposes and mission of the group, and when they stir ... [others] to look beyond their own self-interest for the good of the group." (Bass 1990b, p.21) Bass (1990a) stipulates that this transcending beyond self-interest is for the "group, organization, or society." (p.53) In essence, transformational leadership is a process of building commitment to organizational objectives and then empowering followers to accomplish those objectives. (Patterson, Russell, Stone 2003, p.2)

This kind of transformational leadership engages others, in particular the educators and staff, within a school context, so that the wisdom of the people working in the organization is accessible and best utilized in service to the organizational objectives. A top-down concentration of power flowing from the Administration and/or administrators to the rest of the organization does not facilitate this kind of transformational leadership and, in fact, leads to the existence of tension and conflict between the administration and the faculty. Transformational servant leadership is particularly important in a revolutionary cultural organization like a Waldorf school.[66]

The carrying or management groups in the respective spheres of activity develop and set, or at least approve, policies developed (or sometimes recommended by staff) to guide the work of the staff. This ensures that the gesture of a particular administrative position is clear, the work becomes service-oriented, and the wisdom of the individuals is utilized. For example, a Bursar and a Bookkeeper work in service to one aspect of the middle realm. That aspect is expressed in the formation of a Finance Department, which constitutes the organizational 'respiratory sub-system' of the broader organizational 'rhythmic system.'[67] The Finance Department staff members report and are accountable to the Administrator, who in turn works in service to the broader Governance (Legal-Financial) realm, which embodies the whole middle organizational 'rhythmic system.' The School Administrator reports and is accountable to the Board of Trustees, which is in turn appointed (or elected) by and is accountable to the School Society.[27] The same is true of employees in the other two realms but in relationship to the management staff and groups in their respective realms.

Following is a chart which, while not exactly an accurate depiction because it is two dimensional, represents the overlapping, interconnected and interfacing three dimensional spheres, which in reality are hierarchical in a living systems[68] sense versus a traditional top-down sense. It is presented to clarify the service-oriented threefold approach to administrative

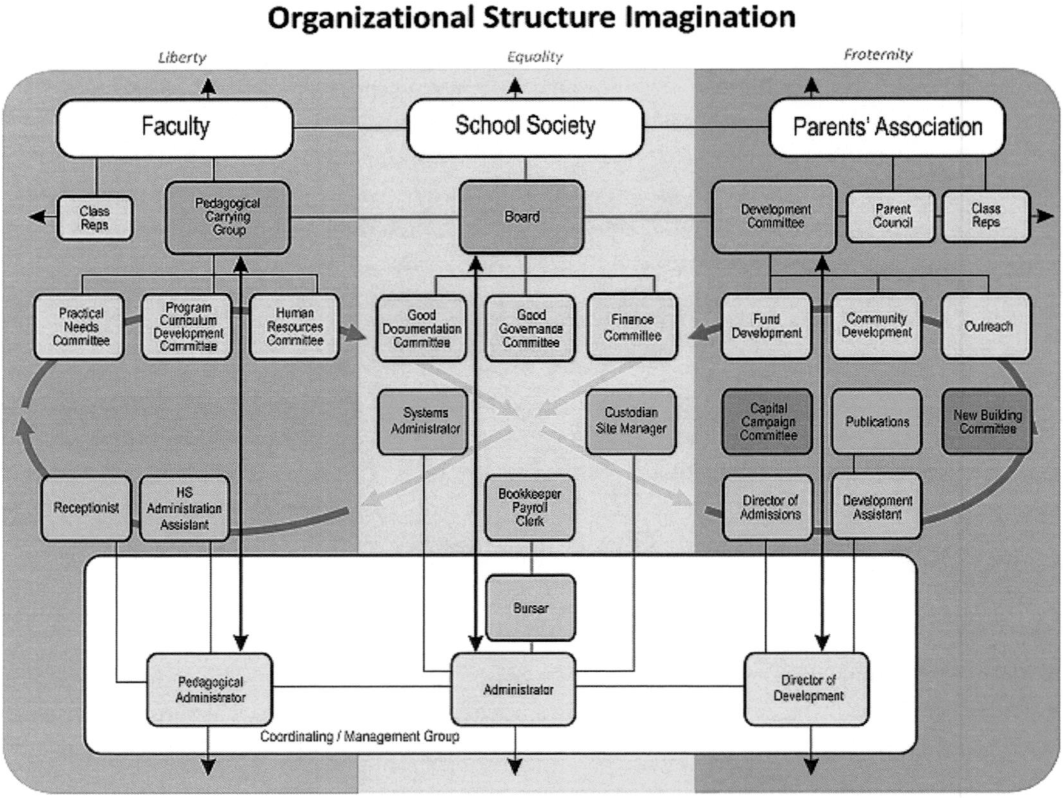

**Figure 27:** *Organizational Structure Imagination*

positions and work. This chart is partially based on how the Vancouver Waldorf School and its Administration differentiated and partly based on the direction I intended to guide its differentiation had I had the opportunity to continue to develop the prototype at the Vancouver Waldorf School. (The process of differentiation was not completed at the School at the time I documented the practical research, and of course how it actually would manifest would be dependent on a collaborative process. So the chart in Figure 27 is a theoretical example only.)

## Step VI    Differentiation of the Community & Resource Development Realm: Establishing an Organizational 'Metabolic System'

### Creating a director of development position and an executive group.

One of the gaps that existed in Administration and not reflected in the previous chart, became apparent very early on when reviewing the Goals[69] document that came out of the re-envisioning work. There was inadequate and poorly organized staffing in the realm of community and resource development. Therefore, in addition to recognizing the need to give authority for the management of the pedagogical life of the School to the Faculty and its newly established Pedagogical Carrying Group, Pedagogical Administrator and committees, another major step the Board of Trustees took was to approve a recommendation to hire a Director of Development to oversee the activities in the realm of Community & Resource Development, the School's 'metabolic system.'

A Director of Development was hired to immediately begin carrying tasks related to the activities of community and resource development, even though there was not yet an official department to manage. Activities, positions and groups had already been in place in this realm prior to the restructuring and consisted of an Enrollment Coordinator, a Building Committee, a Fundraising Committee that hosted an annual auction, and the Class Parents Group that carried and hosted the School's main community fundraising event, the Christmas Fair. Outreach was primarily carried by the Enrollment Coordinator in the form of attending enrollment fairs, hosting open houses, and responding to inquiries. Advertising was arranged by the part-time Registrar, in between completing registration paperwork, with a limited budget and no design, promotion or public relations training or expertise. That was the extent of community and resource development activity in the School. There was no central coordination and no clearly defined or explicitly articulated department. For this reason, at the same time as the Director of Development was hired, the Board of Trustees approved the hiring of an interim employee who was assigned the task of designing a department that would serve the needs of the School in the realm of Community & Resource Development.

Walter Daroshin, a long-time parent, trustee, and the School's Treasurer at the time, took on the temporary position and was given six months to prepare recommendations for creating a community and resource development function for the School. He engaged in six months of intensive exploration, research and analysis of the internal workings of the Vancouver Waldorf School, including extensive case study, many interviews and conversations, and daily participation in the day-to-day operations of the School. While Daroshin was the one who synthesized the information gathered from the experiences that he had, the recommendations were a reflection of the influence and input of many community members.

The original purpose of this work was to provide a roadmap to implement a functioning Community and Resource (financial and human) Development program within the existing structure. As the work progressed Daroshin realized what I also already knew: The existing structure did not reflect the values and ideals upon which the curriculum is built—the same principles that are reflected in a living threefold organizational structure. And he concluded that simply adding a development function would not accomplish the desired results. It became clear that it was necessary that we make changes to the administrative structure and lay a foundation for a Community & Resource Development department, which would provide an organizational 'metabolic system' that would hopefully and literally 'feed' the organization, providing financial and other resources that would enable it to grow, expand and improve.

The Board of Trustees approved the establishment of an Executive Group[70] to oversee and facilitate the effective day-to-day operations of the School, as well as to oversee the restructuring of the administrative unit to reflect the vision, values, mission and goals[71] that were established by the re-envisioning process. This would bring the structure of the administrative unit in line with the living threefolding vision and the inherent principles which were now at the foundation of and driving the School's growth and development. The newly-established Executive Group was comprised of the Pedagogical Administrator, the School Administrator, the newly-hired Director of Development and Daroshin. Additional pedagogical staff and/ or Trustees were invited to participate when specific insight or expertise was needed. This Group became central in facilitating both the restructuring and the growth and development of the School's administrative unit and its staff. It contributed to the effective day-to-day operation of the School and addressed or directed arising issues to the appropriate group for resolution. Many issues of the past reappeared as a result of now having somewhere for them to be resolved. The Executive Group became a juggling act for issues and functioned primarily in the role of directing traffic by referring issues to the appropriate group for resolution or by establishing appropriate task groups to resolve issues.

### Consolidating, redefining and expanding development functions.

The Director of Development, while well qualified to oversee development work, recognized that there was not a department, nor much in the way of development activities, to manage, and instead of taking up management of the non-existent department, she engaged in the process of working with the Executive Group to consolidate what was already in place and re-form and establish a Community & Resource Development Department. This Department would function as the School's 'metabolic system' and nurture the social life of the community, supply the funds and human resources needed to sustain the organizational life and the development and delivery of the curriculum and educational programs. It is what allows the School to pay staff, build buildings, find students, and strengthen programs—in short, to fulfill the vision and mission. Without an adequate development function, one that is appropriate given the current developmental stage, the organization would eventually and fairly quickly find its way to certain death because it can only live on grace and the sacrifice of the pioneers for a limited time.

The reorganization of the existing department resulted in the dissolution of two part-time positions—Enrollment Coordinator and Registrar. A full-time Director of Admissions position was created and filled, and a part-time Publications and Design Specialist and part-time Outreach and Admissions Assistant were hired. Eventually these latter two part-time positions were amalgamated and filled by one full-time person. These changes to staffing in the development realm were accompanied by a whirlwind of other changes, including a redesign of all promotional and enrollment materials and packages—new letterhead, brochures, ads, and an entirely redesigned web site, all of which were professional, modern, beautiful, fresh and appealing.

The Parent Handbook and the weekly information Bulletin were updated. The enrollment and admissions processes and protocols were streamlined, resulting in a professional and user-friendly interface as well as providing clarification of the points of entry for applying families. The tuition and fees structure[72] was redesigned, using the guiding principle that every child's tuition and fees should support every other child's Waldorf education—shifting from the class-centric way fees were structured in the past to a community-centric approach. A new Parent Council structure[73] was designed to augment the already existing Class Parents Group.

A Fund Development Program, which had been launched prior to the Director of Development's hiring and then put on the back burner due to lack of human resources to manage it, was resurrected and relaunched. With a dynamic, experienced and qualified Director of Development in place and the long awaited and much needed 'metabolic system' beginning to form, a short-term plan with a clear goal to strengthen the admissions and enrollment activities and increase and stabilize enrollment was created. The Director of Development recognized that this is the life blood of all schools, allowing for growth, strengthening of programs, paying teachers and staff adequately, and fulfilling the mission as a Waldorf school. Plans were made to expand the plan for the longer term future, and define goals and objectives in the broader development realm such as building and site development, promotion and advertising, fundraising, community development, alumni program and more. The Community & Resource

Development Department was just starting to become established as an integral part of the organizational structure. However, there were still not enough human resources to carry all of the work, even with the changes to the Community & Resource Development Department staffing.

Funds invested in the Community & Resource Development Department are not funds that take away from salaries or the Pedagogical Department, even though some might perceive it that way. Funds carefully invested in the Community & Resource Development Department, in programs staffed and run by qualified and skilled employees will come back in the form of organizational economic and financial health, in balanced budgets and positive cash flow, increases in spending budgets in the pedagogical realm, and increases in salaries and benefits. Paradoxically, growth and increased resources in the pedagogical realm in the form of increased teaching staff, increases in salary, increments, professional development funds and other resources, and improvements to the facility and programs correspond with an increase in size and scope of the Community & Resource Development Department and activities. The very fact that a Community & Resource Development Department was—albeit tentatively—established, almost immediately produced tangible results in the form of strengthened enrollment and increased retention, which led to increased revenue and resources. The introduction of the organizational 'metabolic system' called the Community & Resource Development Department, in conjunction with the changes to the structure and the pedagogical sphere, led to a much stronger economic and sustainable financial base.[74]

The main purpose behind all of the changes to this point was to transform the Vancouver Waldorf School as an organization. Ultimately the education would be the best that it could be through the introduction of order, healthy processes, procedures, protocol, and leadership in a facility that supports the education and with faculty and staff who are adequately remunerated, thereby freeing their highest capacities to work with the children. The one and only vision was to accomplish this by acknowledging the organization as a living entity and by implementing living systems using the guidance of the principles which are at the heart of Steiner's body of research and the spiritual vision of the threefold human being. The result was the emergence of a threefold structure that engaged people with adequate skills, knowledge and attitudes who took up leadership roles in their realms of responsibility.[75] At this point in the School's development, there was leadership effectively differentiated horizontally across and through the organization by virtue of the governance structure, which opened the possibility for future leaders to step up and step in. It was certainly not a fait accompli because a living organization is always in a state of change, responding to its environment, which is appropriate, albeit process intensive, and is what will ultimately keep the organization healthy and not likely to fall prey to the cult of personality.

## Step VII    Consolidating, redefining and expanding legal-financial functions

In the past, development and community development activities were conducted in an ad hoc way with various funds and accounts established outside of the School's accounting and administrative oversight, with money coming from wherever it could be begged, borrowed or scraped. There was no official development department, no staff, and limited development activities and budget. Professional development activities for teachers and staff were funded by virtue of a separate Fair Society established to keep this kind of funding outside of the School accounts. The collection of funds in class kitties or accounts was done so that any accumulation of funds for and spending on supplies, class expenses and field trips could be kept separate from the School operations. Spending of any kind was kept under careful restriction to keep the *per student operating cost* (PSOC) low in order to qualify for government funding. The Ministry of Education has a cap on the *per student cost* of delivering education as part of the formula used to distribute funds to independent schools.

Part of the process of transforming the School's finance department was to develop a system of budgeting and accounting that is in alignment with the principles and a reflection of how the School operates as a threefold organization. Consequently, the chart of accounts was set up as a threefold system. Further, we believed that we needed to work from the whole to the parts and eliminate the compartmentalized, fragmented and 'cup-half-empty' nature of revenue generation and spending. We set out to shift the poverty mentality that had been a part of the culture for so long and replace it with the vision of abundance that would serve the mission of Waldorf education.

In order to consolidate the School accounting, we closed thirty-plus bank accounts that were in various individual's or function's names. We were confident that, by establishing a system of accounting that clearly defined the operating expenses as separate from extra-curricular and community and resource development expenses, we could keep our actual PSOC below the Ministry's ceiling amount, function from a holistic abundance perspective, and begin to nurture the community life, build the development department, and spend money on promotions, events, pedagogical development and other activities that would ultimately enrich and improve the well-being of the organization. We established this new system under the guidance of our auditor and with the support of the Systems Administrator.[76]

In the first year of operating with this system, we spent funds as needed on new development activities and improvements in other areas and on many extra one-time pedagogical development activities to give the entire organization a boost of much-needed resources and nourishment. We ended the year with a large deficit in spending on operations and on development. The next year we leveled the spending again, without incurring the one-time extra expenses, conducted a reasonably successful Annual Giving Campaign and received some large donations from individuals who were beginning to see the improvements to the organization and wanted to support further growth. All of this helped us make it through the second year with a much smaller spending deficit. At the same time we saw a significant increase in enrollment and retention. The year-end audit involved some very tense and intense conversations, presentations, and careful and detailed documentation. The result was that we were able to successfully justify spending on community and resource development expenses as non-essential to the delivery of the education. Therefore these expenses were exempt from the PSOC calculations and we received the highest level of government funding in that year.[77]

The detailed documentation and reports for the auditor secured future government funding because the auditor acknowledged that the community and resource development activities were in fact extra-curricular and therefore could be justifiably excluded from the PSOC. There was a clear structure for identifying and classifying these expenses by virtue of how they are posted into the accounting system. There was no longer a need to be restricted by fear of exceeding the PSOC limit or to compartmentalize spending and fundraising, i.e., create separate bank accounts with funds intended to cover the costs of the non-curricular items. This meant we could now run our organization with complete transparency, without nonsensical bureaucratic restrictions and, at the same time, receive more financial support from the government. We had turned a significant corner: We were spending and investing more in improving all aspects of organizational life and receiving more in return, while significantly increasing enrollment and decreasing attrition.

This was significant in itself, but there was something else that was also different from past years. Previously, the receipt of the highest level of funding was depended upon to pay basic operating costs and keep the School out of a $160,000+ spending shortfall position. Instead, now the extra funding was just that—extra. With a significant increase in enrollment and stabilized retention coupled with careful planning and budgeting, we generated a positive cash flow and year-end surplus with funding at the highest level secured. Also, unlike other years, we qualified for the highest level of funding NOT as a result of tightened spending and a poverty mentality but because of increased enrollment and stabilized retention. Most importantly it was because of *increased* spending on all of the community, resource, and pedagogical development activities, showing a very clear shift to abundance mentality.

The only way to guarantee to continue to receive the highest level of funding was to continue to invest in the Community & Resource Development Department because high enrollment is the only sustainable, viable means of meeting the Ministry's per student operating cost. In fact, with full enrollment the School would not have to worry about the PSOC—it would take care of itself, with receipt of the highest level of funding assured.

With the increase in funding, the Board of Trustees and the Pedagogical Carrying Group had to decide how to spend the extra funds. With careful planning and spending and with continued development activity, the School would be able to maintain the PSOC at current levels and continue to receive the grant with the highest level of funding. This meant that despite the fact that most spending on pedagogical items and salaries increased the PSOC, there was still some room for spending in these areas. Discussions ensued with the Human Resources Committee, the Board Treasurer and the Administrator. It was decided that the first priority was to change the salary increment system to move the range of salary towards a system on par with remuneration for teachers and staff in the public school system. An increment system was designed to be implemented over the next few years with the intention of taking the School in this more equitable direction.

The Executive Group, in conjunction with the Pedagogical Carrying Group, also created a list of spending priority areas for consideration in the budgeting process. The budget group included the three Pedagogical Administrators,[78] the Treasurer, and the Administrator, with systems assistance from the Systems Administrator. Careful planning was necessary with strategic spending because in order to remain a school that qualifies for the highest level of funding and continue to receive that grant from the government, we still had to monitor the spending on PSOC expenses. It was necessary to continue to strengthen the development activities so that retention and enrollment would continue to rise to a level where the PSOC maximum no longer impinged on the ability to meet pedagogical need.[79] The other extremely important step in moving forward was to expand the Community & Resource Development Department's scope of work and institute a reliable fund-development program to provide revenue beyond what could be secured through tuition and the government education grants. This is the only way that the School could increase salaries to an acceptable level on par with the public school sector. The implementation of the new salary grid and increment system was scaled so that the increased cost could be met by the current level of revenue generation. The intention was to implement it at a rate of 100% when a successful fund development program was able to generate adequate revenue to make this possible.

A cultural organization, like a school, does not exist for the purpose of creating a product or service that would ultimately generate revenue for the benefit of its owners, who could then create and sell more product or services that would generate more revenue (Spence 1999, Finser 2007). Rather, cultural organizations are intended to nurture the cultural-spiritual life of human beings, ultimately growing human capacities. In Steiner's view, and in the threefold social order that he hoped would one day manifest, the economic sphere of society was intended to support the cultural-spiritual sphere, which would in turn result in human beings with greater capacities, which would contribute to a stronger economic life and ultimately a stronger society—and so the cycle was intended to continue (Finser 2007). The premise behind this is based on what Steiner called the Fundamental Social Law:

> The well-being of a community of cooperatively working human beings
> is the greater the less individuals demand the proceeds of their work for

themselves or, in other words, the more they make over these proceeds to their co-workers and the more their needs are met not by their own work but from that of others.[80]

Schaefer describes this Law as "complex and awkwardly phrased" but goes on to say that it is "concerned with motives, suggesting that when labor is a commodity and self-interest becomes the motive force of economic activity, suffering, poverty, and want are the result."[81]

The following diagram illustrates at a societal level the dynamic of the three spheres of activity:

## Transformation of Money into Human Capacities

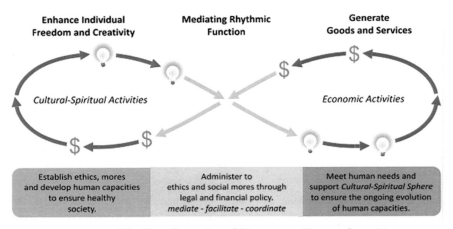

**Figure 28:** *The Transformation of Money into Human Capacities*

Unfortunately, in most cases, economic organizations produce goods and services, not to meet the needs of society, but rather to fill the pocketbooks of the owners, and hence the motive of self-interest is inevitable. In order to compensate for this and to adhere to the principle of the cultural realm—contributing positive human capacities to the betterment of society—the cultural realm of society has to find ways to engage the economic sphere in contributing to and supporting cultural-spiritual life and activities.

In a Waldorf school this means securing donations by finding ways to connect those who are engaged in economic activity to the school's mission so that they are motivated to support the school through their donations of financial, physical and human resources. This will in turn enable the school to deliver an education that builds positive human physical, social-emotional, and intellectual capacities—in particular the capacities of social skills, social sensitivity, and social understanding. Waldorf graduates will go out into the world and contribute to a stronger economic life and a better society. This is another aspect of the transformative, tempering nature of the cultural-spiritual sphere of society, one that will naturally be supported when society is structured based on the living systems threefold principles.

In the absence of conscious working with living systems threefold principles at a societal level, what a Waldorf school can and must do, and what Steiner hoped would happen, is to engage the economic sphere in forming collaborative relationships that support education. In order for this to happen, companies, organizations and business men and women must be engaged in the mission of Waldorf education and be inspired to contribute by giving gifts of money, goods, and human resources that will enable the delivery of the education. This happened with the first Waldorf school, The Free Waldorf School. Emil Molt as the patron provided the economic support, both personally and through the factory where he was the director. This created an essential source of funds for the school's operation. (Steiner 1998) Steiner also expected and hoped for a regular source of support from the economic sphere of society when the original Waldorf School Association was established with the sole purpose of raising funds for the school, and with the establishment of an association of businesses with a mission to contribute substantial revenue from the sale of new products and inventions to Waldorf education. (Molt 1991, Lamb 2007)

By designing and implementing effective accounting, reporting, budgeting and distribution of funds processes, the Finance Department of the Vancouver Waldorf School, which is in essence a sub-department of the School's larger middle organizational 'rhythmic system,' had been reorganized to enable it to better access government funds, and to appropriately and equitably distribute those funds. The funds that came through the development activities of enrolling new students (gifts of tuition[82]), fundraising activities, and donations were also processed by the Finance Department and its new effective systems, and were appropriately accounted for and equitably distributed. This reorganization of the Finance Department's systems and protocols was one step in re-differentiating the middle Governance (Legal-Financial) realm, and thus one step towards defining the organizational 'rhythmic system' had been successfully executed. The Finance Department, as a sub-system within the broader organizational 'rhythmic system,' in essence could be seen as the organizational 'respiratory system,' forming part of and functioning in service to the organizational 'rhythmic system' as a whole.[83]

This limited step in reforming and differentiating the middle realm—the organizational 'rhythmic system'—resulted in more effective financial management, with the beginnings of the establishment of clear legal-financial policies and procedures. This effectiveness was apparent despite the fact that the Finance Department itself was still not fully formed or differentiated, as there was no qualified employee assigned to the role of Bursar.[84] Furthermore, this department as such, even with supportive and collaborative connection to the School's operations through the School Administrator,[85] could do only so much in accessing and maximizing the effective uses of the funds that were available to the School. The amount of revenue generated was and is always dependent on the programs, activities and effectiveness of the School's organizational 'metabolic system,' the Community & Resource Development Department. And because cultural organizations do not, nor are they supposed to, generate their own revenue, the creation and ongoing growth and development of a school's metabolic system is critical to the school's effective operation.

The Vancouver Waldorf School made a tremendous amount of progress in doing just that, and one can actually see it when looking at the organizational structure at the time just before I was hired—BEFORE the vision of a threefolded governance structure was implemented (see Figure 29)—as compared to what existed at this critical point in time after the restructuring was almost complete (see Figure 30):

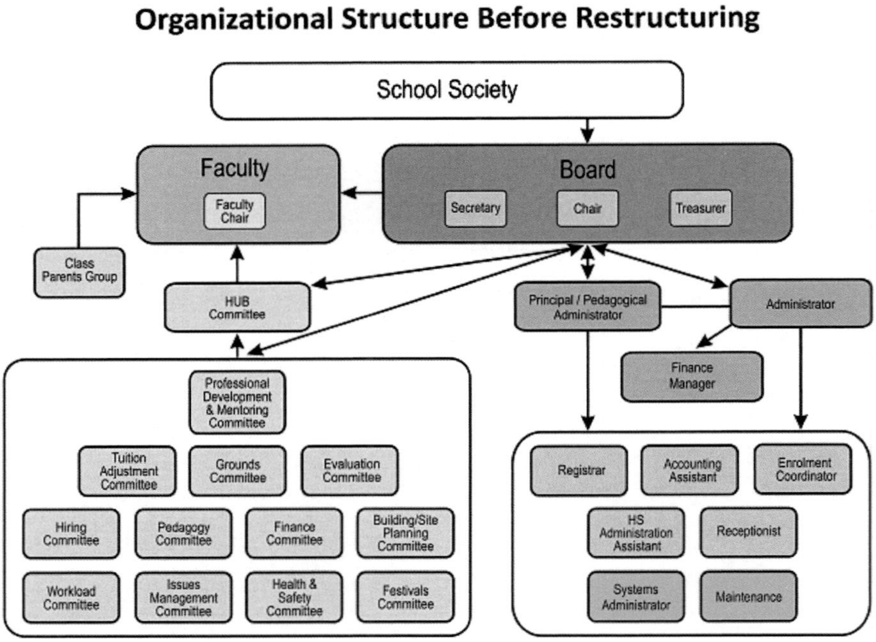

## Organizational Structure Before Restructuring

**Figure 29:** *Organizational Structure before Restructuring*

What was needed now was for the School's newly established 'metabolic system,' the Community & Resource Development Department, to expand its scope of work and develop ways of engaging individuals, organizations and businesses from the economic realm of society in the mission of the Vancouver Waldorf School. A regular source of revenue, over and above the gifts of tuition and the grants, needed to be secured for expansion, improvements, and especially to be able to remunerate teachers and staff such that their human needs are adequately met and so that they are freed for teaching and contributing to the pedagogical development of the School.

# Organizational Structure

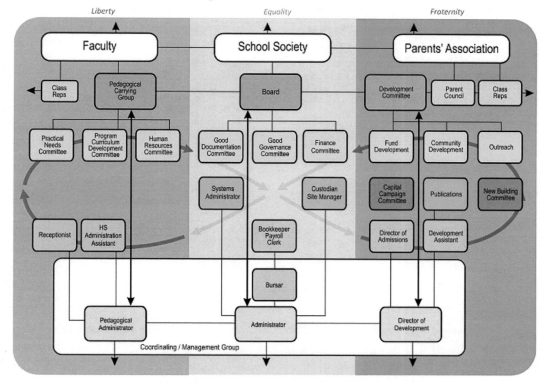

**Figure 30:** *Organizational Structure after Restructuring*

Instead, what happened next appears to take the School down a path that is a departure from manifesting the vision of a living systems threefold structure with unshakable guiding principles that would ultimately result in continued ongoing health and positive growth and development.

The Director of Development was on a positive path in terms of laying down a foundation and planning for the future, in particular through defining goals and objectives in the broader development realm, such as establishing a Development Carrying Group or Committee to manage the tasks and activities of that realm (yet to be fully assembled), building and site development, promotion and advertising, fund development program, community development, and volunteer and alumni programs. The Legal-Financial Department's systems and procedures had been reorganized to best facilitate and administer to the equitable and appropriate distribution of the resources that were to be generated by this dynamic development activity, albeit with a Bursar still required to complete the establishment of an effective Finance Department. The financial and economic health of the School was strong and had improved so much that substantial additional funds had been generated to enable securing significant added pedagogical resources and an increase to salaries with bonuses to faculty and staff. The School seemed poised for a quantum leap in its development. The following table reflects these financial improvements.

| | Revenue | | | | Expense | | |
|---|---|---|---|---|---|---|---|
| Period | College Managed School | Board Managed School | Threefold Managed School | Period | College Managed School | Board Managed School | Threefold Managed School |
| Tuition | 893,996 | 1,173,394 | 1,542,682 | Salaries | 1,017,737 | 1,464,481 | 1,960,197 |
| Grant | 579,587 | 514,547 | 949,063 | Development* | 33,414 | 24,079 | 158,260 |
| Other | 20,162 | 109,764 | 104,170 | Other | 237,888 | 249,147 | 474,801 |
| Total Revenue | 1,493,745 | 1,797,705 | 2,595,915 | Total Expense | 1,289,039 | 1,737,707 | 2,593,258 |

* Development Activities including Pedagogical and Community/Resource Development

**Figure 31:** *Revenue & Expense Comparison over Three Periods of Operation*

This table reflects the significantly improved student retention and attrition rates of 30%, with enrollment going from a static 260 to a stable 306 over a seven-year period. The average salary increased 18% and the top senior salary increased by 19.3%. The number of teachers increased by 46% from a full-time equivalent of 24.3 to the full-time equivalent of 35.4 as of June 2010. These two statistics indicate that there was an overall increase of 72% in payroll paid by the School to teachers. These statistics speak to the positive effect of the aspects of the new living structure that had been successfully implemented over this period.

However, the quantum leap that was anticipated at this point was not to be. Instead, the Director of Development resigned from the position. A hiring process was conducted by the Board of Trustees and a new Director of Development hired.[86] The new Director stepped into a still loosely-formed Community & Resource Development Department, with no dedicated coordinating body for that realm of activities, and no committees formed for building or site development, with few or no programs established in promotion and advertising, fund development, community development, volunteer and alumni involvement. Over the next eighteen months little progress was made in establishing these groups, committees and programs. The consequence was an effective halt in the growth and development of the School's metabolic system. This was serious because this meant that the fund development program that was needed to provide revenue that would enable a continued increase to salaries as planned was not established. This lack of growth threatened the School's financial and economic stability. Cuts to the budget and to spending were implemented, ongoing increases to salaries were limited and bonuses were no longer possible. And while an employee had finally been hired to fulfill the function of a school Bursar, it was intended only as an opportunity to assess whether or not to establish this as a permanent position. It became increasingly difficult and ultimately impossible for the middle realm, the School's 'rhythmic system,' to continue to oversee and manage the financial realm with this kind of 'dis-ease' in the tenuously formed 'metabolic system.' This lack of development contributed to what I experienced as an insurmountable barrier to achieving forward movement. As a result of facing this barrier to forward movement, the work that I had undertaken could not progress further at this point, and I resigned my position as the Administrator.

## Step VIII    Real Time – What Was Next ... What Is Next?

### *The missed step:  re-formation of the governance (legal-financial) realm*

Parallel to all of these developments as the organizational 'metabolic system' was attempting to form and establish itself, as mentioned previously, something else, which contributed to a derailing of the transformation of the School's governance, did NOT happen in relationship to the middle organizational 'rhythmic system.' While it is true that the legal-financial functions were consolidated, redefined and expanded, resulting in the beginnings of the formation of the organizational 'respiratory system,' it was done at a local level, within the Finance Department itself as a subsystem of the larger middle realm—the organizational 'rhythmic system.' The middle realm as a whole was not fully redefined in an intentional or conscious way. As succinctly stated by Lewin (1992), "A characteristic of complex systems [is that] global structure emerges from local activity rules." (p.47) The changes that were happening at the local level in the Department itself, and in the Pedagogical Department, were begging for changes to also happen at a more global organizational level. In retrospect, the Vancouver Waldorf School's organizational 'rhythmic system,'—the realm of the School Society, the Board of Trustees, and the Administrator—should have been the system to be fully and holistically consolidated and re-differentiated after or parallel with the Pedagogical realm, the organizational 'nerve-sense system' was redefined. The wisdom inherent in the differentiation of the human rhythmic system, the second of the three major systems to become visible in a developing human being, provides indications that demonstrate that the organizational 'rhythmic system' needs to be re-differentiated before focus is placed on the Community & Resource Development realm, the organizational 'metabolic system.' Daroshin actually said this to me on two different occasions, but I missed the urgency of the message:

> Hiring a full-time [Director of] Development can no longer be considered a solution. The center of our very being, as a Waldorf school and movement, depends on our awareness, understanding, and practice of threefolding. It permeates the curriculum in its approach to child development, and it speaks to the trinity which makes up most of humanity's collective spiritual consciousness—it's time we incorporate it into our organizational structures. We can do this. We must do this. I have witnessed the profound impact Waldorf education has had on my own children. If a fraction of that fundamental truth finds its way into our organizational structures, we will have served not only our community, but our very humanity. (personal communication, September, 2009)

Throughout the process of transformation, I was aware of the need to extend and apply changes in the middle realm, to the School Society and the Board of Trustees, and ultimately to define the broader leadership role of the School Administrator, but because of the burning needs in so many other places, and because I somehow thought that this piece could wait because I could prop it up—albeit with no explicit leadership authority—in the interim, all meant it did not receive priority. There was some progress made in that a temporary Bursar was hired, a Finance Committee of sorts was reestablished, and a Good Governance Committee[87] was created, but without the changes extending to the School Society, the Board of Trustees, and explicit leadership definition of the School Administrator position, the addition of the temporary Bursar and new committees in the middle realm did not provide the strength, foundation or form in the structure that was needed.

The existing Vancouver Waldorf School Society, with its constitution, parts of which are unalterable, and the bylaws governing its operating structure and approach, was originally created many, many years before based on an traditional top-down paradigm, not on a new leadership paradigm. While there had been some subsequent minor changes to the bylaws, they were not significant. The constitution and bylaws were at this point configured such that the Vancouver Waldorf School Society membership was comprised primarily of parents with a transitory vested interest in what happens in the School rather than on what is actually needed in this constituent group in the middle sphere of a Waldorf school. In fact, what was and is needed in this constituent group are people who are committed to Waldorf education, its philosophical underpinnings *and* social mission, *and, in addition*, have an interest and expertise in the realm of finances, legalities and organizational threefold living systems governance. This Society membership would ideally then appoint a Board of Trustees, qualified in the realm of Governance and Legal-Financial activities and business. A qualified and capable Board of Trustees would have the expertise and knowledge needed to do the business of a management group in the middle sphere, the organizational 'rhythmic system,' of an educational organization specifically in a threefolded Waldorf school structure. This would provide the structural support for the Legal-Financial Department and its staff, and for a School Administrator (or Director as the position is labeled in some schools or non-profit organizations). It also has the potential to provide the structural support for the expansion and implementation of the organizational 'metabolic system,' the Community & Resource Development Department. Perhaps the hiccups that kept happening as that Department at the Vancouver Waldorf School was trying valiantly to establish itself would not have happened at all had appropriate attention to the transformation of the middle system been an earlier focus.

Rather than this redefinition taking place and the leadership authority clarified, what did happen after I left is that the Board of Trustees approved a proposal from the Pedagogical Carrying Group to eliminate the role and position of Administrator, along with the essential and central function of that position, and replace it with a truncated position in the form of a Business and Facilities Manager. This step represents a departure from the threefold living systems vision because it in essence eliminates or cripples the middle organizational 'rhythmic system,' and removes an essential harmonizing holistic organizational leadership function, rather than redefining and strengthening it as should have happened earlier in the process.

The role of the School Society, Board of Trustees, its committees, the Legal-Financial Department staff and the School Administrator in a living systems approach is to function collectively as the organizational 'rhythmic system,' a function that is established early in an organization's development—just as in a developing embryo the human rhythmic system is the second system to develop very soon after the nerve-sense system begins to form.

*Figure 15* provides a picture of the organizational dynamic that must exist between the realms at the poles—development and pedagogical—with the middle realm holding, connecting and harmonizing the activity of the two poles. The three systems working in concert in this way create a living whole. This living systems dynamic is a very different dynamic than the mechanistic one that accompanies the traditional organizational top-down hierarchical leadership paradigm. In a traditional paradigm, the School Society, Board and its Administrator (or Director) would function from the *top, down*, with a *controlling directing* gesture. In the living systems paradigm, the School Society, its Board of Trustees, and the Administrator or Director function from the *middle, out*, in a lemniscate form, with a *weaving, coordinating* gesture. In the case of the Vancouver Waldorf School, the mediation, facilitation, coordination and harmonizing effect that the middle realm should provide—in its place between the two poles (represented in the organization by the other two systems)—was already functioning at a disadvantage by the fact that the School Society, its membership criteria and the bylaws and Board appointment criteria and protocol, had not been redefined and re-formed using the guiding principles of the new threefold living systems paradigm, in the way that the Pedagogical Realm had been re-differentiated. The leadership responsibilities and authority of the School Administrator position were implicit and needed to be explicitly defined. The School's 'rhythmic system' function was being maintained, or propped up as I said, by me, and now with the elimination of the position, and effectively the integrated and integrating middle function, the organizational 'rhythmic system' can no longer function. In the two months that elapsed since my employment ceased, I received two unsolicited communications from employees, which contain qualitative comments providing some affirmation for this description of what has happened with this middle realm. An experienced and longtime teacher at the School said, "The middle doesn't hold without you," and one of the other employee's comments was that "the School doesn't make sense without you." It is important to say that the key issue here is not to do with me specifically being absent from or present in the role of Administrator. Rather, the key issue is that there was now a lack of fulfillment of the particular and important *functions* of the School Administrator and the middle realm in the threefold living systems structure. This creates and created a dysfunction in the whole system.

The function of the School Administrator is to administer to the middle organizational 'rhythmic system,' not only in overseeing the legal-financial activities but also more importantly by establishing and maintaining equity at a greater organizational level through the mediating, coordinating, harmonizing and weaving gesture *in relationship to the other two systems.* The specific challenge in this case is that not only is the School Administrator's position no longer filled, but the middle realm itself has never been appropriately defined and re-differentiated using the threefold living systems vision. That means that now there is effectively no middle realm, with the parts that remain compartmentalized and disconnected from the whole. It also means that the middle realm will not simply and magically begin to function properly with the hiring of a Business and Facilities Manager to take on limited aspects of the middle function. Nor will the issue be resolved by simply hiring a new Administrator. The middle realm in its entirety must be re-formed, redefined and reconnected. This significant and profound insight into the importance of defining the function of the middle realm is now evident, but is it obvious enough to be seen and will action be taken? What is now needed is to redefine and re-establish the middle realm. This means a dedicated process of redefining the Vancouver Waldorf School Society's purpose and membership criteria, amending the bylaws and the role and responsibilities of the Board of Trustees to reflect this clarified purpose, as well as clearly defining the role and responsibilities of a School Administrator in service to this newly defined and differentiated realm. In short, the organizational 'rhythmic system' must be explicitly differentiated and delineated in defining documents and in reality. This must be done in the same manner that the Pedagogical realm in the form of the School's 'nerve-sense system' was successfully re-differentiated and defined with a faculty-defined constitution and membership selection process, an effective Pedagogical Carrying Group, and a Pedagogical Administrator with articulated administrative and leadership functions.

Based on the principles that underpin a threefold living systems structure, in a non-profit organization like the Vancouver Waldorf School, the School Society should appoint (or elect) the non-pedagogical candidates to the Board of Trustees. The Board of Trustees is the management body that ensures that the operations of a school are managed in a financially and legally responsible manner and serve the mission of delivering the Waldorf curriculum, namely, providing educational services based on the philosophy and principles of child development as indicated in the defined educational philosophy. The Board of Trustees monitors, tracks and oversees the yearly budget, ensures that the governance structure is effectively serving the delivery of the education while adhering to the philosophical principles, and ensures that the laws of the greater society are adhered to in the employment of staff and in the operation of the school.

Members of a School Society should have an interest in, understanding of, and support for the philosophical approach of the school and the education. Members should also have an interest in ensuring effective legal-financial and structural operation of the school. Membership eligibility criteria should be clearly defined in the School's Society bylaws, as should the role, responsibilities and expectations of the Board and its Trustees. The appointed Board of Trustees should be qualified and capable in the realm of Governance (Legal-Financial) activities and business of an educational organization,[88] and therefore would have the expertise and knowledge needed to effectively do the business of a management group in this middle sphere.

The role, responsibilities and expectations of the School Administrator also need to be explicitly defined, although the level of practical work that a School Administrator would do depends on the size and stage of development of the organization. The Administrator in a smaller, younger school with a small staff and budget, and simple reporting requirements, would do much more of the nuts and bolts work than in a larger, mature organization, where some of the specialized work that comes with a large complex budget, cash-flow and reporting requirements, demands very specific expertise (i.e., bookkeeping, accounting, financial management) and would be taken up by qualified staff in the form of a Bursar and Bookkeeper. The overriding role of the School Administrator is to provide guidance and support

1. in harmonizing and weaving together all activities that result in a collective manifestation of the school's shared vision, mission and values.

2. in order to ensure the financial health of the school.

3. for the institutional processes, systems, growth and learning that are essential to a healthy, thriving organization.

Working from the principles of transformational servant leadership,[89] the Administrator or Director provides consciousness of the working of the whole organization—through the activity of weaving, coordinating, facilitating and harmonizing—in the area of *legalities and finance*, personnel and *human resource*s management support, *communication, governance* and general *organizational guidance*:

## 1. Legalities and Finance

The Administrator coordinates and oversees the overall functioning of the legal-financial department and staff (i.e., Bursar and Bookkeeper), including the activities of budgeting, accounting, accounts payable and receivable, and reporting, so as to maximize the effective use of funding and revenue. This requires the Administrator to be intimately connected to and involved in the day-to-day working of the school in all departments, in particular the Board, the Development Committee and Pedagogical Carrying Group and committees and task groups. The Administrator must have a strong sense of the financial needs of the school, in particular in the pedagogical realm and then work closely with the development department, in particular the Director of Development if one exists, to support the development and implementation of a strategic plan for enrollment growth, outreach and fund development that will provide the revenue to adequately meet those needs.

### 2. Human Resources

The Administrator participates in and provides administrative support for all human resources activity, including the work of the pedagogical Human Resources Committee and any other human resources task groups in all departments, ensuring that all processes comply with the internal organizational and broader societal rules, regulations and laws.

### 3. Communication

The Administrator is responsible for coordinating, developing, maintaining, and approving all internal and external communication. In addition, the Administrator facilitates communication between the Board of Directors, the Community & Resource Development Department and the Pedagogical Carrying Group in the development of policies for the school to ensure interconnectedness, consistency and professionalism.

### 4. Governance

The Administrator administers to the work of maintaining and manifesting the broader governance vision for the entire school and in monitoring and responding to the overall health of the governance system. This work could be best carried by a Board of Trustees-mandated Good Governance Committee, with the Administrator administering to and supporting it in its responsibilities.

### 5. Organizational Guidance

The Administrator provides coordinating, synchronizing, harmonizing leadership for all administrative/business functions of the school including financial issues, legal issues—including pedagogical legal issues—monitoring fund development and enrollment to ensure that there are adequate resources being generated by that department and those activities, information technology, facilities maintenance and use, and human resources.

Through active participation in the management of operations, on all key carrying groups and in committee business processes, and in the development of all policies, procedures and protocols, the School Administrator is responsible for monitoring, administering to and supporting the successful realization of the broader school mission, goals, aims and objectives and holding the consciousness that the goals, aims and objectives in all departments are collectively in alignment with and contributing to the manifestation and furtherance of the broader collective vision. The School Administrator does *not* direct others from a top-down gesture, nor does the School Administrator necessarily decide how to successfully realize and manifest any of this but rather works from the middle out through transformational servant leadership and active participation and collaboration.

### Compromised structure and an underdeveloped organizational 'metabolic system'

At the Vancouver Waldorf School, at this point, with the School Administrator function replaced by the limited role of a Business Manager position, the administrative structure is now looking not like a three-legged stool,[90] nor even like a stronger and stable four legged stool,[91] but like a lopsided two-legged stool with a third shorter truncated leg that does not touch the ground.[92] This also leaves the School with the Community & Resource Development Department still unformed and not generating the essential financial and human resources needed for the School to thrive. Questions remain: Will the focus on the broader role of operating a school and guiding its development and growth be appropriate and adequate? Will the required knowledge, skills, and attitudes needed to provide this kind of bigger picture oversight and coordination—something that a School Administrator would, or at least most certainly should possess—be present? Hiring someone to fill the role of a Business and Facilities Manager will provide specific and much needed expertise in managing the finances and business aspects of the School and will fill a gap that exists in taking care of the physical plant, but will this provide the Management Group or the School as a whole with the expertise and kind of leadership from the middle needed to successfully operate a non-profit organization, in particular a Waldorf school, in today's environment?

So the future unfolds for the Vancouver Waldorf School—time, financial statements, enrollment and retention statistics, and staff satisfaction will tell whether it will find its way to future health and positive growth. And for the threefold living systems approach to organizational development, a strong foundation on which to grow has been established and the ongoing development of a working prototype will undoubtedly continue at another time, in other places.

*Chapter 5*

## Conclusions and Next Steps

*The trouble with our times is that the future is not what it used to be.*
— Paul Valery

The hypothesis put forward here is that an organization is a dynamic living organism able to learn and grow though phases of organizational development. Furthermore, and unlike in other either amorphous[93] or traditional top-down hierarchical structures, the intentional implementation of a living systems governance and operating structure that unites the understanding of Steiner's threefold ordering of society and social organizations with the new living systems paradigm rooted in quantum physics will transform an existing organization and its governance structure. The suggestion is that implementing such a living systems structure will create successful organizational forms and result in an effective governance structure at a local level. Additionally, it may also be co-evolutionary at a global level. Now the questions remain: Did the application of the living structure at the Vancouver Waldorf School result in effective organizational governance? And if so, will the effect extend to a broader societal level?

The development and implementation of a threefold governance and operating structure using the unique and intentional approach described to this point resulted in a transformation of the entire Vancouver Waldorf School organization and a remarkable and notable improvement, with both qualitative and quantifiable results at many levels within the organization. To a large extent, after the implementation was well underway, the sense of constant chaos and crisis management, which had existed in the organization in the period before the reorganization process began, had dissipated. Before the threefold structure was implemented, there were many symptoms of a struggling organization including one to three staff members on stress leave at any given time, a very serious lack of financial and human resources to provide for the needs of the School, a disproportionately low student retention rate, no clear or satisfactory avenue for addressing parental concerns and an organizational closet full of unresolved issues with no mechanisms in place to clear them up. Many procedures and protocols were implicit only and subject to individual interpretation with regard to adherence to them and how they were applied. Minutes at most meetings were not recorded or distributed such that information flow was limited, obstructing interconnection and collaboration.

Despite the good work and good will of the countless pioneers who dedicated many years of their life's work to building and maintaining the Vancouver Waldorf School, the approach to organizational governance and the operating structure were no longer serving healthy development; it was not based on a conscious understanding of organizational development or what is needed for healthy living systems. For the most part, the human beings responsible for creating and maintaining the structure did not know what they did not know. The organization had remained too long in a pioneering phase of development, and the structure, forms and processes were no longer serving it. The organization was surviving on the good intentions, good will, desire to succeed and hard work of committed individuals but without a unified vision of how it could grow and develop in a healthy way.

Significant change was necessary for the organization to grow and thrive. A paradigm shift to a new way of seeing organizations as living entities could provide this lifeline, one based on an understanding of living forms and living systems that would serve the healthy development of the organization.

Walter Daroshin, drawing from months of interviews and conversations with community members, years as a school Trustee and Society Treasurer and from his personal experience of living through the three years of operating under the imposed Board mandated-model system, reported to the Board of Trustees about what had been happening up until the new vision for a threefold structure was introduced to the School:

> What soon became clear to me was that the [Vancouver Waldorf School of the past] was built on a theoretical realization of a threefold social order, yet as an operating entity, was principally engaged in two of its three folds. In fact, for the last number of years it seemed as though there was a struggle to wrest control and moral authority away from one fold, the cultural realm (the College of Teachers), and place it into another, the rights realm (the Board [of Trustees]). During this time of reorganization, which included the implementation of a … 'mandated' system of working, we neglected to pay sufficient attention to the common good. The work that was being done was indeed of good intention and an important part of our evolution, and I am grateful for having played a small role in how we have come to where we are today. It was however self-centered.

> …We all knew what was in front of us, yet something was blocking our forward movement. … Our enthusiasm for taking advantage of perceived windows of opportunity, or possibly fear of being accused of inaction, led to decisions which in hindsight might be considered expedient. However, my due diligence suggests that it was a lack of organizational structure, represented by the philosophies [the threefold principles] written into our constitution and held within our curriculum, which created these 'blocks.' The VWS is structured much like any other top-down hierarchical organization:

| Vancouver Waldorf School Society | |
|---|---|
| **Vancouver Waldorf School Board of Trustees** | |
| **Management** Administrative Coordinator Finance Manager Principal | **Mandated Committees** |
| **Administration** | |
| Accounting Assistant Computer Services Enrollment Officer Enrollment Assistant | Junior Accountant Maintenance Receptionist Registrar HS Administrative Assistant |

This model grants the Board the moral authority (through the selection process of the Society) and the legal authority (dictated by the laws of British Columbia) to govern and manage the VWS. I mentioned previously that the hiring of a Director of Development to perform specific task oriented activity can work only if it is married to a restructuring of our organization. We needed to reflect an understanding and a practical approach to a threefold way of working. The diagram above illustrates the relationship our mandated committees have with our management team and administration. The mandated committees report directly to the Board …. The Board reports to the Society. Management reports to the Board and Administration report to various members of Management. There is no place under this type of structure for either the pedagogical realm or the development realm to plant an effective seed. Everything flows through the rights realm. The responsibility for all activities within the School falls to the Board. Not only is this contrary to any preordained threefold social order, it is completely unrealistic, and the reason why the policies and governance needed to provide the School with vision and proactive forward thinking have failed to be realized. There is no accountability, or seeming responsibility, in many areas of school life, not because of a perceived 'flat' or 'non-hierarchical' way of working, it is because we are structured to nurture self-interest, not the common good. (personal communication, n.d.)

The introduction of the threefold vision, married with an organizational living systems paradigm, shifted and reorganized the structure that Daroshin describes above. It began with the differentiation and redefining of boundaries between realms. The Pedagogical Realm has now completed its differentiation and is functioning effectively and efficiently for now. The Governance (Legal-Financial) Realm and the Community & Resource Development Realm are waiting in the wings for their turn at completing definition.

The Administration was reorganized and employees are now clear about their responsibilities and accountabilities via detailed job descriptions, and there is clarity about the impulse and gesture out of which their work is generated and which realm they serve. There was a recognized attempt to ensure that staff members were appropriately qualified to do the work for which they were hired, although you will see from my conclusions that more should have been and needs to be done in this regard, including increasing salaries in order to successfully attract and retain those qualified employees.

There is now in place a clearly differentiated Pedagogical Realm with experienced Waldorf educators serving on the Pedagogical Carrying Group and in the role of Pedagogical Administrator. Explicit, documented policies and procedures were developed and approved in the appropriate realms through collaborative processes, and which are subsequently adhered to by staff. The financial and economic foundation was improved to the point that vibrancy and health was just beginning to become apparent in such a way that is indisputable.

There is undeniable quantifiable evidence that supports the conclusion that grand improvements took place in the School as a result of the new threefold living systems structure and, despite the missed step and the subsequent missteps, I can therefore conclude that it is possible to transform an existing governance structure through the implementation of and the intention to continue to implement the described threefold form. This aspect of the hypothesis holds true at the local organizational level. This is supported by what follows.

One dramatic piece of supporting evidence is reflected in the Revenue & Expense chart, which compares revenue and expenses prior to and after implementation of the threefold structure, from the two periods prior to my arrival at the Vancouver Waldorf School to the most recent budgetary year. (See *Figure 31: Revenue Expense Comparison over Three Periods of Operation*, p.94.) The numbers show that the financial and economic foundation of the School greatly improved over time compared to the period before the implementation of the threefold living systems structure when it was managed with different approaches. By the end of this documented period of development, in which time the development and implementation of a threefold living systems prototype for the operation and management of the Vancouver Waldorf School was mostly realized, the budget increased by $1.1 million.

If money is the equivalent of organizational 'blood,' then it can be said that the Vancouver Waldorf School's 'blood' had become rich with health-giving nutrients. This richness resulted in a significant increase in the total number of staff, primarily teaching staff, as well as improved staff retention, improvements to hiring processes, mentoring, professional development funding, training requirements, and higher salaries. Prior to the implementation of the new structure, the average teacher salary was static at $34,600 with a top senior salary of $37,280 per annum. In a relatively short period of time the average salary increased 18% to a current average of $40,760 per annum. The top senior salary increased 19.3% to $44,482. The other significant statistic is that the number of teachers has increased by 46% from a full-time equivalent of 24.3 to the current full-time equivalent of 35.4.[94] Together these two statistics resulted in an overall increase of 72% in payroll paid by the School to teachers.

Improvements in many other areas are equally indisputable. Before the implementation of the threefold living systems structure, the enrollment numbers were unchanging with an average of 260 students in Preschool through Grade Twelve. Recently the enrollment numbers were holding steady at approximately 310, and the retention and attrition rates improved significantly by up to 30%. The Vancouver Waldorf School has never had difficulty attracting interest, with moderate success enrolling new students; however the challenge in the past was with satisfaction and retention. At one point just before the new structure was implemented with a total enrollment of 260 students, the statistical reports show 100 students withdrawn and another 100 new students enrolled from one school year to the next. In contrast, the retention rate is currently excellent. In a recent year, out of a total enrollment of 306 only 24 in total withdrew or did not return, with an additional 27 new students projected to enroll. Increased enrollment and increased retention have been the current trend, demonstrating student and parent satisfaction.

The other significant indicator of improved working conditions is the retention and attraction of well qualified and excellent teachers. Prior to the implementation of the new structure, there were at any given time one to three staff members on long or short-term disability leave for stress. This is no longer the case. Insurance premiums have been reduced or remained static several years in a row because of the lowered use of this benefit, despite the significant increase in total number of employees enrolled in the program.

There are indications that the quality of the work environment also improved. Qualitative comments and feedback (received up until June 2010 just prior to the writing of this book) indicate that something was different, the School environment was experienced as positive and uplifting, and the relationships between faculties, staff, departments, individuals and groups less strained and more collegial. Qualified, highly trained and experienced teachers have been attracted to and accepted positions at the School and have remained employed despite the still unsatisfactory salaries. We heard from these teachers that the positive work environment and collegial atmosphere are attractive.

The following quote by Dieter Brüll (1997) is an explanation of what happened as a result of the design and implementation of this threefold principle-based organizational structure at the Vancouver Waldorf School:

> If threefoldness is derived from what is human, as Steiner says, then why should one not consider it when building institutions? Is it not true that humans place their whole being to these? Whether one calls this threefold social life, or whether one reserves this term for the macro-sphere [at the

society level] is a question of semantics and not of concepts. ... Three organs are created to form, as it were, a shell and, thus, structure what the [teachers, staff, trustees, and community members] [bring] to the school as [their] very own impulses. (p.15)

What Brüll is saying here is that the threefold structure provides the vessel in which all individuals can participate with enthusiasm and a sense of fulfillment, contributing their gifts, their expertise and their best work. The vessel also provides the form and structure that can temper and provide a check and balance for the self-interest of the individual in the interest of the greater good of the whole organism. The clarity provided by a structure born out of the principles inherent in three overlapping spheres of influence and in the day-to-day dynamic, reflecting the systems or the living structure of the threefold human being, results in a healthy, responsive, growing, developing organization. My colleague, Walter Daroshin, who, working alongside me and others during the most intensive period of development and implementation of the threefold structure, said:

We are building a critical mass of understanding of our individual roles and responsibilities. Working from within, through service and the tempering of self-interest, we will be the change we wish to see in our school.

The seams or overlaps, when deficient, can manifest in illness—both physical and structural; however, those same seams or overlaps, when recognized and understood, will create a brave new world for us from which to work. (personal communication, n.d.)

The positive effect of the implementation of the threefold structure guided by the vision described in this book is evident. However, perhaps more is possible and necessary. Throughout this book I have touched on the fact that in the mainstream corporate world there is a growing new consciousness of the importance of working in new ways in organizations, while at the same time the *form or structure* remains in an old form, that of an owner/operator top-down hierarchical leadership paradigm. The focus of this research has been on *new forms and a structure* within which such a *new consciousness* can exist, and I am confident that the implementation of the threefold living systems structure has had, and could by itself in another context have, a positive outcome.

I cannot conclude without touching on the work of Dr. C. Otto Scharmer (2007). Just as the work documented in this book cultivates an understanding of *new forms and organizational structure*, so too does Scharmer's work on a new social technology, which he calls Theory U, advance the work on the *new consciousness* that has been developing in the corporate world. It is important to mention his work here because the vessel that is created by the implementation of the new threefold ordering of an organization is waiting for a new consciousness. While it is true that simply implementing the new structure has had a significant positive impact on the effectiveness of the Vancouver Waldorf School's operation, and perhaps this *has* resulted in a raising of the organizational consciousness to a degree, I cannot help but wonder if the effect is similar to what happens when one smiles. Even when the smile is not generated from the inside in response to genuine feelings of joy, it is almost impossible not to feel happy when one is smiling. This living systems form, which is an alternative to both an amorphous flat structure and to a top-down leadership paradigm, naturally necessitates collaborative, cooperative, associative working relationships resulting in certain level of consciousness of the need to work in new ways. This organic threefold living systems governance structure with its natural network-based hierarchy that shifts the authority depending on the specific expertise and particular function needed in a given context, does not require that a collegial environment be artificially created by a leader at the top of a hierarchical structure. Rather, the structure itself ensures that creativity, innovation, and collaborative, cooperative teamwork are present and active throughout the system.

Theory U provides processes, practices, and tools that enable a new intentional consciousness and approach to working that would fit the vessel created by a threefold structure like a glove. Unfortunately, exploring the possibilities that could be created by working with Theory U is not possible within the context of this book, but it is important to at least mention it in the concluding comments because the use of these practices *in conjunction with* the implementation of a threefold structure could very well expedite and exponentially increase the ultimate effectiveness of implementing a threefold living systems structure. It could provide a much needed injection of consciousness that could boost the transformative effect of implementing the threefold structure.

It is also remarkable (and likely not coincidental) that Theory U is based on a threefold picture, which in essence involves the development of the ability at "personal, group, institutional, and global" levels for "deep seeing" or "sensing." (Scharmer 2007, p.7) This new social technology that supports the development of deep seeing involves three core stages, or movements as Scharmer calls them, when responding to issues, challenges, or a call for advancement, change and improvement. Scharmer describes the basic actions or movements:

- observe, observe, observe
- retreat and reflect
- act in an instant

These three core movements give an individual, a group or an organization access to an inner knowing through a different kind of non-judgmental listening that requires and engages an open heart *and* an open mind. It approaches and deals with issues at a systemic root level rather than simply addressing symptoms with quick fixes. Scharmer emphasizes the importance of learning the capacity to work with an open mind and an open heart, but he also talks about a third capacity—an open will. He says, "While an open heart allows us to see a situation from the whole, the open will enables us to begin to act from the emerging whole." (p.12) He notes that it is easy to understand the concept of an open mind, which is possible to achieve by approaching from a gesture of inquiry rather than from judgment based on past experience and knowledge. The capacity to open the heart is developed through practicing genuine empathic listening. Opening the will, on the other hand, is the most difficult concept to grasp and capacity to develop. Scharmer describes the experience of the process of opening the will as it was described to him by Danish sculptor and management consultant Erik Lemcke:

> After having worked with a particular sculpture for some time, there comes a certain moment when things are changing. When this moment of change comes, it is no longer me, alone, who is creating. I feel connected to something far deeper and my hands are co-creating with this power. At the same time, I feel that I am being filled with love and care as my perception is widening. I sense things in another way. It is a love for the world and for what is coming. I then intuitively know what I must do. My hands know if I must add or remove something. My hands know how the form should manifest. In one way, it is easy to create with this guidance. In those moments I have a strong feeling of gratitude and humility. (p.12)

These three capacities of open head (or thinking), open heart and open will are conditions that must be present when individuals, groups and organizations are working on unfolding the future. Scharmer goes on to describe leadership capacities that he says must also be cultivated by a group before the process defined by Theory U can be successful. The capacities include suspending all judgment and exercising pure objective observation with deep openness, sensing and awareness, while seeing and acting—or providing prototype solutions—from the whole and beyond to the greater whole. In summary, Scharmer says, "[C]onnecting to one's best future possibility and creating powerful breakthrough ideas require learning to access the intelligence of the heart and the hand—not just the intelligence of the head." (p.13) If these process-oriented techniques, tools and practices could be utilized by the people working within the complementary structural framework that a threefold form provides, the quantum leap that I have referenced as possible and necessary for social renewal would have a much greater chance to manifest than if either is attempted in isolation.

Regrettably, the implementation of the threefold living systems structure at the Vancouver Waldorf School was not completed. The end of the story described in Chapter 4 marks the end of the action-based research documented here and defines the point of interruption of the process at the Vancouver Waldorf School of developing a prototype for a threefold living systems structure. With the lack of development in the Community & Resource Development department and with little movement or headway gained in terms of fund and resource development programs and activities over the past two years, I experienced a serious stall or interruption in the School's development. For the first time since I began my work at the Vancouver Waldorf School, I was not successful in finding a way to facilitate forward movement. I thought perhaps I was enabling the lack of movement by remaining in my position—perhaps people were relying on me to carry the consciousness of the living systems threefold vision. Perhaps there was reticence to move forward and define the leadership, because of a fear of giving authority to that leadership, or possibly there was simply no collective will to continue. The reason for the resistance to move forward with the ongoing development of the threefold living systems structure was not obvious to me—I knew only that movement had ceased. With this in mind I stepped back with the hope and intention that it would provide a catalyst for forward movement.

I sincerely held the hope that the faculty, staff and involved parents and community members would respond by taking up the task identified by Daroshin. "The seams or overlaps, when deficient, can manifest in illness—both physical and structural; however, those same seams or overlaps, when recognized and understood, will create a brave new world for us from which to work." The task of recognizing and understanding the roles and responsibilities of individuals and the seams and overlaps of the threefold vision needs to be taken up with intention in order to enable a broad explicit consciousness and understanding of how to maintain and continue the healthy development of the living organism that was mobilized at the Vancouver Waldorf School, in particular at this point in relationship to defining and empowering leadership, as well as the reformation and redefining of the Society and Board of Trustees, and specifically to leadership in and development of the Community & Resource Development Realm. With a broader consciousness and the explicit *shared* understanding of the threefold vision underpinning the entire development, refinement and implementation of the threefold structure, the vision could continue to inspire and guide the School's organizational development.

Engaging in a transparent process of looking at the ramifications of my departure, a process that in particular would have involved the Full Faculty and Pedagogical Carrying Group could provide the possibility of broadening the understanding and consciousness of the threefold principles and relationship to a living systems approach to governance and management. This is what was needed. Out of that broader understanding and consciousness, a transition plan could have developed. A quantum leap in the School's development was still within reach.

However, this is not what happened next. Instead, the remaining management staff and leadership groups chose to take a different tack and sever the relationship to the threefold living systems vision, which is described in detail in this book and that was collaboratively developed over time, guiding the School through its transformation to this point. There will be no replacement Administrator hired. Instead, in a return to a former approach to managing the School's middle realm, the position has been truncated, taking the form of a Business and Facilities Manager. It will be the responsibility of the person in this position to manage legal and financial business and oversee maintenance of the facility. The mediating, facilitating, coordinating rhythmic function carried by the Society, Board of Trustees, its committees and a School Administrator, functioning collectively as the organizational 'rhythmic system' (Governance [Legal-Financial] body), working in service to the organization, between the two poles represented by the other two systems occupied by the Pedagogical body and the Community & Resource Development body, will no longer exist in the middle. This function, which is an essential function in a well-established organization that is in the differentiation phase of development, was partially developed as the restructuring progressed; but unfortunately, it did not develop to the point of having strong roots. It appears as though I was holding the middle in place and this was clearly not sustainable. As mentioned in Chapter 4, the explicit reformation and redefinition of the Society, its Board of Trustees, and the confirmation of the role of the Administrator needed to happen earlier.

It appears as though there will no longer be a centralized School Administrator, holding the consciousness of the whole and coordinating the operational and administrative activities in the other realms, weaving it all together into a harmonized whole in service to the organizational mission. Instead, it has been proposed that the management group for the Pedagogical realm (Pedagogical Carrying Group) can provide this greater rhythmic function for the entire organization, while the financial management aspect of the middle realm will continue to be managed by the Board of Trustees and its new Business and Facilities Manager. If this happens, it could constitute an impingement of the spiritual-freedom realm on the realm of equality. If Karutz's (2001) understanding of what happens when there is impingement at a social level is accurate, and in fact an impingement of freedom on the equality realm takes place, "then all rules are undermined, bringing insecurity and chaos." (p.28) This could be the effect of such a step, regardless of whether the step is conscious or unconscious.

As indicated in *Figure 32: Dynamic of the Pedagogical Realm*, the Pedagogical Carrying Group, with its Pedagogical Administrator working in service to this body, is the coordinating, regulatory (rhythmic) body for the *Pedagogical* realm of activity and NOT for the whole organization. The coordinating, mediating role for the entire organization is the function of the middle *Governance (Legal-Financial) body*, the Board of Trustees and its Administrator, while the coordinating function for the pedagogical realm is the role of the Pedagogical Carrying Group and its Pedagogical Administrator.

The decision not to replace the School Administrator, but rather to hire instead a Business and Facilities Manager, with limited oversight of aspects of the middle realm, means that the structure will now have management groups with administrators serving only two of the three realms, with a financial and business management skill-set specific manager in the

## Dynamic of the Pedagogical Realm within the Whole

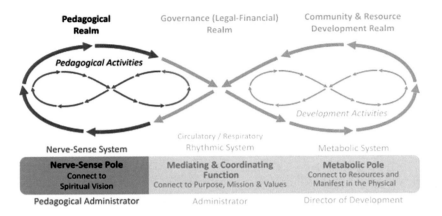

## Dynamic of the Pedagogical Realm in Detail

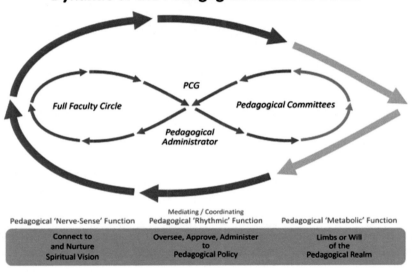

**Figure 32:** *Dynamic of the Pedagogical Realm*

third realm overseeing only a portion of the activity of that realm, the legal-financial business. No one will provide the greater organizational coordinating mediating function of the middle realm except perhaps the Pedagogical Carrying Group and the Pedagogical Administrator, by stretching beyond pedagogical boundaries and attempting to provide this broader school function. Instead of the envisioned four-legged stool supporting and serving the threefolded organization, it will be a two-legged stool, which has a truncated third leg in the form of the concept behind a Business and Facilities Manager.

Furthermore, only one of the three envisioned folds or spheres of activity (the Pedagogical sphere) has been clearly differentiated, while the other two spheres remain amorphous. This step in the School's development was not inspired or guided by the threefold living systems vision which developed over time through collaborative working as described in detail in this book. I can offer some ideas about why this change of course or regression has taken place. It is possible, even likely, that the School was experiencing a crisis of the differentiation phase of development and that the challenges at that moment are a result of resistance to or fear of going through the developmental eye of the needle, which is part of transitioning to the next phase of development, the mature integrative-associative phase. Instead, there is a return to old, familiar or comfortable ways of working that may (or in some ways may not) have been satisfactory and somewhat successful in the past. Schaefer (1996) in *Vision in Action* talks about the crisis of the differentiation phase of development. "The trick in the integration phase is to see the organization as a process organism and to restructure it to enhance the central processes." (p.51)

The following insights and suggestions regarding enhancing central processes related to the greater whole could guide the School through this transitional phase and into the mature integrative-associative phase of development:

1. There is confusion or disagreement about—and therefore a need to clarify and confirm—the role of the Pedagogical Carrying Group in relationship to the rest of the Pedagogical realm ('nerve-sense system') and its relationship to the whole organism.[95] It is also necessary to reaffirm, redefine and re-differentiate the role of the middle realm ('rhythmic system'), which includes the Administrator, finance department staff, the Society and its Board of Trustees, again in relationship to the whole.

2. There is a lack of—and therefore a need to institutionalize—widespread consciousness and understanding of both the new quantum physics paradigm and the view of social organizational development as a reflection or expression of the threefold human being (as described in Chapter 1) as the guiding vision. There are indications of a lack of understanding of the function of the middle realm and therefore the result was a reaction that seemed to reflect a fear of impingement or loss of control should the Administrator position remain as part of the structure. This fear would be eliminated if there is a genuine and widespread understanding of the new paradigm and the threefold living systems vision.

3. When administering to the holistic unified operation of a Waldorf school, there is a need to ensure that appropriate skills and competency exist in the individuals in leadership positions who work in the administration in service to the three realms of the school.

This suggestion that the School is in a transitional phase and experiencing the crisis of the differentiation phase of development, in conjunction with the recent developments and the insights I have highlighted above, causes me to reflect on what I would do differently if I could return to various points during the implementation, and also causes me to consider what I have learned from what has happened. It is important to consider this so that the next opportunity to develop the prototype can be that much more successful, constructive and refined.

1. I would be more insistent on organizing ongoing presentations for Society members, Trustees, Faculty, Pedagogical Carrying Group members, parents and friends, and staff to share the threefold living systems vision and to provide updates on progress and challenges.

2. I would make a better effort to ensure that decisions and changes in direction are transparent and process-driven and that challenges are shared with the faculty and staff, in particular with the Pedagogical Carrying Group members, so that the educators have the greatest possible opportunity to provide the kind of input and direction regarding the administrative life and structure of the School that Steiner (1998) insisted is essential. Steiner insisted this collaboration is essential if education as a cultural-spiritual activity is to retain the kind of autonomy that is needed for the cultural life to achieve its purpose, and ultimately achieve its social mission and have a transformative effect on the rest of society.

3. I would be more attuned to the need for adequate process in relationship to hiring administrative staff, ensuring that the staff members hired possess adequate and appropriate qualifications. Again, for example, this would ensure, in the case of hiring of administrative staff, that the educators who form the organizational 'nerve-sense system' have adequate opportunity to give important input and appropriate direction to the selection process.

4. In concert with the implementation of the threefold living systems structure, I would engage the use of the tools, practices and processes that bring a heightened level of consciousness to the whole organization, such as those defined by the new social technology of Scharmer's Theory U. This combination of a revolutionary living systems *structure* with an equally revolutionary living systems *consciousness* in relationship to social reform may just be what generates a quantum leap on all levels, and in particular what could carry a School through a transitional crisis phase to become a mature process-oriented organization.

5. And finally, I would focus even more on my own personal development, inner work and healthy threefold development because, as Karl König (n.d.) said:

> Dear friends, only this—and again I say something which I feel is of great importance, and so I repeat the words which Rudolf Steiner used time and again—only this will make it possible for a true threefold social order to become established where you work. For the threefold order in the social realm is not something which can be superimposed on any social organism; it has to grow from within. It is the result of the effort of the single human being to learn to live with an understanding of the threefold being of man. The more you concern yourself with the concept of threefoldness, not in the social realm but in the being of man, the more directly, immediately, the social structure will turn into a threefold existence, because you order it from within. You order it from within, magically. Magically, dear friends, it will emerge, whether you like it or not, and suddenly you will see: It is the threefold social order. So it is. (König, [n.d.], Karl König Archive Aberdeen, UK)

In my final analysis and to conclude: A modern revolutionary approach to creating living organizational structure and form has birthed out of the research and out of the application of the theory over the time that I was at the Vancouver Waldorf School. The results show that the effect on the health of the organization, when approaching it with the new consciousness of organizations as living entities, utilizing Steiner's threefold approach to understanding life with its threefold principles as the essential properties, is positive and transformational. Whether I can go so far as to say that it has a co-evolutionary effect on other social organizations and the rest of society would only be conjecture at this point. Much more work needs to be done, a way found to either take up again and continue the work at the Vancouver Waldorf School, or alternatively at other schools or in other organizations, and to study the long term results of that work and observe and quantify the effects beyond the schools or organizations themselves. However, the insight that suggests that the implementation of the revolutionary living systems structure could happen along with intentionally heightening the living systems consciousness gives me new hope for the realization of Steiner's hope—that the Waldorf movement will serve as an example for how society could order itself, thereby providing an antidote for that which ails humankind. Perhaps as Jantsch said, "sociocultural man in co-evolution with himself actually does have the possibility of 'creating the conditions for his further evolution.'" (p.251) And perhaps that further evolution will be a positive one for humankind.

# Appendix A

# Summary of the Five Disciplines of a Learning Organization Detailed in *The Fifth Discipline* by Peter Senge (1994)

## 1 Systems Thinking

Senge (1994) describes systems thinking as a "discipline that involves approaching problem solving and addressing issues, not by focusing on isolated events or parts of the whole but rather by looking at the patterns and events as interrelated parts that effect and are affected by each other and that collectively make up a unified and inseparable whole." (p.7)

## 2 Personal Mastery

"Personal mastery is the discipline of continually clarifying and deepening our [the members of the organization's] personal vision, of focusing our energies, of developing patience, and of seeing reality objectively." (p.7)

## 3 Mental Models

"Mental models" are deeply ingrained assumptions, generalizations, or even pictures or images that influence how we understand the world and how we take action …

The discipline of working with mental models starts with turning the mirror inward, learning to unearth our internal pictures of the world, to bring them to the surface and hold them rigorously to scrutiny. It also includes the ability to carry on "learningful" conversations that balance inquiry and advocacy, where people expose their own thinking effectively and make that thinking open to the influence of others. (pp.8–9)

## 4 Shared Vision

The practice of shared vision involves the skills of unearthing shared "pictures of the future" that foster genuine commitment and enrollment rather than compliance.

## Team Learning

The discipline of team learning starts with "dialogue," the capacity of members of a team to suspend assumptions and enter into a genuine "thinking together." … The discipline of dialogue also involves learning how to recognize the patterns of interaction in teams that undermine learning. The patterns of defensiveness are often deeply engrained in how a team operates. If unrecognized, they undermine learning. If recognized and surfaced creatively, they can actually accelerate learning. (pp.7–10)

# Appendix B

## Summary of *Old Board-Mandated* Mandate System

(in operation prior to the implementation of a threefold living systems approach)

For three years prior the whole school community was involved in a change of governance and organizational structure which transferred the authority from the former College of Teachers to the Board of Trustees. Under this mandate system, the daily running of the school was carried out by the administration and mandated committees (which also included teachers and parents). This process of changeover was guided by a consultant.

This new style of governance takes time to evolve in an organic and healthy way. It is now the third year of operation under this system and time to review it. It is timely to think about what was successful, what needs adjustment and what has been unsuccessful. Here is the existing structure.

*The Board*, composed of parents, teachers and alumni parents (and Administrator and Principal, ex-officio), is responsible for the legal, financial and structural wellbeing of the school.

*The Hub*, composed of a parent and a teacher rep from each section of the school plus the Administrator, receives reports from all mandated committees and reminds about timely action.

*The Administrator*, a full-time position responsible for the day-to-day running of the school in all its aspects.

*The Principal*, a part-time position to support the Administrator and take responsibility, along with the Pedagogical Committee, for the needs of the teachers in relation to Waldorf pedagogy and the Ministry of Education. Monitors the Issues Management System and chairs the Hiring Committee.

*Mandated Committees in each of the following areas*: Hiring, Professional Development (including Mentoring), Pedagogy, Health and Safety, Grounds, Workload, Evaluation, Finance, Festivals, Issues Management, Tuition Adjustment, Site Planning and the Class Parent Group, all accountable and responsible to the Board of Trustees.

*Chairperson of each Faculty*: Kindergarten, Grade School, High School and Full Faculty: organize meetings and follow through on recommendations from Coordinating Hub.

*Administration & Services*, composed of two full-time employees and seven part-time employees to run the day-to-day affairs of the school.

Administrator, Principal, Receptionist, Enrollment Coordinator, Systems Administrator, Maintenance, Registrar, High School Administrative Support, Finance Manager, Accounting Assistant, and Janitorial service

A visual representation of this system is being created, which will be on display when complete.

# Appendix C

# Hub Coordinating Committee Mandate—Old Mandate System

## Mandate-Coordinating Hub

### Brief summary of committee's task

The Coordinating Hub is designed to serve as the central body of awareness and to maintain a broad overview of the workings of the various committees and their functions in the school in support of the mission statement. It is to serve as a communication conduit to help the community be aware of important information and to maintain the goal of transparency in the workings of the school. It is an important function that the Hub will share information with all parties in matters that may have an impact upon them.

1. To serve as communication conduit for all committees and mandated groups in the school.

2. To help ensure that the work of the school's committees and mandate groups is done, through direct and regular contact as agreed upon between the Hub and the particular mandate group or committee.

3. To set the agenda on a consultative basis with the faculty and facilitate the Full Faculty Meeting.

4. To help ensure the steering and coordination of matters of a more general nature that are of importance to the faculty and the community at large.

5. With respect to item 4 above, to help streamline the workings of the school to avoid duplication of task and foster efficient and timely functioning.

6. To help ensure that evaluation of each committee and the whole system of administration occur in conjunction with the Board. This may involve assistance from external sources.

### To whom does the committee report?

1. The Hub will be responsible to the Board of Trustees.

2. The Hub will report to the Board at the regular meetings and meet with the Board as a full group at least twice annually.

3. The group will report to and consult with the faculty at Full Faculty meetings.

## Meeting times and timeline

The Hub will meet for 1½ to 2 hours weekly to discuss reports and activities of the Board and set the agenda for the Full Faculty Meeting. This meeting will occur at least two days before the Full Faculty Meeting.

Faculty members responsible for setting the agenda and facilitating the Full Faculty Meetings will need to meet at a separate time to plan and prepare this meeting. It is expected that this will involve a minimum of 1 hour.

## Criteria for membership *(including required skills)*

Members are to be from the general School community in good standing. Individual members need to possess the following in order to work effectively with this group:

a) Strong communication skills
b) The ability to carry the vision of the required operations of the School
c) The ability to set goals and determine priorities
d) The ability to synthesize complex issues
e) The ability to delegate

## Number of members *(min. and max.)*

Seven (7) members are required from the following areas of the School:
1) a Kindergarten teacher
2) a Grade School teacher
3) a High School teacher
4) the School Administrator
5) a Board member
6) a Parent representative
7) a seventh to be selected by the Hub on the basis of skills needed

In the event that full membership is not attained or maintained at any given time in the working life of the group, members must be actively sought out complete membership. The Board must be made aware of such a circumstance and approve the continued operation of the Coordinating Hub despite any shortfall in membership.

## How are committee members selected?

a) Parent: Selected by the Class Parent Group although this parent need not be a Class Parent
b) Faculty: One from each individual department as recognized within specific faculties
c) Board: A member of the Board as recognized by the Board
d) Administration: The Finance Manager or School Administrator

e) The Seventh: to be selected by the Hub members on the basis of skills needed

f) Final membership of the Hub will be confirmed by the Board.

## Terms of Service

The member's length of service shall be a minimum of a 1- or 2-year term. Changes shall occur in such a way that a maximum of 50% turnover occurs each year in order to maintain continuity.

Rotation on and off is recognized as needing flexibility, except for the Administration position. However, terms of service will begin in mid-January.

Notice must be given by November 1st of the previous year to allow time for new members to be selected and form a transition into the group.

## What major decisions is the committee responsible for?

The Hub will have no decision-making responsibilities except in the setting of the agenda and facilitating the Full Faculty Meetings.

## What specific proposals/recommendations will the committee make?

The Hub will make proposals and recommendations to other mandated groups, committees, Board and Faculty as the need arises.

## How, how many, and when "input loops" are required

There is continuous movement (loops) between the community elements, and more specifically the Board that provides the mandated committees/individuals with input, advice, support, guidance and affirmation.

The principle of the communication function of the Hub is that selected, important information is to be presented to the Hub through its respective liaison members. The Hub then will help facilitate the information flow such that it moves through established links or help to form those links when necessary, to other relevant groups, thus enhancing the communication in the School. Communication is to be made in writing and needs to be in the form of a synopsis rather than a lengthy report or request. It is particularly important that a report maintain confidentiality where appropriate.

The Hub will designate its own contact person(s).

## Communication loops

a) The Board member will communicate information to and from the Board.

b) The Business Administrator will communicate information to and from the administrative staff.

c) The Teacher representatives will communicate information to and from their respective departments.

d) The Parent representative will communicate information to and from the Class Parent Group.

e) There will be a designated individual within the group who will communicate with designated contact persons (i.e., Chairs) of the various committees.

f) Individuals can give input or make requests through the designated contact person(s).

g) The communication will be weekly or as per meeting schedule of the designated group (a minimum of once monthly) in writing. In addition, this communication may occur in person or by invitation to the Hub meeting.

h) Listing of current discussion items and pertinent information will be made available to the community through the Parent Bulletin and/or through posting on a bulletin board.

i) Memos will be sent to specific groups as required.

### How and when is the committee and its function evaluated?

A self-evaluation must be completed no later than April 30th of each year after the new membership has been established and been in operation. This is seen to take the form of a conversation outlining what is working and what is not and contain constructive criticism and suggestions, which are to be written and made public.

The Board will conduct an evaluation at its discretion.

# Appendix D

# Mandate System Review Committee Mandate

## VWS Mandate System Review Steering Committee

**Purpose (Mandate):**

To guide a process of reviewing the mandate system, which has been in place for three years, following the timeline, and make recommendations for changes and refinements to be brought to a meeting of community members before the end of June, and then to generate a report for the Board's approval, with recommendations, before the end of June.

**Summary of Tasks:**

1. Design a questionnaire that will allow for both group and individual input and that will have a clear covering letter to give intention, timeline, areas of responsibility in the process, and expected outcomes. The questionnaire will include a cover letter that identifies areas of known gaps/flaws in the system so that people can focus on giving feedback on what we do not already know. The questions must be simple and ask for examples of 2 or 3 positive and 2 or 3 negative or frustrating experiences in relation to the existing system/structure.

2. Identify and interview key people/groups who are active in the various committees and within the school to obtain information about gaps that will aid in the refinement process.

3. Include others, when and where needed, on the Steering Committee for input at each step depending on the skills, knowledge, or attributes that are needed

4. Analyze the information collected, find patterns and gaps and make recommendations for refinements, changes, and adjustments that will make the organizational structures more responsive to needs of members and of the school

5. There will be two types of recommendations: i) short-term practical refinements, and ii) big-picture envisioning in the fall.

6. Plan a meeting with community members with the goal of reviewing and revising changes and finalizing recommendations and changes.

7. Ensure that the process takes place in a timely manner (see timeline, to be revised as required once process has gathered information)

**Meeting Times:**

Wednesdays at 5:45–6:45 and as needed at the discretion of the group

**Timeline:**

1. Mandate submitted to Board for next meeting (by April 5 to Secretary)
2. Questionnaire completed by April 8 to 22
3. Distribute and collect questionnaire April 22 to May 6
4. Analysis and collation, and recommendations to be done by May 22nd
5. Community meeting dates, for those who will work to affirm and make changes, to be May 22nd at full faculty meeting time and May 23rd in the evening

**Committee Membership Criteria:**

Knowledge needed:
1. History of the school and of mandate system
2. An understanding of Rudolf Steiner's Threefold Worldview and its relationship to the Waldorf School movement
3. Relationship to the being of the school, and willingness to work with this aspect
4. Knowledge of other types of organizations and their management

Skills needed:
1. Ability to listen, to communicate
2. Ability to delegate, ask for help
3. Good analytical skills
4. Good writing skills
5. Ability to form concise questions, to work with clarity

Attributes/attitudes:
1. Forward looking, and committed to this school's future and its well-being
2. Time to do the work

MANDATE OF CORE GROUP IS TO DRAW IN OTHERS AS NEEDED TO FOCUS THE WORK, NOT TO DO IT ALL.

**Decisions to be made:** Decide on information gathering methods and processes including survey questions and interview questions for selected individuals. Create a report and decide on final recommendations

**Input Loops:** All Faculty, Administration, Board, and Community, Individuals with past involvement in the school

**Review:** A self-evaluation of the committee's process will be carried out after the process is complete.                    **Mandated by:** The Board

# Appendix E

# Initial Review Process Findings and Recommendations

The following are identified general areas of strengths, concerns and gaps identified after three years of operation under the Board-mandated committee system:

## Achievements

-more transparency

-mandates established to describe areas of work

-responsibility in each mandate group allows for decision making

-Hub was created to be a group to carry consciousness of flow of information/ decisions, & to monitor effectiveness of committees

-Issues Management process established

-greater unity amongst faculty, working together in day-to-day individual faculty meeting & full faculty – artistic/study/business

-meetings of committees documented with minutes with more follow-up possible

-processes & procedures are being developed & reviewed in various committees

## Gaps and Areas of Concern

-sense of working alone without unity, or a shared vision that connects the parts to a whole, that informs the work, roles, and decisions

-lack of pedagogical management group that, with a clear pedagogical vision, can manage pedagogical committees and consider, & resolve pedagogical questions and issues

-lack of clear, effective interface between committees

-lack of clarity around final authority

-lack of communication skills

-lack of clarity about input loops; getting info from others in order to make informed decisions

-lack of trust in group processes, falling back on a desire for hierarchical authority

-communication with parents; introduction to & education about our pedagogical ideals is lacking

-lack of clear links between Board, Faculty, Mandate Groups, Parents

-Principal (pedagogical head) swamped with issues; as an individual it is too much

-role of admin in school not clear; definition of individual roles and interaction with parents and faculty unclear

-no Development Officer or development plan

-lack of volunteer plan – volunteerism is down

-large turnover of student population

-lack of long range financial planning

-poor facility, poor salaries

The numbers of issues, challenges and gaps within the structure and systems of the school are many, so time is required to establish recommendations. For example, the parents' surveys contain reference to specific unresolved issues and these need to be resolved somehow. Questions were asked and answers are expected. However, an attempt has been made to formulate some immediate recommendations that will allow for more efficient and effective operation of the school.

**Recommendation:**

*Background: The school vision is still very much implicit and is not consciously used to drive decision-making or actions. In order for a vision to be the driving force and the school's immune system, it must become explicit and be kept alive in every working group within the school. The school needs a big picture or tableau that helps direct the development and implementation of short- and long-term goals, aims and objectives.*

Develop a Plan out of a whole community process of re-envisioning with the intention of making explicit what is implicit within the members of the school. Out of this process would emerge vision and mission statements, a statement of values, and an action plan that will help identify short- and long-term goals and objectives. A comprehensive Development Plan would be developed from this larger picture. This process could begin with the full faculty in the August meetings.

**Recommendation:**

Based on a threefold vision, it is suggested for the long term, that the school establish three umbrella groups, one in each sphere—pedagogical, governance (legal-financial), community & resource development (economic)—to guide, steer, and coordinate the activities and nurture the impulse of each sphere. Umbrella groups will be responsible for identifying the need for mandate groups, will define each mandate, and select committee members. They will ensure that each committee has adequate and clear policies and procedures and that these are part of the mandate document. They will receive minutes and reports, monitor and ponder these, and evaluate the effectiveness and/or need for the committees at regular pre-determined intervals. These groups will take input, suggestions, and feedback from the larger body associated with its specific sphere and consult with the other spheres when appropriate. They will delegate task groups or individuals that will take up other pedagogical, governance (legal-financial), and community & resource development tasks as needed.

The immediate need, however, is to establish a Pedagogical umbrella group that would carry the pedagogical area in the above manner. The feedback indicated that this is a step that requires immediate implementation and that the full faculty will need to create this group.

# Appendix F

# Nine Propositions in Search of the Threefold Social Order

By Christopher Schaefer

*What kind of institutions must exist for people to be able to have the right thoughts on social matters, and what kind of thoughts must exist that these right social institutions can arise?*

Rudolf Steiner

In a series of lectures called "Education as a Force for Social Change," Rudolf Steiner describes three great dangers for modern humanity: the mechanization of the spirit, the vegetablization of the soul, and the animalization of the body.[1] Since his time, these dangers have become ever more pronounced through a media-driven, consumer-oriented global society, promoted by the market capitalism of the West. His response to these dangers was to promote the ideas of the threefold social order, arguing that a healthy social life and healthy human beings depend on grasping the principles of threefolding, "socialism for economic life, democracy for the life of rights, and individualism for spiritual life."[2]

As we come to the end of the [20th] century and the unquestioned global triumph of the democratic capitalist model of society, we need to recognize how few of Steiner's social ideas have found an echo in our broader culture and how, even in our own circles, his social imaginations and concerns have elicited limited interest and response. I believe that this limited interest and activity among individuals and groups otherwise interested in spiritual science is due largely to the fact that we see Steiner's social ideas as a program or a utopian model to be imposed on reality, rather than as an actual description of what is already present in reality, although unconsciously. For this reason, I have chosen to elaborate, in a very brief manner, nine propositions about Rudolf Steiner's social insight and the principles of the threefold social order as a spur to dialogue and action.

## 1. The social world is a humanly created world.

The natural world of mountains, sunsets, and grazing deer is given to us by a divinely created world. We are part of that creation. We, however, create the world of road signs, living room conversations, post offices, amusement parks, and multi-national corporations. Evermore in this century, we inhabit the humanly created world of office buildings, highways, shopping malls, and urban landscapes.

## 2. The social world both reflects and shapes human consciousness.

What kind of consciousness is expressed in the cathedrals placed in the center of European cities in the 13th and 14th centuries, and how did the many pictures and ceremonies of the drama of human salvation shape the medieval mind? What do office buildings, sports arenas, and parking garages in the center of American cities say about our consciousness? How does the work world of functional specialization, information technology, and production timelines affect our consciousness?

I recently attended a research conference on education and heard Barry Sanders, the author of *A Is for Ox*, ask the question, "If the text [manuscript or book] has been an organizing principle of human consciousness since the 13th century through the structure of words, sentences, and paragraphs, what impact will the new organizing principle of the TV and computer screen have on us?"[3]

## 3. Humanity's power in transforming the natural world and creating the social world necessitates a growing responsibility for creating a healthy social order.

In this century, we have moved from a predominantly rural lifestyle, lived in connection to nature and the seasons, into an urban, industrial or post-industrial society. In the past, instinct, tradition, and religion guided the greater portion of humanity in creating families, villages, and towns—in creating the fabric of social life. The rapid growth of technology and our new capacity to control and exploit the earth suggest a new responsibility in co-creating the natural and social worlds. For me, the testing and use of atomic weapons proclaimed a new age of human social responsibility. Rudolf Steiner describes this new responsibility as the need to replace fading social instincts with a new, spiritually-based social understanding.

## 4. As human beings are threefold in nature, all social creations (groups, institutions, and society) have a threefold character.

If we create society, and our fundamental nature is threefold in that we have a body, soul, and spirit, and possess the faculties of thinking, feeling, and willing, then these characteristics are built into all social forms. In conversation, we can notice ideas, feelings of like or dislike, and intention or motive. In groups, we can observe the dance of words, of relationships through speaking and listening, and of procedure, or the common will life of the group. In organizations, there is a realm of identity or *spirit* that comes to expression in the mission, purpose, and history of a company or school; of *soul* expressing itself in the quality of internal and external relationships (in the culture of the organization); and of *body*, as experienced in the buildings, machinery, and product flows. When working with organizations, I often ask, "How is the dialogue with spirit? Is it alive and shared through celebration, mutual learning, future planning, and mission clarification? How is the dialogue with people, both within the organization and with the broader culture? How is the dialogue with the earth—with buildings, maintenance, machinery, and resources?"

If we turn to society as a whole, we can clearly discern the realm of spirit as expressed in the language, literature, history, and gestures of a nation. The cry of manifest destiny in 19th century American politics is still with us in our dealings with Iraq. The desire to make English the official language is an effort to understand and defend our uniqueness, as was the unsuccessful French effort to keep EuroDisney out of France.

The soul realm, the realm of rights and responsibilities, is being continuously renewed through new laws, and new legal battles. Will Congress renew the Independent Counsel Act after what we have been through with Kenneth Starr? Does affirmative action legislation continue to reflect the sense of right of the American people?

With regard to economic life, we can't help but be aware of the Dow Jones Industrial Index, the policies of the Federal Reserve Board, or our own worries about right livelihood. Indeed, the production, distribution, and sale of goods and services for maximum profit have become the dominant fixation of our culture.

Threefoldness is therefore not a theory, but a formative principle in all social reality. The challenge is to see and understand it, and to form social relationships in accordance with its underlying qualities.

## 5. Threefoldness and the qualities relevant to each sphere are a set of empirical propositions that govern social health.

Independent thinking, a sense for the rights and responsibility of self and other, and action dedicated to service are the hallmarks of a healthy individual and a healthy society. For Steiner, the interdependent physiological functioning of the nerve sense system, of the heart-lung rhythmic system, and of the metabolic limb system are the prototype for a new society. The more cultural life is free, expressing different cultural norms, and the more it fosters the free unfolding of individual capacities, the more it will provide creative solutions and ideas for the future. Many philosophies of education, many different schools, and educational choice with equal access will do more for our society than national standards or bureaucratic guidelines. When the state restricts itself to the defense of public safety and the formulation and administration of rights through the legal system, it exercises its proper mandate. An economic system dedicated and organized to provide goods and services to meet true human needs will produce maximum well being if it is truly service-oriented and structured in an associative manner through promoting a dialogue between producers, consumers, and traders.

The same principles hold good for any organization—the more a school, company, or therapy center fosters individual creativity within the context of a clearly shared organizational mission, the more it cultivates a culture of shared rights and responsibilities, and the more it focuses on true service to customers or clients, the healthier it will be.

## 6. There are seven social laws that govern social life.

Rudolf Steiner articulated at least seven different social laws or principles during his lifetime. As social laws, they focus on the interplay of human consciousness and social forms, indicating a realm of choice.

a) In 1898, Steiner formulated what he called the Basic Sociological Law: *At the beginning of culture, humanity strives to create social arrangements in which the interests of the individual are sacrificed for the interest of the whole. Later developments lead to a gradual freeing of the individual from the interests of the community and to an unfolding of individual needs and capacities.*[4]

This law, or principle, exists in time, in all likelihood covering the whole of known history. Certainly, when one ponders the sweep of history and the gradual emergence of individual rights from Greco-Roman times to the present, it appears justified and points to one of the central aspects of historical evolution: the emergence of individual consciousness. Based on my observation of institutional development, I would say that it also applies to the life cycle of institutions, which require the energy and sacrifice of individual interests in order to be established and are then, in later years, more able to respond to the needs of individual members.

b) In 1905, Steiner described a second principle, calling it the Fundamental Social Law: *The well-being of a community of cooperatively working human beings is the greater the less individuals demand the proceeds of their work for themselves or, in other words, the more they make over these proceeds to their co-workers and the more their needs are met not by their own work but from that of others.*[5]

This complex and awkwardly phrased law is concerned with motives, suggesting that when labor is a commodity and self-interest becomes the motive force of economic activity, suffering, poverty, and want are the results. To what degree is the poverty in the Third World or in our inner cities the result of this social law not being understood in the developed world? What will be the long-term social consequences of a modified capitalist system appealing to self-interest?

There are numerous curative communities, shared income groups, and schools working with Steiner's Fundamental Social Law. The resulting appeal to service, to true motives, and to community interest is evident. Do such arrangements produce "well-being"? Steiner not only argued yes, but suggested there would be less mental and physical illness because individuals would then make life choices based not on income considerations, but on an assessment of their real capacities and interests. Such laws are empirical propositions, accessible to reason and experience, as well as capable of being tested. Although I am not aware of systematic studies having been conducted to prove the validity of either of the above laws, there is considerable experience in working with the Fundamental Social Law—efforts that have in common the separation of wages from work.

c) The principles of the threefold social order were elaborated by Rudolf Steiner in many lectures between 1918–1922 and in his book, translated as *Toward Social Renewal*.[6] While he did not directly formulate the Threefold Social Order as a law except by inference, it could be expressed in the following way: *The health of a group, institution, or of society is the greater the more it works with principles of freedom in cultural life, equality in the sphere of rights and responsibilities, and brotherhood and sisterhood in the area of work or economic life.*

If this is true, groups, institutions, and societies working with these principles will be characterized by higher levels of creativity and greater health and will produce higher levels of commitment and satisfaction among their members and their clients. Health is not synonymous with efficiency or profitability, although such factors should also be considered.

Christof Lindenau, a German sociologist, has formulated these principles in more detail as follows:

d) *The meeting of human needs within a group, institution, or society of cooperatively working human beings is the greater the more it is based on the practice of brotherhood or sisterhood.* [Refers to economic life.]

This principle refers to the conscious division of tasks within an institution or society based on competence, in which each person contributes his or her talents to serving the needs of the whole and to a wage system based on need as opposed to power or influence.

e) *Agreements on rights and responsibilities within a group of cooperatively working human beings are most binding and effective the more they are based on the practice of equality.* [Refers to rights life.]

This principle suggests that a conscious rights life—spelling out the rights and responsibilities of, for example, parents, teachers, and Board within a Waldorf school, or of members and council within the Anthroposophical Society—is most effective when based on dialogue and consensus.

f) *The creative working together of people in a group or an institution is most fruitful when it can proceed from the exercise of freedom.* [Refers to cultural life.][7]

When individuals are granted substantial autonomy or freedom of initiative within a generally accepted mission or set of goals, they will be more creative on behalf of the whole.

It is important to note that there is an inherent tension within each sphere: in economic life between service and efficiency; in rights life between rights and responsibilities;

and in cultural life between individual freedom and a set of cultural norms or institutional goals. An inner balance between the polarities is essential for health.

In working with a wide variety of institutions over the years, I have also experienced an essential interdependency between the three spheres. If the goal or mission of an organization is not clear or shared (cultural life), the rights life suffers in the sense that power plays and personality conflicts become more pronounced (social life), which in turn makes the trust or delegation required for an effective work life based on brotherhood and sisterhood more difficult (economic life). Equally, if the resources in economic life are continuously too limited, it will over time erode both the relational and spiritual life of the organization or of society at large.

g) In addition to the Basic Sociological Law, the Fundamental Social Law, and the Laws of Threefoldness, Rudolf Steiner articulated a Motto of the Social Ethic, which is often worked with in our institutions:

*The healing social life is found when in the mirror of the human soul the whole community finds its reflection and when in the community the strength of each one is living.*[8]

This motto captures the essential relationship between the individual and the community, describing the need to develop new social capacities through inner schooling in order to perceive the needs of the community. It also suggests that the virtue or strength of each one can live only if the community is organized in a conscious, threefold manner. The individual needs a threefold organizational and societal form in order to bring to consciousness the three soul forces of thinking, feeling, and willing in a healthy manner, in order to offer these capacities in service to the greater whole.

Reflection on these seven principles suggests that there are, in all likelihood, hundreds of such propositions operative in social life. For example, the larger and newer the group, the more structured the leadership required to have an effective group process; or its reverse, the smaller and older the group, the less structured leadership is required. Another example is that the more an institution is willing to learn from its history and experience— the more it delights in being a learning community—the more successful it will be in coping with the future. Such principles have the quality of enhancing insight while at the same time making an appeal to consciousness.

## 7. Through action learning—in the realm of practice—we have the opportunity to experience and discover principles for a healthy society.

Steiner suggested that social understanding requires jumping into the test tube, or what my profession refers to as "action learning." It is estimated that there are some 9000 groups and institutions connected to anthroposophy, ranging from the burgeoning Waldorf school movement and community-supported agriculture projects (CSAs), to farms, shops, therapy centers, colleges, and companies. What an incredible opportunity to experiment, learn, and share! How do we really foster a free spiritual life in our institutions? How does the economic life of the Anthroposophical Society come to expression and how can we foster it? Why haven't we developed a more conscious service orientation toward parents in Waldorf schools? What would it really mean to have a conscious rights life in an adult education center? The ongoing testing of insights and principles would allow us to create a community of social learning among the network of cooperatively-run institutions indebted to Rudolf Steiner's work. It would also lead us into a more fruitful dialogue and collaboration with the many groups and institutions sharing similar social and spiritual concerns. Lastly, it would give us the experience and insights to speak with authority on a broader range of cultural, social, and economic issues affecting our society.

## 8. In addition to action learning, we have the possibility of testing the principles of threefoldness through empirical research.

Three years ago I was given an article from *The New York Times* reporting on a health study, which found that in those communities in the U.S. where income inequalities were highest, the rate of physical and mental illness was higher among both rich and poor than in comparable communities with lower income differences. The truth of the Fundamental Social Law is here expressed in conventional research terms: The well being of a community is greater when individuals do not take the proceeds of their work for themselves. Is evidence of illness less in Waldorf schools and Camphill communities than in similar but more conventional organizations? I expect so.

In this testing of laws and principles, I could imagine comparing the growth rates and other social measurements of different societies during the last century in order to see how those that come closest to the principles of the threefold social order have fared.

Daniel Jones, a management professor in England, studied Toyota's lean production principles and has co-authored two best-selling books with James Womack of MIT, *The Machine that Changed the World* and *Lean Thinking*.[9] They found that a company's real commitment to maximizing customer value and service and to eliminating waste is key to economic performance. Looked at carefully, this approach embodies essential aspects of an associative economic life.

The research I have been doing over the last few years leads me to believe that practice is ahead of theory—that many individuals and organizations are engaged in wise practices embodying the laws of threefoldness. Our challenge is to perceive, practice, and articulate the lawfulness that is already present in the social world.

**9. If we can consciously work with principles of threefoldness in our lives and institutions, and if we are able to see and articulate these formative principles at work in society, then we will be able to promote social healing in the world.**

The laws of threefoldness that Steiner began articulating at the beginning of this century are the formative principles of the social future. They are not an experiment that failed in 1922, but the road to building a healthy society in the 21st century. It is because of the urgency of perceiving and articulating these social laws and principles that I have been involved in creating a non-profit research and educational institute called High Tor Alliance: Resource for Organization and Community Renewal. We see our task as that of creating a partnership of practitioners, researchers, and consultants to discover and formulate the essential connection between the inner world of the human being and the outer world of work, to articulate the threefold laws of social creation.

## Notes

1. Rudolf Steiner. *Education as a Force for Social Change,* Anthroposophic Press, 1997, p.9.

2. Ibid., p.10.

3. Barry Sanders. *A Is for Ox: Violence, Electronic Media and the Silencing of the Written Word,* Pantheon, 1994.

4. Contained in GA 31, 166, p.147. Translation by the author.

5. Contained in GA 34, 1960. Translation by the author.

6. Rudolf Steiner. *Toward Social Renewal,* Rudolf Steiner Press, 1987.

7. Christof Lindenau. *Soziale Dreigliederung,* Verlag Freies Geistesleben, 1983.

8. Rudolf Steiner,. *Verses and Meditations*, Rudolf Steiner Press, 1985, pp.116–117.

9. James Womack and Daniel Jones. *The Machine that Changed the World*, Simon and Schuster, 1992, and *Lean Thinking*. Simon and Schuster, 1996.

Christopher Schaefer, PhD, is a founding member of the Social Science Section of the Goetheanum School of Spiritual Science in North America, a former faculty member at Sunbridge College, and Director of the Waldorf School Administration and Community Development program. He is also an organization development consultant and the Executive Director of High Tor Alliance, 823 Chestnut Ridge Road, Spring Valley, NY 10977 (914) 426-1293, e-mail: hta@hightor.org.

# Appendix G

# Community Forum Envisioning Conference Agenda

**Evening '1'**

19:00     Verse

         Welcome
              Background, How did we get to this place?
              Intentions/Goals
              Introduce facilitators & Community Development & Planning Committee

19:15     Getting Started

         Responsibilities:
            Participants
            Community Development & Planning Committee
            Facilitator

         Preview of Agenda

         History-Building Group activity w/ handout

19:45     Values – cross sectional small groups        Facilitator
         Lower School Teachers
         Kindergarten/early childhood teachers
         High School Teachers
         Administration
         Board
         Parents

20:30     Reporting

         4 or 5 key values or beliefs from each group
         e.g., educating the whole child, cultural diversity     Reporters

20:50     Identification of Common Themes        All

21:00     Closing

**Day '1'**

09:00     Singing

         Verse

09:15 Mission Statement: What do we commit to achieve?
Small groups by discipline
e.g., provide an appropriate education for each stage of child development, provide ongoing opportunities for the professional development of teachers and staff

10:00 Reporting          Reporters
4 or 5 key commitments that show how we reflect our values in action

10:25 Identification of Common Themes     All
3-sticker exercise

10:30 Break

11:00 Review of 3-Sticker Exercise

Vision Statement: Personal writing exercise    All

3 sentences, 50 words: Describe the purpose of our organization, the values that we reflect, and how we will achieve our vision.

11:15 Small group activity – cross sectional groups

Place personal writing in the center of the table, select one and read it to the small group while others take notes. Draft a vision statement using the best of what has been shared in your group, and any new inspirations that come through discussion.

12:15 Reading of small group vision statements   Reporters

12:30 Lunch – CD&P Committee meet with facilitator

14:00 Long Range Plan
Small Groups by Area of Passion:
e.g., curriculum
   facilities
   professional development
   community building
   development and fundraising
   outreach
   government interaction
   financial and administrative strength

What will we have achieved in this area by 2015?

What stakeholders/resources will be needed to deliver these goals?

15:00 Reporting          Reporters

| 15:30 | Break |
|---|---|
| 16:00 | Next Steps: Where do we go from here? <br> Suggested Action Steps |
| 17:00 | Verse |
| | Closing |

# Appendix H

# Vision, Values, Mission

## VISION

The Vancouver Waldorf School

- endeavors to offer an academic, artistic and practical education that integrates independent thinking with social responsibility in a way that will enable its students to fulfill their life tasks and contribute to world renewal.

- using the Waldorf curriculum, works out of a recognition of and respect for an understanding of the human being as a spiritual being as indicated by Rudolf Steiner.

- envisions a school community where each individual participates and contributes to the school's vision and mission while working out of its shared values.

## VALUES

Out of a commitment to Waldorf education, and a recognition of and respect for the understanding of the human being that underlies it, we value

- an education that integrates body, soul, and spirit — thinking, feeling, and willing, that inspires confidence in oneself, social feeling for others, and respect for all living things, that awakens independent thinking and enables our graduates to fulfill their life tasks.

- Rudolf Steiner's understanding of child development and of the unique destiny of each child as a spiritual being.

- an educational environment that awakens the child's moral awareness and safeguards his or her healthy development through the actions of the school community's adult members.

- the recognition of the spiritual essence of the human being and an environment and education that nurtures reverence for that essence.

- a school community in which the integrity of each member is respected, a diversity of gifts is recognized, and the participation in service to the school's vision and mission is encouraged.

- the individuality and integrity of each and every person within the social fabric of the school and the skills that each individual can bring to the school's life and mission.

**MISSION**

- deliver Waldorf education using Rudolf Steiner's understanding of child development and the Waldorf curriculum to enlighten and inform our teaching

- provide an environment that nurtures childhood through rhythm, ritual, relationships, reverence and respect, which supports the incarnating spirit

- provide a curriculum that balances academic with artistic and practical learning and integrates the faculties of thinking

- provide and sustain a beautiful and healthy environment that supports the education of the children

- support and nourish the teachers through providing opportunities for spiritual and professional development

- recognize the reality of different learners and provide the professional development needed to serve these children

- provide opportunities for parents to deepen their understanding of Waldorf education

- ensure that Waldorf education is available to any child regardless of financial circumstances

- support the teachers by providing financial security

- operate out of financial stability and abundance and create an environment that fosters the spirit of giving

- operate out of a recognition of life's threefold principles and create a school that is a living, evolving organism

- foster strength of community between teachers, parents, children, alumni and friends

- promote a greater public awareness of the values of Waldorf education

- actively enhance cultural, social and financial diversity within the life of the school.

# Appendix I

# Goals

## Goal 1    Pedagogical

### *Goal 1a*

To have and define the expectations of a full Waldorf curriculum in all grades to ensure retention of students and to result in waiting lists for all grades. Elements of a full curriculum would include:

- At least two foreign languages;
- A full music program, including Grade School and High School choirs and Orchestra;
- A full arts and crafts program;
- A full physical education program, including spatial dynamics;
- A gardening program;
- A pattern of community service integrated into the curriculum.

Strategic steps needed:

- Create a functional curriculum overview document that will provide the basic information that teachers will require in order to implement the curriculum

- Find and retain teachers trained in Waldorf pedagogy who are capable of bringing the Waldorf curriculum to the students

- Maintain and expand a professional development program to support teachers in their continuing learning—pedagogically, emotionally, spiritually

- Deepen the understanding of the therapeutic aspects of the curriculum and of those children whose learning needs challenge us to re-think our approaches to teaching

- Ensure that teachers have the financial support necessary for them to continue teaching.

### *Goal 1b*

To establish a continuing education program in Waldorf education for parents, including opportunities to understand the implications of the threefold principle in the operation of a Waldorf school.

### *Goal 1c*

To support the West Coast Institute for Studies in Anthroposophy, in concert with other Waldorf schools in the Pacific Northwest, in establishing a grade school teacher training program.

## Goal 2    Facility

To have a facility for Early Childhood to Grade 12 which supports a full curriculum, housed in an aesthetically pleasing, ecologically responsible setting, a showcase for Waldorf education.

To meet our goals we need:
- A comprehensive strategy for development and fundraising.
- Sustained enthusiasm and commitment to support and maintain our vision
- Purchase properties, find partners as necessary
- Ensure that what is built is what is needed and wanted.
- Expanded Building Committee/Site Development Committee
- Development Office
- YES! from community.

## Goal 3    Community Development

### Goal 3a

To establish a Community Development Program that generates commitment from community members to furthering the mission of the school and includes
- Parent Education program
- Alumni Program with database
- Volunteer Coordination program
- Realistic and informed communication channels between school and school community
- Community events

and results in informed parents, committed and willing volunteers, and active alumni.

### Goal 3b

To have ten consecutive years of increased enrollment, resulting in full classes with waiting lists for all classes.

## Goal 4    Financial Health
- Have a financial plan.
- Support the teachers by providing financial security.
- Operate out of financial freedom, vitality, and stability and create an environment that fosters the spirit of giving.

## Goal 5    Administration

To implement and maintain an administrative structure that clearly defines the boundaries, overlaps, communication links, and accountability within and between the three areas of operation within the school.

# Appendix J

# Pedagogical Carrying Group Constitution – Example '1'

## Preamble

The Pedagogical Carrying Group (PCG) is designed to serve as the central pedagogical body of awareness and to maintain a broad overview of the workings of the various pedagogical committees and their functions in the school. It is to serve as a communication hub to help the community be aware of important information, and it is to maintain the goal of transparency in the workings of this sphere of the school. It is an important function that the PCG will share information with all parties in matters that may have an impact upon them.

## Purpose

To carry the spiritual impulse underlying the pedagogy of the Vancouver Waldorf School and provide pedagogical direction and initiative using consensus as its method of decision-making.

## Summary of the Pedagogical Carrying Group's Task

1. To be the body that mandates groups or strikes committees as deemed necessary to perform functions for the healthy pedagogical life of the school. To ensure that the work of the school's pedagogical mandate groups and related committees is done and that a review and evaluation of each occurs on a regular basis.

2. To serve as a communication hub for all pedagogical mandate groups and related committees in the school and to be the pedagogical 'sense organ' of awareness through which matters of a general pedagogical nature (i.e., program, overall well-being, etc.) are steered and coordinated.

3. To establish general pedagogical policy through the following means:
   a. by requesting policies from pedagogical groups and ensuring their fulfillment
   b. by ratifying policies of a pedagogical nature that help streamline the workings of the school
   c. by clarifying tasks and fostering efficient and timely execution of these tasks

4. Where questions of employment (human resources) arise, the PCG will stand behind each Mandate Group's due processes. As such, the PCG will receive recommendations from pedagogical mandate groups (Evaluation, Hiring, Professional Development and Workload) and either

a. support and minute the recommendations as a final decision,

b. return the issue for further work, or

c. refer issues to an Issues Management Process (IMP).

Such referrals will report the outcome of the IMP to the PCG.

5. For issues *not* related to Human Resources or the IMP, where due process has been followed through committees or mandate groups, the PCG will arbitrate and resolve matters outstanding.

   *[A general reporting mechanism of IMP activities by the Pedagogical Coordinator to the PCG is important in relation to safeguarding children and Waldorf education.]*

6. Consult and solicit input from the Faculty.

7. Support and ensure facilitation of the Full Faculty Meeting.

8. Act as a support and advisory body for the Pedagogical Coordinator.

9. Serve in the support of teachers and excellence in their work.

10. Act in good faith on behalf of the Faculty and work cooperatively with the Board, the Finance, Administration and Development areas of the School.

## Accountability and Reporting

1. The PCG is accountable and reports to the Faculty and The Board of Trustees.

2. The PCG's activities will be reported and consultation sought at the meetings of the Faculty, Finance and Development.

3. The PCG will provide regular reports to the Board at the Board's regular meetings and meet with the Board as a full group at least thrice annually.

## Meeting Times

The PCG will meet three hours weekly on Thursday afternoons three times per month.

## Membership Requirements

Both Faculty members selected from the Mandate and Faculty Groups and the Community member are to have at least two years of experience in the school. All candidates are to respond in writing as to how they feel they meet the criteria by completing a form using the items from the Membership Criteria. This will then be used in the Selection Process (see below).

## Membership Criteria

Members must commit to attending all scheduled meetings of the PCG.

### Skills

- Experience with Waldorf pedagogy
- Interpersonal skills, cooperative working, maintaining confidentiality, directness
- Clear thinking
- Ability to be transparent in relation to the functioning of the group

### Knowledge

- Of Waldorf pedagogy, Waldorf curriculum, anthroposophy
- Of School policies

### Attitudes

- Willingness to serve on this group
- Commitment to the Vancouver Waldorf School
- Commitment to deepening the understanding of the spiritual nature of the human being, particularly as it relates to child development
- Commitment to self-development
- Willingness to work with the process of consensus
- To recognize and acknowledge anthroposophy as the spiritual foundation of the Vancouver Waldorf School and to work with this impulse

### Assets

- Knowledge of Waldorf courses and curriculum development that are available
- Knowledge of developments in education and related research

## Number of Members and Composition of PCG

Twelve members are required. Recognizing that duplication will occur, the PCG is to have at least one member from each of the following areas of the school:

1. Professional Development Mandate Committee
2. Evaluation Mandate Committee
3. Hiring Mandate Committee
4. Workload Mandate Committee
5. a Kindergarten teacher
6. a Grade School teacher
7. a High School teacher
8. Faculty members at large
9. a non-teaching community member
10. the Pedagogical Co-coordinator
11. the Administrative Coordinator (ex-officio)
12. the Development Coordinator

Collaborative/cooperative links (liaisons) are to be made with the following areas:
1. AWSNA delegates
2. Finance

3. Board of Trustees
4. Development
5. Issues Management
6. Mentoring

In the event that full membership is not attained or maintained at any given time in the working life of the group, members must be actively sought out to complete membership. The Faculty and Board must be made aware of such a circumstance and approve the continued operation of the PCG despite any shortfall in membership.

## Selection Process

Members will be selected from within their respective mandate or faculty group in 'Number of Members and Composition of PCG'] on the basis of collegial recognition using the criteria outlined in 'Membership Criteria' above. Candidates are to have completed the Membership Criteria form. This is to be circulated amongst the members in the selecting group, and a full discussion is to follow on the basis of the responses of the candidates and the questions of the members. In the case of the community member selection, to evaluate the Membership Criteria form, an ad hoc group will be established, to be composed of two Faculty members and two Community/VWS Society members who have a record of long standing service in the community.

PCG members chosen must recognize that they will carry the consciousness of and provide input from the group from which they have been selected. In the event that all representation is accomplished without attaining full membership in numbers (7), a 'member at large' may be added to complete the seven-member constituency. The full membership will be finalized by Full Faculty consensus.

## Terms of Service

There is no fixed length of time for member to serve on the PCG. However, membership shall be reviewed annually. A re-recognition from a member's representative group must occur and a re-commitment by the member must be made in the form of a written statement to the Faculty. Changes need to occur in such a way that a maximum of 45% turnover occurs each year in order to maintain continuity.

Rotation on and off is recognized as needing flexibility. However, terms of service will generally commence in mid-August and mid-February. Notice must be given three months prior to these times to allow time for new members to be selected and transition into the group.

## Raison d'etre

The PCG will make recommendations for and ratify pedagogical policy. In cases where due process has been followed through committees or mandate groups and when requested, the PCG will arbitrate in (resolve) matters outstanding that are of a pedagogical nature. Such a request may come from a group or individual; however, the Full Faculty must be informed that such procedure is being undertaken.

## Input Loops

The principle of the communication function of the PCG is that selected, important information is to be presented to the PCG through its respective members. The PCG then will help facilitate information flow, such that it moves through established links. It will help to form those links if they do not exist, thus enhancing the communication in the School. Communication is to be made in writing and needs to be in the form of a synopsis rather than a lengthy report or request. It is particularly important that a report maintain confidentiality where appropriate.

The PCG will designate its own contact person(s) where appropriate.

A PCG member will be designated to liaise with the Faculty Chair(s) to provide input for setting the Full Faculty agenda and to coordinate consultative processes, receive input and share information necessary to bring to the Full Faculty Meetings.

## Communication Loops

Each PCG member will report to his/her group at their regular mandate/departmental meetings on matters being taken up by the PCG that pertain to it. Contact persons (liaisons) will be established with all relevant committees who are not directly represented in the PCG (i.e., Class Parent Group, Maintenance, etc.). Regular contact and timing will be agreed upon by the PCG and a particular committee.

The appropriate forum for communication to the community is to be worked out. (such suggestions as regular summaries in the Parent Bulletin, etc.). Listing of current discussion items and pertinent information will be made available to the community through the Parent Bulletin and/or through a posting on a bulletin board.

## Documentation

Minutes will be kept in writing, outlining the items discussed, decisions, actions and requested statements. Memos will be sent to specific groups as required in writing.

## Evaluation

An evaluation must be completed no later than April 30th of each year after the new membership has been established and is in operation. This is seen to take the form of formal input from the Faculty and Administration as in a questionnaire so that an outline of what is working and what is not can be identified and reported upon. The group to conduct this will be struck by the Full Faculty.

## Recall

Any member or members may be recalled to discuss his/her/their place as a member(s) of the PCG with the Full Faculty. This would have to be done through application to the Full Faculty Chair(s) who will then consult with the Mandate Chairs before a meeting takes place with the member(s) in question with this same group. If unresolved at this level, a meeting with the Full Faculty and the member(s) would need to take place.

## Consensus Decision-Making

Decision-making is to be made using the process of consensus. The PCG is not to resort to decision by vote or any other 'democratic' decision-making process. Should consensus be unattainable with respect to a particular issue, the issue shall be referred to the Full Faculty for assessment of both the issue and the functioning of the PCG. In such cases, the Full Faculty shall reserve the right to instruct the PCG as to how it shall move forward.

The following definition of consensus is to serve as the basis for PCG decision-making:

Consensus is a group decision which all members feel they can live with, support and commit themselves not to undermine. The decision is arrived at through a process whereby the issues are fully aired. All members feel they have been adequately heard, everyone has equal power and responsibility so that all are satisfied with the process. The process requires the members to be emotionally present and engaged, frank in a loving, mutually respectful manner, sensitive to each other; to be selfless, dispassionate, and capable of emptying themselves; and possessing a paradoxical awareness of the preciousness of both people and time. This includes knowing when the solution is satisfactory, and that it is time to stop, with a willingness to reopen the discussion at such a time as the group determines a need for revision.

(Adapted from *A World Waiting to Be Born* by S. Peck)

# Appendix K

# Pedagogical Carrying Group Constitution – Example '2'

The Pedagogical Carrying Group (PCG) is designed to serve as the central pedagogical body of awareness and to maintain a broad overview of the workings of the various pedagogical committees and their functions in the school. It is to serve as a communication hub to inform the community and to maintain the goal of transparency in the workings of this sphere of the school. The PCG will share information with all parties in matters that may have an impact upon them.

## Purpose

To carry the spiritual impulse underlying the pedagogy of the Vancouver Waldorf School and provide pedagogical direction and initiative using consensus as its method of decision-making (see definition of consensus).

## Summary of the Pedagogical Carrying Group's Task

1. To be the body that mandates work and strikes committees through one of the three Pedagogical Committees as deemed necessary to perform functions for the healthy pedagogical life of the school. Its role is to ensure that the work of the school's Pedagogical Committees and task groups is done and that a review and evaluation of each occurs on a regular basis.

2. To serve as a communication hub for all Pedagogical Committees in the school and to be the pedagogical 'sense organ' of awareness through which matters of a general pedagogical nature (i.e., program, overall well-being, etc..) are steered and coordinated.

3. To establish general pedagogical policy through the following means:

   a. By requesting policies from Pedagogical Committees and ensuring their fulfillment

   b. By ratifying policies of a pedagogical nature that help streamline the workings of the school

   c. By clarifying tasks and fostering efficient and timely execution of these tasks

4. To consult and solicit input from the Faculty

5. To support and ensure facilitation of the Full Faculty Meeting

6. To act as a support and advisory body for the Pedagogical Administrators

7. To serve in the support of teachers and excellence in their work

8. To act in good faith on behalf of the Faculty and to work cooperatively with the Board, Executive Group, Administration, and Development areas of the School

9. The PCG will consider and ratify pedagogical policy. In cases where due process has been followed through committees or mandate groups and when requested, the PCG will arbitrate in (resolve) matters outstanding that are of a pedagogical nature. Such a request may come from a group or individual; however, the Full Faculty must be informed that such procedure is being undertaken.

## Accountability and Reporting

1. The PCG is accountable and reports to the Faculty and the Board of Trustees.

2. The PCG's activities will be reported and consultation sought at the meetings of the Faculty, Board, Executive, and Development.

## Meeting Times

The PCG will meet weekly for at least two hours.

## Membership Requirements

Faculty members selected from the Faculty Groups are to have at least two years of experience in a Waldorf school. All candidates are to respond in person at a PCG meeting as to how they meet the Membership Criteria listed below.

## Membership Criteria

Members must commit to attending scheduled meetings of the PCG.

### Skills

- Experience with Waldorf pedagogy
- Interpersonal skills, cooperative working, maintaining confidentiality, directness
- Clear thinking
- Ability to be transparent in relation to the functioning of the group

### Knowledge

- Of Waldorf pedagogy, Waldorf curriculum, anthroposophy
- Of School policies

### Attitudes

- Willingness to serve on this group
- Commitment to the Vancouver Waldorf School
- Commitment to deepen the understanding of the spiritual nature of the human being, particularly as it relates to child development
- Commitment to self-development
- Willingness to work with the process of consensus* (see below)

- To recognize and acknowledge anthroposophy as the spiritual foundation of the Vancouver Waldorf School and to work with this impulse

**Assets**

- Knowledge of Waldorf courses and curriculum development that are available
- Knowledge of developments in education and related research

## Number of Members and Composition of PCG

Recognizing that duplication will occur; the PCG is to have at least one member from each of the following areas of the school:

1. Program and Curriculum Development Committee Chair
2. Human Resources Committee Chair
3. Practical Needs Committee Chair
4. Kindergarten teacher
5. Grade School teacher
6. High School teacher
7. Faculty members at large
8. The Full Faculty chair
9. Pedagogical Administrator(s)
10. Administrator (ex-officio)
11. Development Director (ex-officio)

In the event that full membership is not attained or maintained at any given time in the working life of the group, members must be actively sought out to complete membership. The Faculty must be made aware of such a circumstance and approve the continued operation of the PCG despite any shortfall in membership.

## Selection Process

Members will be nominated to the Pedagogical Carrying Group after being suggested by either the Full Faculty, Pedagogical Carrying Group or individuals on the basis of collegial recognition using the criteria outlined in 'Membership Criteria' above. Pedagogical Carrying Group members chosen must recognize that they will carry the consciousness of and provide input from the group from which they have been selected. In the event that all representation is accomplished without attaining a membership of seven, a member at large may be added to complete the seven-member constituency.

## Conscientious Objection

Following the nomination, the candidate will be announced in Full Faculty Meeting, whose membership has three business days in which to submit to the Pedagogical Carrying Group any written confirmations or objections to the nomination of a member to the Pedagogical Carrying Group. If there are one or two objections, these objections will be referred to the Pedagogical Carrying Group. A person can be confirmed as a member under these circumstances. If there are three (3) members of the FF who submit objections, the prospective member must stand aside from membership until the PCG has reviewed and resolved the issues raised. If no objections are submitted, the Nominee is appointed in the next Full Faculty Meeting by its Members.

## Terms of Service

There is no fixed length of time for member to serve on the PCG. However, membership shall be reviewed annually. Changes need to occur in such a way that a maximum of 45% turnover occurs each year in order to maintain continuity.

Members who intend to stand down from the PCG are asked to give three months' notice to allow time for new members to be selected and transition into the group.

## Input Loops

Selected, important information is to be presented to the PCG through its respective members. The PCG will help facilitate information flow such that it moves through established links. It will help to form those links if they do not exist, thus enhancing the communication in the School. Communication is to be made in writing. It is particularly important that a report maintain confidentiality where appropriate.

The PCG will designate its own contact person(s) where appropriate.

## Communication Loops

Each PCG member will report to his/her group at their regular departmental or committee meeting on matters being taken up by the PCG that pertain to it. Contact persons will be established with all relevant committees that are not directly represented in the PCG (i.e., Class Parent Group).

## Documentation

Minutes will be kept in writing, outlining the items discussed, decisions, actions and requested statements. Memos will be sent to specific groups or individuals as required in writing.

## Evaluation

An evaluation must be completed no later than April 30th of each year after the new membership has been established and is in operation. This is seen to take the form of formal input from the Faculty and Administration as a questionnaire so that an outline of what is working and what is not can be identified and reported upon. The group to conduct this will be struck by the Full Faculty.

## Recall

Any member or members may be recalled to discuss his/her/their place as a member(s) of the PCG.

## Consensus Decision-Making

Decision-making is to be made using the process of consensus. The PCG is not to resort to decision by vote or any other 'democratic' decision-making process. Should consensus be unattainable with respect to a particular issue, the issue shall be referred to a task group within the PCG for further work and proposals and brought back to the PCG for discussion. The following definition of consensus is to serve as the basis for PCG decision-making: "Consensus is a group decision which all members feel they can live with, support and commit themselves not to undermine. The decision is arrived at through a process whereby the issues are fully aired. All members feel they have been adequately heard, everyone has equal power and responsibility so that all are satisfied with the process. The process requires the members to be emotionally present and engaged, frank in a loving, mutually respectful manner, sensitive to each other; to be selfless, dispassionate, and capable of emptying themselves, and possessing a paradoxical awareness of the preciousness of both people and time. This includes knowing when the solution is satisfactory, and that it is time to stop, with a willingness to reopen the discussion at such a time as the group determines a need for revision." (Adapted from *A World Waiting to Be Born* by S. Peck)

# Appendix L

# Pedagogical Carrying Group Membership Selection Process Example

## Membership Requirement

PCG members are to be Faculty members with at least two years' experience at the school. *All Members must commit to attending all scheduled meetings of the PCG.*

## Selection Process

All prospective members must go through the following process. Prospective members are, to a greater or lesser degree, to meet the criteria listed in order to create an effective PCG.

Each qualifying member is to
1. carefully read the attached copy of the constitution of the PCG and,
2. complete the form prior to the selection meeting with the Full Faculty.

The Full Faculty then enters into a process that carefully and seriously considers each qualified member as a potential PCG candidate. This process would include:
- a review of the completed forms
- conversations in the Full Faculty with each individual sharing insights on aspects of the completed form
- receiving and asking questions
- giving and receiving feedback from each other

*Note: A process to allow for conscientious objection is detailed in the Pedagogical Carrying Group Constitution.

**Please describe your personal relationship with the following criteria.**
**Give examples; use separate page if needed.**

### *Skills*

- Experience with Waldorf pedagogy

  _____

  _____

- Interpersonal skills, cooperative working, maintaining confidentiality, directnes

  _____

  _____

- Clear thinking

  _____

  _____

- Ability to be transparent in relation to the functioning of the group

_____

_____

## Knowledge

- Of Waldorf pedagogy, Waldorf curriculum, anthroposophy

_____

_____

- Of School policies and procedures

_____

_____

## Attitudes

- Willingness to serve on this group

_____

_____

- Commitment to the School

_____

_____

- Commitment to deepen the understanding of the spiritual nature of the human being, particularly as it relates to child development

_____

_____

- Commitment to self-development

_____

_____

- Willingness to work with the process of consensus

_____

_____

- To recognize and acknowledge anthroposophy as the spiritual foundation of the School and to work with this impulse

_____

_____

## Assets

- Knowledge of Waldorf courses and curriculum development that are available

_____

_____

• Knowledge of developments in education and related research

_____

_____

***Please complete the following questions relating to your participation in the PCG:***

• What can I offer?

_____

_____

• What are my limitations?

_____

_____

• What is my reason (motive) for joining this group? (Do I have a personal agenda?)

_____

_____

• What is my relationship to the 'Being' of the School?

_____

_____

• In what ways do I see myself working with anthroposophy within the PCG group?

_____

_____

• In what ways do I engage in Anthroposophical study and pedagogical research?

_____

_____

# Appendix M1

# Faculty Meeting Agenda – Hypothetical Example
## *before* a PCG is established

### Full Faculty Meeting

2:50     Opening Verse

             Attendance

             Thorns & Roses

3:00     Workload Proposal

3:15     Room Use Proposal and Questions

3:25     Shepherd's Play time and director

3:30     Standing Reports:
             High School
             Grade School Kindergarten Administration
             Board
             Finance
             Site Planning
             Principal
             Hiring
             Pedagogical Carrying Group
             Mandate Groups:
             Professional Development
             Evaluation
             Hub
             Workload

3:50     Announcements: Gems

4:00     Closing Verse

4:05     Mandate Groups (individually arranged)

### Future Agenda Points:
- Finance: pro-rating of Salaries/Tuition adjustment for faculty
- Typing of minutes
- Faculty reports to Bulletin
- Evaluation proposal
- Pro D/Mentoring proposal

# Appendix M2

## Faculty Meeting Agenda – Hypothetical Example
### *after* a PCG is established

**OPENING VERSE**

*We have been joined by destiny together*
*To unfold powers which are to serve a good creative work.*
*Wisdom itself will teach us,*
*As we walk on the soul's path,*
*That greatest things can be achieved,*
*When souls who give each other spirit certainty*
*Unite in faithfulness toward the healing of the world.*

Benedictus, Portal of Initiation

Mystery Drama, Rudolf Steiner

**AGENDA**

| | |
|---|---|
| 2:45–2:50 | Welcome, Attendance and Verse Regrets |
| 2:50–3:00 | Personal Biography sharing |
| 3:00–3:10 | A Look Back: Professional Development Summer and Fall |
| 3:15–3:45 | Eurythmy |
| 3:50–4:00 | Meditative work of the teacher |
| 4:00–4:15 | Full Faculty Chair nominations (see qualities & skills list below) |
| 4:15–4:25 | Faculty Support Fund nominations (see notes below) |
| 4:25–4:30 | Pedagogical Carrying Group Nomination |
| 4:30–5:00 | Faculty Meal |
| 5:00–5:15 | Clean up for non-Pedagogical Carrying Group members |

**ANNOUNCEMENTS**

• Pedagogical consultant will be here next week.

## REPORTS

### Programs and Curriculum Development Committee

- PCDC met Monday as a full committee. We had a fruitful discussion about when and how to split large classes. Next meeting we will bring all of this work together and try to craft a proposal for the lower school, middle school and high school.

- Task groups:

- Pro-D: AWSNA Feb. conference is close so we will strive to send as many faculty and staff as possible. In the future if the AWSNA conference is far away the school will host one.

- Adult Education: Clarity needed on what this task group should be working on. Some adult education is being done on an administrative/development level and is not the work of this group.

- Trips: A report outlining the present budget numbers is forthcoming.

- Gardening: Report forthcoming.

### Practical Needs Committee

- Task groups working independently on specific assigned tasks

### Human Resources

- Screening Waldorf Applicants for Grade One 2010

### Pedagogical Carrying Group

- Prepared next Full Faculty meeting

- Discussed parent proposal about room use

- Discussed the work with "Toward the Deepening of Waldorf Education"

- Made changes to the Intake Policy. Further discussion needed

### High School

- Local poet will speak at this week's High School assembly.

- Social event on Saturday evening was a wonderful success—thanks to all the organizers and performers.

- Friday's pizza party for the soccer team went well and celebrated the end of the season.

- The High School student council met for the first time this week. Updates to come.

- Some of the exchange students spent Sunday visiting Granville Island and went on a Falls Creek Ferry trip.

- Nothing planned for Halloween at time of writing.

- Grade 12 continue with main lesson in the lab.

## Grade School

- Continued art of Goethean Conversation

- Making arrangements for Remembrance and Martinmas events

- Class teachers have agreed to be flexible with play dates to make room for grade six and to accommodate High School plays.

- songs for Monday assemblies to continue.

- Grade School meetings will begin with three minutes of singing instead of Eurythmy.

- Class teachers are preparing for in-class Halloween celebrations on Friday, October 30th.

## Early Childhood

- Study: Education of the Child

- Review of the Early Childhood Parent Handbook

- Meeting with Aftercare teachers; discussed the transition from morning programs to Aftercare

- Puppet show rehearsals have been planned

## QUALITIES OF A FULL FACULTY CHAIR

Ideally, a Full Faculty Chair would

- be connected to all three faculties

- see this task as part of his/her journey as a Waldorf teacher

- have an inclination towards social responsibility

- have a strong grounding in anthroposophy

- be a good communicator, most especially a good listener

- have the ability to be decisive

- carry the respect of the group

- be able to come from a position of neutrality, i.e., be able to set aside his/her own views in order to be open to the views of others

- have integrity

- not be coming from an 'empty cup' position, would have a strong class

- have the quality of discernment, the ability to discern what is needed at a meeting

- have a firm commitment to maintaining confidentiality

- be willing to give up a bit of his/her own individuality in order to function as a representative of the group

### Skills of a Full Faculty Chair

- Ability to maintain confidentiality

- Humility, ability to subsume the ego for the good of the group

- Facilitation skills: function as a facilitator for the meetings, ensuring that everybody is heard

- Ability to delegate

- Member of the PCG, or would become one upon appointment and thus must meet requirements

- Flexibility re: timing if a pressing issue arises

- Organizational skills

- Ability to recognize own areas of challenge and seek support/guidance where appropriate

The Full Faculty Chair position would be considered to fulfill the person's committee work responsibilities.

### FACULTY SUPPORT FUND

*Question* – Has it not served the faculty in the past?

It was shared that the support fund money has shifted its focus and how it is administered. It is now for extraordinary reasons, whereas in the past it could be a support to teachers' income.

*Question* – Who should be on this committee?

***General Comments:***

- Ideally teacher vs. a parent should chair the committee.

- A retired teacher still has the trust of the faculty

- It is important to the have the fund.

- Is it also important to have an outside view of 'reality'?

- Does anyone feel called to be on this committee as 'part of their journey'?

- There is something about the experience of applying for assistance that is very exposing, and if there isn't a dialogue with the SF committee and one can get 'twisted out of shape.'

- It is a good time to re-evaluate the composition of the committee.

- It is easier to share finance picture with a colleague than with an outsider.

- This is not the role for a parent.

- The full amount of $10,000 is allocated every year from the fund.

- The difficulty of exposing oneself to a parent was again expressed.

- Emergency fund – Is it necessary to write down one's complete financial profile?

- Another voice supporting this committee living in the faculty vs. the parent body.

# Appendix N1

# Pedagogical Carrying Group Agenda – Hypothetical Example '1'

**ATTENDANCE, STUDY**

## 1. REVIEW OF MINUTES

   1.1   Follow-Up

   1.2   Review – Tracking Items

   1.3   Follow Up – Action Items

## 2. ANNOUNCEMENTS

## 3. AGENDA APPROVAL

## 4. REPORTS

   4.1   Full Faculty Chair

   4.2   Development Committee

   4.3   Social Inclusion Committee

## 5. CURRENT ITEMS/ REQUESTS *(items in italics have been previously circulated)*

   5.1   ECE Intake Policy – ratification

   5.2   Due date midterm report cards

   5.3   Knit-a-Thon

   5.4   Torch Relay

   5.5   Report from SCIG and proposal. Questions

   5.6   Report from Grade 8

## 6. FUTURE AGENDA POINTS

   6.1   Mentoring Colloquium

   6.2   Fundraising Grade 12

   6.3   Health and Safety Manual

   6.4   Funding protocol for PC funds

## 7. REMINDERS, CLOSING VERSE

*Our rightful place as educators*
*Is to be removers of hindrances.*
*Each child in every age*
*Brings something new into the world from divine regions,*
*And it is our task, as educators,*
*To remove bodily and psychical obstacles out of his/her way,*
*To remove hindrances so that his/her spirit may enter*
*In full freedom into life.*

Rudolf Steiner: *The Spiritual Ground of Education*

# Appendix N2

# Pedagogical Carrying Group Agenda – Hypothetical Example '2'

**ATTENDANCE**

**1. REVIEW OF MINUTES  August 31**

    1.1   Follow-Up

    1.2   Review – Tracking Items

    1.3   Follow Up – Action Items

**2. ANNOUNCEMENTS**

    2.1   Ministry

**3. AGENDA APPROVAL**

**4. COMMITTEE REPORTS**

    4.1   PCDC

    4.2   PNC

    4.3   SI

**5. CURRENT ITEMS/ REQUESTS** *(italics are items with previously circulated material)*

    5.1   Faculty Support Fund

    5.2   Grade School students in High School sports teams

    5.3   All Souls Day

    5.4   Class size

    5.5   School hall

    5.6   New faculty on committees

    5.7   Handwork proposal

    5.8   Anthroposophical Society booking

    5.9   Review of Intake Committee and selection process for members

    5.10  Children after school

## 6. FUTURE AGENDA POINTS

6.1   Review of Grade School PE program needs, specifically lessons required

6.2   Soccer Uniforms to be continued . . .

6.3   ECE staff remuneration

6.4   Booking an event at the School

6.5   Heating policy

6.6   Serving alcohol on school premises at evening or weekend adult-only events

## 7. REMINDERS, CLOSING VERSE

*Our rightful place as educators*
*Is to be removers of hindrances.*
*Each child in every age*
*Brings something new into the world from divine regions,*
*And it is our task, as educators,*
*To remove bodily and psychical obstacles out of his/her way,*
*To remove hindrances so that his/her spirit may enter*
*In full freedom into life.*

Rudolf Steiner: *The Spiritual Ground of Education*

# Appendix O

# Pedagogical Administrator Job Description

## Position Summary

The PA brings leadership and support to the pedagogical work of the faculty of the Vancouver Waldorf School and supports the processes and decisions of mandated committees. As a member of various committees and groups, including the Full Faculty, the Pedagogical Carrying Group (PCG), the Operations Management Committee, the Board of Trustees and the Development Committee, the PA actively participates in the healthy functioning of the school. This role is to be combined with teaching duties. The administrative title of Principal, for Ministry liaison purposes and for official communication requirements, will be assigned to the PA.

## Reporting Relationships

The PA reports to the Pedagogical Carrying Group and works closely with the Administrator, the Director of Development (DoD), the Faculty and the administrative team, as well as with parents.

## Position Information

This is a full-time position.

## Position Accountabilities

- Brings leadership and support to all teachers, including assisting in the provision of necessary resources to accomplish pedagogical tasks

- Actively participates on and attends all meetings of the Board of Trustees (BoT), Operations Management Committee (OMC), the Full Faculty (FF), PCG, the Human Resources Committee (HRC), Social Inclusion Program Coordinating Committee, and Discipline Management Group and participates in other mandated committees of the PCG as required. Attends the three faculty departmental meetings on a rotational or as requested or required basis.

- Supports the processes and decisions of the PCG- and Faculty-mandated committees

- Liaises with the Ministry of Education, oversees the preparation for inspections by the Ministry and ensures the completion and submission of Prescribed Learning Outcome documentation (PLOs) and all other Ministry documentation as required by Ministry guidelines

- In conjunction with the HRC Chair, administers to the tasks of the HRC:

  - attends HRC meetings regularly

  - holds teachers accountable for meeting their professional commitments

  - in conjunction with the Administrator, ensures that necessary government requirements for certification of teachers and reporting are met

  - ensures that all teachers are evaluated after their probationary period and then as per the HRC schedule

  - coordinates mentoring for teachers as determined by the HRC

  - in conjunction with the Administrator, implements HRC and PCG decisions regarding the hiring and dismissal of Faculty

- Trouble-shoots substitution issues

- Together with Administrator and Director of Development, implements and maintains all school policies and procedures

- As the key pedagogical member of the Operations Management Committee, acts as a point person for pedagogical issues and for receiving concerns or issues: listens impartially to concerns from both faculty and parents, takes issues raised to the Operations Management Committee and/or PCG to ensure that they are addressed appropriately and expeditiously by the appropriate body, as well as monitors and oversees the process leading to the resolution of these issues

- Oversees the implementation of the three primary pedagogical policies/protocols and participates as a member of the Discipline Management Group, the Social Inclusion Coordinating Committee, and remedial task group (if created and as required)

- Makes an immediate decision, when needed, regarding situations that threaten the wellbeing and safety of children, faculty and staff

- Ensures reporting of suspected Child Abuse and other Ministry of Education reporting requirements

- Writes correspondence pertaining to Ministry and Pedagogical matters

- When no mandated committee has been established to take on a particular task vital to the running of the school, the PA, in collaboration with the Operations Management Committee, may take responsibility for ensuring that those tasks are taken up.

## Administrative Responsibilities

- Reads and acts on the Ministry e-board as required

- Ensures the Prescribed Learning Outcome (PLOs) documentation is in good order

- Ensures that the Grad 2004 documentation and marks are in good order and submitted as required by the Ministry of Education, and that the VWS transcripts are created, distributed and kept on file, as requested

- Applies for Special Education (SE) Grants and, in conjunction with the Class Teacher and task group (if created), creates and administers Individual Education Plans for SE students

- In collaboration with the Pedagogical Committee Chairs, the Administrator and the DoD, prepares the PCG meeting agenda and ensures the meeting is facilitated. Ensures minutes are taken, distributed and kept on file.

## Position Qualifications

- BC certified and experienced Waldorf teacher

- Relevant work experience with a demonstrated track record of working with Faculty, a Board of Directors and an Administrator

- Ability to function and multitask under pressure; ability to supervise and delegate

- Excellent pedagogical and communication skills

- Competency with computers

- Ability to work within the processes of Government and Ministry of Education

- A thorough understanding of Waldorf education

- Compatibility with existing Faculty and administrative staff

## Hiring and Evaluation Process

The PA(s) is hired by a Hiring Task Group or the HRC as designated by the PCG. The PA(s) is evaluated on a yearly basis by the PCG.

## Important Notes: Essential Duties

Job descriptions are designed and intended only to summarize the essential duties, responsibilities, qualifications, and requirements for the purpose of clarifying the general nature and scope of a position's role as part of the overall organization. Job descriptions do not list all tasks an employee might be expected to perform, and they do not limit the right of the employer to assign additional tasks or otherwise to modify duties to be performed—even if seemingly unrelated to the basic job. Every employee has a duty to perform all assigned tasks. It should also be noted the order of performance responsibilities as listed in the job description is not designed or intended to rank the duties in any order of importance relative to each other.

# Appendix P

# Pedagogical Committee Mandate – Example

**Practical Needs Committee**

## 1. Objective of the Practical Needs Committee

The Practical Needs Committee is dedicated to ensuring the proper delivery of Waldorf education by securing adequate physical spaces, tools, and systems.

## 2. Matters of the Practical Needs Committee

Ongoing Year-Round Work

- Facilities and Site Planning

- Health and Safety

Regular and Defined Work

- Classroom and Pedagogical maintenance and upgrading

- Room Use and Room Allocation

- Furniture

- Storage Space Oversight

- School Pictures

- Teacher Resources

- Supplies

- Pedagogical Budgeting

Occasional Work

- Acknowledgements

- Ministry Visitation Days

- Bus Program Management

- Snack Roster for Meetings

## 3. Summary of the Practical Needs Committee's Role

The Practical Needs Committee is designed to serve under the PCG as an active committee undertaking the actions. making decisions and policy recommendations that relate predominantly to the practical and logistical needs in the pedagogical operations of the VWS. Aspects of the items that must be addressed and monitored are generally described in this mandate. The PCG reserves the right to modify, amend, and further determine this description.

The Committee keeps procedures for the regular Task-Groupings within its mandate (see the Task-Group Mandates for Teacher Resources, Facilities, Supplies, Budgeting, Maintenance and Upgrading, and others).

The Committee refers issues beyond the scope of the work of the Committee to the PCG, to the Executive Group, or to both.

## 4. Practical Needs Committee Membership

At least eight members make up this committee, drawn from the following pools:
a. Full-time Faculty (around eight members)
b. Part-time Faculty
c. Employees of the School
d. Parents at the School
e. Members of the VWS Society

Members will commit to attending all scheduled meetings of the Practical Needs Committee.

All members will exhibit good interpersonal skills and the ability to work cooperatively and maintain confidentiality. Directness and a living understanding of anthroposophy and Waldorf education are necessary.

In the event that full membership is not attained or maintained at any given time in the working life of the group, members will be actively sought out to complete membership. The PCG will be made aware of such a circumstance and must approve the continued operation of the Practical Needs Committee despite any shortfall in membership.

## 5. Terms of Service

### Full-time Faculty (to 0.75)

There is no fixed length of time for members to serve on the Practical Needs Committee. In the interest of continuity, it is desirable that a faculty member remain in one committee unless pressing matters urge his/her involvement on one of the other two committees.

### Part-time Faculty (0.2 to 0.7)

There is currently no requirement for Part-time Faculty to serve on committees, but they are welcome to become core members. (This should be accompanied with a commitment to remain on the committee for a year or more.) Part-time Faculty members may be requested to assist in undertaking certain tasks of the committee. In this case they would be involved only in addressing the particular issue and for a limited and pre-determined time period.

### Other VWS Employees

Other employees may be requested to assist in undertaking certain tasks of the committee (i.e., on specific task-groups). In particular, the Administrative and Development Coordinators may be asked to join the task-groups or committees for input pertaining to their realms of activity.

### Parents and Society Members

With approval of the committee and PCG, parents and community members may be invited to become core committee members. This should be accompanied with a commitment to remain on the committee for a year or more.

## 6. Practical Needs Committee Chair and Co-Chair

The Practical Needs Committee is chaired by one full-time Faculty Member. The Chair is the representative of the committee to the PCG and Full Faculty. The Chair is assisted by a Co-Chair, who will take the chairing position in case of absence. It is the responsibility of the Co-Chair to oversee the Committee Binder usage and to provide input into the written communications, agendas, and other chairing activities.

Both Committee Chair and Co-Chair must have at least two years' experience working in the school and be mandated by the Committee Members following a consensus process allowing input from all members (including absent members). (The workload consideration of the chair and co-chair positions will be assessed, evaluated, and determined by a workload task-group within the Practical Needs Committee.)

## 7. Ending Committee Service

Committee Service may be terminated by a Committee Member following the protocol outlined below:

- Member will simultaneously submit to the Committee, the PCG, and the Executive Group, a written request to end service to the Committee.

- Member may not end services without probationary period of one month, during which the alleged reasons for termination of service will be assessed by the above mentioned groups.

- Upon acceptance of termination by the above mentioned groups, Member will be assigned a more suitable committee responsibility or task, the progress of which will continue to be monitored by the PCG.

If a Member of the Committee is identified as not honoring his/her commitment, not fulfilling his/her mandate, or not meeting the needs of the group or of the identified tasks, the protocol outlined below will be followed:

- Allegations and concerns will be directly discussed first with the individual.

- Allegations and concerns will be brought to the Committee and the PCG. The situation will be discussed first in the presence of and then in the absence of the individual.

- If it is felt that an immediate resolution is necessary, Committee members may, through unanimous (consensus) decision, suspend membership. It is understood that the individual in question will not participate in the consensus.

- The PCG will monitor the situation by engaging either in Issues Management process, re-integration of the individual on the Committee, or termination of membership.

- In the case of termination of membership, the PCG are responsible for assigning a new committee membership or designating a new task more suitable to the individual, in accordance to terms of employment.

## 8. Accountability, Documentation, Communication and Reporting

The Practical Needs Committee is accountable and reports to the PCG. In addition to permanent representation of the Practical Needs Committee on the PCG through PCG membership of the Committee Chair, the Committee will participate in an annual joint meeting with the PCG.

Communication to and from the Practical Needs Committee is to be made in writing. It is particularly important that reports and minutes highlight issues of confidentiality and be circulated only to the PCG or effected groups. The Chair of the Committee is the central contact person, while the Co-Chair proofs reports and other communications.

Minutes are kept in typed format, outlining the items discussed, decisions, actions and position statements, in accordance with communication protocol. Decisions and position statements will be extracted and published separately and communicated to the PCG. Each meeting's minutes will be copied digitally to the Pedagogical Administrator,

Administrator and Director of Development. Minutes are kept in a specific committee binder for the academic school year.

Memos originating from the work of the group will be sent to specific groups or individuals as necessary in writing and will be documented in the committee's binder.

The Practical Needs Committee's activities will be reported at all meetings of the Full Faculty via their PCG Representative.

## 9. Meeting Times

The Practical Needs Committee will meet from 3:30–5:00 pm Thursdays for regular meetings. These meetings allow for reporting and group decisions, although there is flexibility to allow for independent 'task-work' to take place within this timeframe.

Tasks requiring longer effort or further research will take place outside of this meeting time.

## 10. Committee Evaluation

A method of evaluating the work of the Committee will be provided by the PCG. An initial evaluation will enumerate the frequency and manner of future evaluations.

## 11. Method of Decision-Making: Consensus

All decisions will be made using the process of consensus. The Practical Needs Committee is not to resort to decision by vote or any other 'democratic' decision-making process. Should consensus be unattainable with respect to a particular issue, the issue shall be referred to the PCG for assessment of both the issue and the functioning of the Practical Needs Committee. Such communication will be conducted in full consideration of the timelines attached to tasks. In such cases, the PCG shall reserve the right to instruct the Practical Needs Committee as to how it shall move forward.

The following definition of consensus is to serve as the basis for Practical Needs Committee decision-making:

> Consensus is a group decision which all members feel they can live with, support and commit themselves not to undermine. The decision is arrived at through a process whereby the issues are fully aired. All members feel they have been adequately heard, everyone has equal power and responsibility so that all are satisfied with the process. The process requires the members to be emotionally present and engaged, frank in a loving, mutually respectful manner, sensitive to each other; to be selfless, dispassionate, and capable of emptying themselves, and possessing a paradoxical awareness of the preciousness of both people and time. This includes knowing when the

solution is satisfactory, and that it is time to stop, with a willingness to reopen the discussion at such a time as the group determines a need for revision.

Adapted from *A World Waiting to Be Born* by S. Peck

## 12. Task-Group Work

Groups or individuals undertaking a specific task are mandated for their work by the Committee using consensus. The issues on which they are to work will be clearly identified in the Committee's minutes or in a mandate document. A timeline for completion of the work will accompany each task-grouping and will be provided by the Committee. Ongoing tasks have a separate Task-Group Mandate (below) and may require further coordination (agendas, chairing, composition of memorandums, etc.).

Much of the task work will necessitate collaboration with other committees; members may have to attend other meetings for presentations and feedback on issues or invite or appoint individuals or groups of people to collaborate with them on various tasks. Likewise, administrative staff may be asked to attend committee meetings or planned sessions with a task-group.

### a. Members and Composition

Task-group membership is based on skills, knowledge, and attitude. Task-groups consist of anywhere from one to five members serving on the Practical Needs Committee, as well as other faculty, staff and school community members, who may be regular task-group members based on approval from the Practical Needs Committee.

The Committee Chair will track and coordinate a review of the workload of the members on the different Task-Groups to ensure equity of work distribution.

### b. Terms of Service

Task-group membership is assigned by consensus on an as-needed basis. Membership is not necessarily continuous or static. In selecting the task-group membership, the committee members must strive for a balance between a new member's unique input and the experience that prior task-group membership provides.

### c. Positions on the Task-Group

One member will be selected to represent the task-group to the committee. All other tasks such as writing communications and undertaking contact with others can be assigned within the task-group as needed.

### d. Accountability, Documentation, Communication and Reporting

All task-groups are accountable to and report to the Practical Needs Committee.

Communication within and from the task-group will be in accordance with communication protocol. For example, actions from the task-group such as memorandums or meetings must be documented in the committee binder (via meetings minutes or by documentation). Similarly, feedback, recommendations, or proposals from the task-group to the committee are to be kept in the committee binder.

### e. Task-Group Evaluation

Members of the Practical Needs Committee will provide feedback to task-group members following their completion of a central task by way of recommendation and/or final documented feedback, immediately after completion or within 14 days of completion, to allow for further reflection on the process.

# Appendix Q

# The Cult of Personality

By Walter Daroshin

In defining an operating structure at the VWS, it is fair to say that the quality of humanity often plays a role in decision making. This respect for the needs of the individual flows naturally from the work in the classroom and is complemented by our collective efforts in 'striving together.' In defining more clearly a development impulse within our organization, I have been met consistently with questions around 'how we work.' The comments offered are not exclusive to understanding systems, policies, or procedures. There seems to be a real and palpable distress over workload and lack of definition around lines of communication. There is a clear imbalance between what is being asked of those individuals employed at the VWS and the resources with which we ask the work to be done. This often presents a challenge that those drawn to work in spiritual-based institutions take on as part of their own journey. Working through adversity, whether the challenge is financial (underpaid staff), or operational (too much work and not enough staff) can lead one to great heights of achievement. Everybody within our existing organizational structure faces challenges. How those challenges are met helps to define us as individuals. While celebrating the humanistic need for growth within the experience of adversity, we have replaced institutional memory with the cult of personality.

So much of what we do relies on the character and personality of those who are charged with doing it. Parents, for the most part, do not question the technical qualifications of teachers but rather focus on their relationship to them. We teach an intuitive brand of education that builds 'capacities' and aims to 'develop' our children, preparing them for their future lives. Things seem to work out somehow, as if by providence. This attitude permeates not only what we do, but who we are. The lack of clarity and understanding that many parents feel in regards to the curriculum is similar to the lack of clarity and understanding that many teachers feel in regards to administration. However, it all seems to work because we are all in this for the same reason—the children. This basic premise, a faith-based relationship between consenting adults, is the foundation on which our administrative life has been built. In defining administration I am speaking to the larger work of groups and individuals, both staff and volunteer, in meeting our operational needs. We need to clearly define the positions required to operate the school as well as the requisite job descriptions of each position.

We need to clearly define lines of communication, accountability, and responsibility. An evaluation process needs to be in place which will effectively monitor whether individuals are meeting the expectations of their job descriptions. We need to encourage individuality and recognize the work of each other; however we must also be clear in setting workload boundaries. By doing so, we create a category of work which is considered as required, and will either be taken up as extraordinary or volunteer. In either case, it will be acknowledged. In respecting our individual journeys, we have to drop the burden of expectation from our daily working lives and make decisions on extraordinary activity out of free will. Michael Spence writes in his book *Freeing the Human Spirit* that in order to fulfill its purpose in accordance with spiritual reality, a Waldorf school must be structured and make its administrative decisions based on that same spiritual reality.

Currently we employ a hybrid organizational structure of threefold social awareness (only two folds of which are in place) mixed with conventional business economic thinking. We don't seem to be doing either with the strength of conviction we seemingly exhibit towards the curriculum. By bringing clarity to what we do and how we do it, we will set each other free to do it according to our own spiritual path. Those who take on the extraordinary will be acknowledged, as will those who perform their predetermined tasks with ability and enthusiasm.

# Appendix R1

# Tuition & Fees Terms and Conditions of Agreement – Example

### Terms and Conditions of Agreement

The School does not discriminate on the basis of race, sex, religion or national origin and welcomes all applicants for enrollment.

In consideration of the School's enrolling my child(ren) as student(s) on the terms set forth in this agreement and accompanying attachments, and that the School will provide an education so long as the conduct of the student and/or parents/guardians does not warrant termination of the enrollment, we agree as follows:

[ ]     1. Any decision regarding my child(ren)'s acceptance, and continued enrolment, at school is entirely within the discretion of the School. The School reserves both the right to request that my child(ren) be withdrawn and the right to dismiss my child(ren) during the school year at its discretion without forfeiting tuition fees.

[ ]     2. I/we agree to the terms and conditions set forth in the School's current Tuition & Fees Agreement – Terms & Payment Requirements in addition to the current year's Tuition Schedule and Tuition & Fees (Tuition Detail) Reports.

[ ]     3. Subject to agreement on any approved tuition adjustment, I/we agree to be jointly and severally liable for the payment of tuition and fees calculated in accordance with the terms and conditions set out in item 2.

[ ]     4. I/we agree to abide by the current policies and procedures of the School Society and the School *Parent Handbook*, the most current copy of which I/we have received. I/we understand and agree that any failure to abide by the policies and procedures or the terms and conditions set forth in this agreement may result in the School's exercising its discretion to dismiss my child(ren).

[ ]     5. Personal information including personal data and photographs will be used and disclosed, including personal information published in the School's community phonebook and other publications not withstanding any existing consent agreements, in accordance with the School Personal Information Privacy Policies. If you have any questions about the collection, use and disclosure of this information, consult the School Personal Information Privacy Policies in the *Parent Handbook* or contact the School Privacy Officer.

_____

SIGNATURE                    DATE (YYYY.MM.DD)

_____

PARENT/GUARDIAN NAME (PLEASE PRINT)


_____

SIGNATURE                    DATE (YYYY.MM.DD)

_____

PARENT/GUARDIAN NAME (PLEASE PRINT)

# Appendix R2

## Tuition & Fees Agreement – Terms & Payment Requirements – Example

### 1. Tuition Payments

A child is permitted to attend class when tuition payment(s) are received and the family's account is in good standing.

### 2. Method and Terms of Payment

#### Resident Payment Requirements
**Option 1**
Full payment is due by the latter of: 1) the signing of the Agreement, or 2) May 1.
You may claim a 2% Early Payment Discount (minimum 5 month contract).
Payments can be made in cash, by cheque, debit, VISA or MasterCard.
Early payment discount is not available to accounts with adjusted tuitions.
**Option 2**
Pay in monthly installments with the first payment occurring on the latter of:
1)      the signing of the Agreement, or
2)      May 1, and with the final payment occurring on April 1.
Monthly payments will be processed as automatic debits from your bank account.

#### Non Resident Payment Requirements
Tuition must be paid in full prior to receiving an official letter of acceptance. Payment may be made via bank transfer, certified check, international money order, VISA or MasterCard.

### 3. Midyear Admission

Students enrolling after May 1 will be required to make tuition payments in accordance with the schedule outlined in item 2 Method and Terms of Payment.

### 4. Admission Fee

A non-refundable admission fee of $200 per student is paid each year by all successful new applicants and any currently enrolled students who did not, if required by item 5, provide a commitment deposit on or before the Commitment Deposit deadline.

### 5. Commitment Deposit

A non-refundable deposit of $200 is required for each returning student in all fully enrolled programs in order to secure a space in the class. This deposit due date is the first Friday in March.

## 6. Development Fee

Each student is charged a development fee which is used to fund school community, promotional and educational events and activities. These events and activities are provided to community members in addition to and separately from the student's education and include festivals, educational lectures, workshops and programs, and social and promotional events.

## 7. Tuition Insurance

Tuition Insurance is mandatory for registered resident families who make monthly payments and for all registered non-resident students. Tuition Insurance may entitle both resident and non-resident students who withdraw mid-year to a partial refund of tuition in accordance with the terms of item 10.

The purchase of Tuition Insurance is only optional for resident families paying full tuition using the early payment method. Should early payment resident families choose NOT to purchase Tuition Insurance and subsequently decide to withdraw their child(ren) mid-year, NO tuition will be refunded.

### Exceptions

Children attending Parent and Tot classes are not required to purchase Tuition Insurance.

### Payment

The $300 per family premium will be automatically added to the first tuition payment for those families who use the monthly payment option. For families choosing the early payment option, the fee will be added to the total tuition and fees payable for the school year.

## 8. Bus Transportation

Bus fees for students who require bus service are incorporated into their families' tuition payments. All students using the bus service are subject to the terms of the Bus Agreement.

## 9. New Students

Each student's acceptance is provisional; for all new students there is a three-month probationary period. The teacher will observe and assess the student's needs and abilities during this probationary period. The teacher may recommend that the student be placed in a grade commensurate with the developmental level of the student, and/or the parents may be required to provide academic, ESL, language, remedial, and/or therapeutic support as a condition of remaining in the class. The school reserves the right to ask for withdrawal (see item 10).

## 10. Withdrawals/Refunds

### Residents

Families enrolled in all programs and services wishing to withdraw are required to provide written notice of withdrawal. Following receipt of notification of withdrawal, a withdrawal fee in the amount of 10% (one month's tuition) of full year tuition and fees will be retained. The assessed withdrawal fee is payable in full together with tuition & fees assessed up to and including the later of the dates of receipt of written notification of withdrawal and the last day attended in the program, and apply to all students who withdraw after the first payment date of May 1. Refunds will be granted for any payment received in excess of assessed tuition, fees and withdrawal fee based on written notice of withdrawal. Families who have made early payment and have chosen not to purchase Tuition Insurance receive no refund of tuition or fees (see item 7).

### Non-Residents

Before the student has attended, refunds are granted upon submission of evidence of government denial of student authorization. Upon receipt of such evidence, the school will retain a minimum fee of $500 and will refund remaining paid tuition. Refunds are also granted depending upon the proportion of the stay completed. If a student withdraws during the first quarter of the intended stay, 50% of the total fees paid will be refunded. If a student withdraws after the first quarter of the stay, 25% of the fees will be refunded. Once a student has completed half of the stay, no fees will be refunded. No refund is granted if a student is expelled. The school reserves the right to ask for withdrawal of a student as outlined in the Tuition Agreement.

## 11. Accessible Tuition Program

Tuition is adjusted based on financial need and is solely granted through application to the Accessible Tuition Program. Pre-school aftercare and bus transportation fees are not eligible for adjustment.

Tuition reductions or adjustments will not be granted based on partial attendance due to the implementation of Individual Education Plans, such as athletic, artistic or learning needs programs.

## 12. Loss of Student Government Grant

If due to holidays or reasons other than illness a child does not attend 600 hours of school between the first day of school in September and May 15, the school will lose a portion of the government Education Grant. Parents will be responsible for replacing the lost grant funds unless a doctor's certificate justifying an extended absence can rectify the situation with the Ministry of Education.

### 13. Late Payments & NSF Charges

Accounts in arrears may be charged a fee of $10 per communication required to bring the account into good standing. The finance office will notify the account holder by email or letter of an impending charge to provide the account holder with the opportunity to bring an account into good standing and avoid the charge.

A charge of $25 will be applied for any check or automatic debit that is returned to the School by your financial institution because of insufficient funds. The family must make immediate arrangement for replacement of refused payments. If acceptable arrangements are not made, the account will be considered to be in arrears and the student may be asked to withdraw (see item 1).

### 14. Costs Included in Tuition

Costs for items normally purchased and distributed to students by the school on behalf of the parent(s) and or guardian(s), are included in Tuition & Fees. This includes items purchased in bulk such as flutes, filtered water, gym strips, most handwork & practical arts supplies, main lesson books, some Fine Art supplies, specialized Waldorf art and writing supplies, and field trips expenses. These costs are included in and apportioned out of the tuition fees each year. Any shortfall will be covered from an amount reallocated from the fees paid during that school year and no request for further fees will be made (see note 15 for exceptions). Any surplus will be used to purchase classroom supplies and/or equipment as needed and no refund will be given.

### 15. Costs Not Included in Tuition

Some materials, particularly those used in the High School, will be not be purchased and supplied by the school because they are selected by the students based on personal preference and are not materials normally purchased in bulk by the school on behalf of the students. This includes such items as musical instruments (except recorder flutes), material for individualized handwork projects, binders, binder paper, notebooks, writing implements and pencil crayons. While the cost of field trips is covered by Tuition, the purchase of medical insurance coverage over and above BC Medical Services Plan coverage for field trips outside of BC, is the responsibility of the parent or guardian. Additional medical coverage will not be covered by Tuition and will not be purchased by the school.

# Appendix S

# Parent Council Mandate – Example

## 1. Purpose

The purpose of the Parent Council proposal is to define the ways in which parents of the School are participating in the social, organizational, and spiritual unfolding of the school's mission and of its day-to-day operations, in view of implementation in the second half of the school year and subsequent school years.

## 2. Objectives

- Design of Parent Council, its structure, responsibilities, and activities

- Integrate the participation of parents in a welcoming, respectful, inspiring, and systematic way

- Enable transition from Parent Group to Parent Council within period from November 2 to January 1

## 3. Timeline

- Proposal is presented to the existing Parent Group on November 2 for input in the perspective of the Strategic Plan and towards the aim of consensus approval.

- Upon receiving consensus approval, recommendation is made within 10 business days (November 16) to the Executive Group presently acting as the Development Carrying Group (DCG) who will ratify the recommendation and make if effective January 1.

- Existing Parent Group will implement the transition to Parent Council in the period between November 19 and January 1 with the support of the Executive Group acting as DCG.

## 4. Decision

- After due consideration of Parent Group input, decision will be made by the ExecutiveGroup (acting as DCG). This decision is not subject to consensus and is irrevocable.

# Parent Council Structure

## 1.   Vision

Parent Council embraces the vision of an engaged and valued parent body in service of the actualization of the school's mission.

## 2.   Mission

The mission of the Parent Council is to design, hold, guide, and facilitate the participation of parents in the unfolding of the school's mission and its day-to-day operations in accordance with stated values and in the context of the Strategic Plan.

## 3.   Core Values

The Parent Council adopts as its fundamental values a commitment to working in synergy with the underlying principles of Waldorf education as expressed in the Strategic Plan and as developed through the Executive Group, and a commitment to generate, welcome, and honor parents' participation in the life of the school.

## 4.   Structure

The Parent Council is directly connected and accountable to the Development Carrying Group, and is composed of parent volunteers who are willing and able to commit to a minimum of a two-year term (calendar year). Participation as a member of the Parent Council stands as fulfillment of volunteering guidelines as defined in the Volunteer Program. Parent Council meetings occur on the second Tuesday of every month from 7:30 pm to 9:30 pm, and regular communication occurs as needed via email, phone, or in person. Members of the Parent Council hold the following specific responsibilities.

- Parent Council Chair  also serves as a member of the Executive Group
- Parent Council Co-Chair/Development Coordinator
- Volunteer Program Coordinator
- Social Events Coordinator
- Fairs and Special Events Coordinator
- Community Fund Coordinator & Treasurer
- Adult Education Coordinator
- Class Representative Liaison
- School Beautification

## 5.   Membership Term

- Parent Council membership is for a 2-calendar year term.

- Parent Council members bear the responsibility to search for, evaluate, and train prospective members within 9 months of their decision to end their term, and in fully disclosed terms. They are responsible for informing the Parent Council of all desired changes in their level of involvement within a minimum timeframe of 3 months, and in consideration of training potential replacing members as outlined above.

## 6.  Responsibilities

### Chair Acts as Secretary

- develops agendas from Parent Council members' input
- holds minutes, extracts decisions, and communicates to Faculty and Board of Trustees accordingly and in systematic collaboration with Co-Chair/Development Coordinator
- Participates in weekly meeting of the Development Carrying Group (DCG)
- Develops Volunteering/Social life section of the annual Community Survey
- Manages all correspondence

### Co-chair / Development Coordinator

- Ensures that the Parent Council projects and events are in agreement with and serve the Development Carrying Group plans
- Is responsible for Communication from the Parent Council to the school community via the Bulletin

### Volunteer Program Coordinator

- Designs yearly Volunteer Program in accordance with the needs of Parent Council projects and events
- Manages the Volunteer Program: prepares documentation and processes outcome;.ensures that all needs are met
- Attends and holds April re-enrolment evenings for Volunteer Sign-up
- Communicates volunteer lists to Event Coordinator
- Prepares and sends Volunteer Thank You notes

### Social Events Coordinator

- Prepares calendar of social events

- Organizes and Coordinates Social Events

- Manages Social Events volunteers

- Prepares Event Summary and Evaluation Reports

### Fairs and Special Events Coordinator

- Designs Christmas Fair, May Fair, and Special Events

- Prepares Event Summary and Evaluation Reports of all events

- Prepares proposals for events modifications

- Coordinates and ensures the presence of due representation at all Special Events in collaboration with Enrollment/Admissions Director

### Community Fund Coordinator & Treasurer

- Serves as the treasurer of the School Association

- Acts a treasurer of Parent Council

- Prepares and holds Parent Council budget

- Makes budgetary recommendations to Finance Committee via Executive Group

- Allocates Community Fund resources as requested by Faculty

- Monitors Community Fund and prepares monthly reports

### Adult Education Coordinator

- Designs yearly calendar of events: workshops, lectures, study groups, Q&A sessions, in collaboration with the Parent Representative Liaison

- Researches and books speakers and study group facilitators with the assistance of Faculty

- Organizes and coordinates all Adult Education sessions

- Manages Adult Education volunteers

- Prepares and manages Adult Education program budget with treasurer

### Fundraising Coordinator

- Researches fundraising activities as defined in the fundraising policy in support of the operating budget

- Manages and monitors existing fundraising activities such as HEARTof.com and Shopfunds

- Motivates the community to participate in fundraising activities by communication in the Bulletin and in collaboration with the Development Coordinator

- Maintains a clear understanding in the community of the distinctions between fundraising activities (scrip and e-scrip programs, RMM) and Community Fund activities (Fairs and Special Events)

### Class Representative Liaison

- Acts as a liaison between the Class Representatives and the Parent Council

- Communicates the needs and observations of the parents in the areas of fundraising, volunteering, activities, social life, and adult education to the Parent Council

- Communicates the vision and decisions of the Parent Council to the class representatives

### School Beautification and Hospitality Coordinator

- Acts as liaison with the Buildings & Grounds Committee

- Manages community activities related to school beautification such as Community Workdays

- Manages Community Workdays volunteers

## 7.   Projects

### COMMUNITY FUND

#### *Purpose*

The purpose of the Community Fund is to generate funds in support of the school's out-of-classroom curricular activities such as class trips and field trips. The Community Fund serves the needs of the entire community of students, as well as the needs of a developing Waldorf school in a developing country.

#### *Objectives*

- Meet the Community Fund-approved fundraising budget as defined by the Parent Council in response to Faculty requests for out-of-classes curricular activities

- Generate, cultivate, and maintain collective enthusiasm and constructive effort in support of the entire body of students' experience

- Create, cultivate, and maintain a legacy of care, responsibility, and accountability toward the Waldorf school movement, particularly towards courageous Waldorf initiatives that currently lack financial support

- Create and maintain financial support to a Waldorf initiative abroad

- Create, develop, and sustain awareness in the students and parent body of the impact of their participation in community activities

### Activities

The Community Fund generates funds by engaging in community-oriented activities including but not limited to the Christmas Fair and the May Fair.

- The primary objective of these events is to raise funds.

- Their primary audience is the extended community, i.e., the portion of the population that is not currently part of the parent body. Therefore, the events are designed and marketed according to this above mentioned focus.

- These activities are designed in accordance with the principles and values underlying Waldorf education as understood and developed by the community. Therefore, the events express respect and understanding of the values and are mission-appropriate.

- Events call on the parent and the student volunteer efforts to participate in the enhancement of the students' curricular experience.

- The activities related to the Community Fund are collective and collaborative in nature.

### Operations

The Community Fund is managed by the Parent Council, its account(s) are held by the School Association and managed by the Parent Council treasurer. The Community Fund is established by and with the transfer of all existing Class bank account balances into the School Association bank account.

#### Current School Year

All class bank accounts are transferred to the Community Fund during the week of November 22, with the exception of Grades 8 and 12 which are authorized to contnnue fundraising activities for the current school year provided that:

- a fundraising activities plan for the remainder of the year is proposed to the Parent Council and the Executive Group (acting as the DCG) prior to November f6.

- no fundraising activity take place prior to Parent Group and Executive Group decision of December 2,

- fundraising activities are in accordance with the fundraising principles as outlined in point 2 of section c) above.

- funds expected to be raised are exclusively reserved to the funding of Class trips

- the absence of a written fundraising proposal for Grades 8 and 12 on or before the above mentioned date will render these exceptional arrangements null.

**Subsequent School Years**

- All out-of-class curricular activities in Grades 1 through 12 are financed by the Community Fund.

- Parent Council Treasurer informs the Faculty of the level of funding likely to be available for the subsequent school year by February 15.

- Faculty requests for out-of-classes curricular activities funds are submitted to the Parent Council on or before the first Thursday of April in preparation of the April Parent Council meeting. Faculty request consists of a detailed plan ratified by the Pedagogical Carrying Group. Detailed plan includes length of trip, frequency, cost analysis (transportation, housing and food, fees).

- Funds are allocated yearly by June 15 in accordance with Faculty requests. In the event that requests exceed budgeted funds, the proposal will be returned to the Faculty for further adjustments within the above mentioned timeframe.

- Funds allocated for out-of-classes curricular-related experience are not to be used for any other purpose, however important, urgent, or unforeseen. However, Faculty reserves the right to alter and modify plan of activities to accommodate for unexpected opportunities. However, there will be no modifications to the Community Fund allocations to reflect these changes.

## VOLUNTEER PROGRAM

### Purpose

The purpose of the Volunteer Program is to clarify, define, communicate, and manage the needs of the school for volunteers in all sectors of activities and to provide parents with a clear understanding of the expectations of the School in the area of parental involvement and volunteering.

### Objectives

- to ensure that the needs of the school for volunteers are met

- to evaluate, monitor, and develop a sustainable level of volunteerism

- to ensure that all events are staffed adequately

- to guarantee that parents will not be asked to volunteer for activities outside of their commitment to the Volunteer program

### Activities

- In the absence of contractual requirements, parents are asked to volunteer for 40 hours per year, in the capacity of their choice, and for activities they select on the listing designed by the Volunteer Coordinator with the support of the Parent Council Co-Chair.

- Listing of Volunteer opportunities include but are not limited to fairs, fundraising events, special events, participation on committees and working groups such as Grounds and class representative

- The Volunteer Program is established in direct relation with the school's calendar of events, which is prepared in April for the subsequent school year in preparation for the April reenrollment days.

- Faculty needs for volunteers beyond class representatives are to be communicated to the Volunteer Program Coordinator prior to April 1st for subsequent year. Faculty members are encouraged to develop a clear understanding of the volunteering program and of its implications on the lives of parents, in order to limit unplanned class requests to a level that is considerate of parents planned involvement.

## SOCIAL EVENTS

### Purpose

The purposes of social events are to develop and sustain a sense of living community among students, their parents, and their teachers, and to create and nurture a culture of openness, sharing, and care within the school community.

### Activities
- New school year community picnic and school year-end community picnic
- Halloween parade
- Community dance
- Community workdays and potlucks

## FAIRS AND SPECIAL EVENTS

### Purpose

The purpose of Fairs and Special Events is to generate funds to meet the Community Fund budget.

### Activities
- Christmas Fair
- May Fair
- Any other events involving the community that holds as its stated purpose the raising of funds for the Community Fund

### Operations

- Fairs and Special Events are scheduled in the yearly school calendar in April for the subsequent school year.

- They are organized and coordinated by the Fairs and Special Events coordinator, member of the Parent Council.

- They are produced and staffed by volunteers in accordance with the Volunteer Program specifications.


## ADULT EDUCATION PROGRAM

### Purpose

The purpose of the Adult Education Program is to support the research, understanding, and applications of the philosophy underlying Waldorf education and the School.

### Objectives

- To engage in and nurture an ongoing dialogue between faculty, existing parents and new parents, about Waldorf education and all related fields pertaining to human development

- To design a program of lectures, workshops, study groups, and activity groups that meet the needs of the parent body and the community

- To provide a context for deepening the community's understanding of the particularities of Waldorf education and the philosophy underlying it

- To provide parents and teachers with a local and accessible resource center

### Operations

The Adult Education Program is managed by the Adult Education Program Coordinator, a member of the Parent Council, in close collaboration with the Pedagogical Carrying Group.

- The components of the program are scheduled in April within the context of the School calendar of events.

- An Adult Education Program brochure is generated with the Development Coordinator, as well as advertising and promotion.

- The seed budget for the Adult Education Program is allocated by the treasurer from the Community Fund. The program aims to be self-supportive.

## CLASS REPRESENTATIVES

### *Purpose*

The purpose of Class Representatives is to provide a vital line of contact at the class level.

### *Activities*

- Support the teacher with activities such as class plays, field trips, class meetings

- Communicate class needs to the Class Representative Coordinator

- Acts as link to the parents of their class: to share with other parents what is new, what is happening, what is needed, so everyone can participate in the life of the school

- Meet with the Parent Council group in September and March to discuss life in the classes they represent

### *Terms*

Class Representatives volunteer for one calendar year term (January to January), to ensure that the needs of their class are met and communication is ongoing immediately after the beginning of the school year. They are responsible for searching for, evaluating, and training their replacement(s) at the end of their term.

## SCHOOL BEAUTIFICATION

### *Purpose*

The purpose of the School Beautification activities is to ensure that the school buildings and grounds are maintained in a way that meets safety, cleanliness, and esthetic standards conducive to the proper functioning of the school and to a satisfactory level of pride in parents, students, and faculty members.

### *Activities*

- Community Workdays organized in collaboration with the Social Events and Buildings and Grounds Committees

- Monitoring of the cleanliness and beauty of the classrooms and common areas at school events

# Appendix T

# Development Committee Mandate

## Development Committee

### Raison d'etre

The Board of Trustees of the school currently has a dual management responsibility at the school. Alongside fiscal responsibility it holds responsibility for Community and Resource Development (Development) activity. The Board has delegated the responsibility for coordinating and managing development activities to a Development Committee and has approved its mandate. Development activities generate financial and human resources, nurture community life and relationships, and maintain and develop the physical plant and site. Development activities include site maintenance and development, admissions, marketing, public relations, community development, parent participation, alumni, and fundraising. The essential and ongoing work of the newly formed Development Committee is to define criteria and select and retain adequate membership on the Development Committee, design and establish a functioning and effective development department, and approve, oversee and ensure adequate management of specific development related projects and initiatives.

### Mandate

The School works with a threefold departmental model of management, with three distinct spheres of activity and with management bodies responsible for overseeing the work unique to each realm. The three departments are Pedagogical, Governance (Legal-Financial), and Community & Resource Development, each with its own administrator(s) and support staff. The Development Committee is a committee of the Board of Trustees and serves as the management body for Community & Resource Development. The Director of Development is the administrator for that realm.

### Tasks

- To work with the Director of Development to create a coherent vision of community and resource development at the School and to establish priorities and goals for that work

- To create sub-committee task groups that take up specific work to meet goals and priorities

- To support and oversee the work of the Director of Development

- To provide opportunities and the means for the parents, alumni, donors and friends of the school to participate in community and resource development at the school and to channel and direct their interest and support of the school

## Reporting and Accountability

- The Development Committee is accountable to the Board of Trustees.

- The Development Committee, through its Director of Development, will provide a written monthly report to the Board of Trustees and the PCG.

- The Director of Development will report at each meeting of the Development Committee.

- The Development Committee will set annual objectives for the Director of Development and will evaluate the Director of Development annually with respect to the achievement of those objectives.

## Meeting Times

- The Development Committee meets every second week.

## Membership

- All parents, alumni, donors and friends of the school are eligible as candidates for membership. Membership criteria will be determined by the Committee and approved by the Board.

- All members must be approved by the Board.

- At least one member of the Development Committee shall be a member of the Board of Trustees.

- The School Administrator and Pedagogical Administrator shall be ex officio members.

- Membership will be a minimum of 3 and a maximum of 7 members.

- The Director of Development shall serve as Chair of the Committee. Duties include preparing and sending out agendas and ensuring minutes are taken, distributed and filed appropriately.

# Appendix U

# Good Governance Committee Mandate

**Raison d'etre**

The School works with a threefold departmental model of management, with three distinct spheres of activity and with management bodies responsible for overseeing the work unique to each realm. The three departments are Pedagogical, Governance (Legal-Financial}, and Community & Resource Development, each with its own administrator(s) and support staff (collectively, "the Management Bodies") each with its own administrator/manager (collectively, "the Operations Management Committee [OMC]") and support staff. The OMC manages the day-to-day operations of the school, and the Management Bodies carry the vision for each department. The GGC is the committee that carries the broader governance vision for the entire school and monitors and responds to the overall health of the governance system.

**Tasks**

- To review, on an ongoing basis, the functioning of the different governing bodies, monitor the relationships/connections and communication between them

- To review and monitor that all mandates, constitutions, job descriptions, and evaluation and performance reviews for staff, operating, communication and reporting policies, procedures, and protocols are in place and utilized as required

- To create a calendar that outlines the regular review of all aspects of the governing structure of the school

- To make and implement recommendations for improvements, changes and developments regarding points 1–3

- To keep the various groups within the community informed about governance

- To keep a pulse on the status of short- and long-range planning

**Reporting and Accountability**

- The GGC is a committee of and is accountable to the Board of Trustees.

- The GGC will report through the Chair to the Board at every Board meeting.

- The GGC will provide annual reports to the Board of Trustees on its accomplishments.

## Meetings

- The GGC meets every second week and more often as necessary.

- GGC meetings shall be open at all times to all members of the Management Bodies.

## Membership

- The Chair of the GGC shall be a member of the Board.

- The Administrator shall serve as a member of the GGC.

- One member of the PCG shall serve on the GGC.

- Members/Chair of the GGC shall be selected based on their interest in and experience with good governance and management practices, particularly as related to Anthroposophical institutions.

- The number of members of the GGC shall consist of a minimum of 3 and maximum of 7 members.

- Members shall be members of the School Society.

## Membership Selection

- The Board of Trustees appoints the Chair of the GGC.

- The Pedagogical Carrying Group shall appoint one member (to help ensure that the philosophical approach and the work is consistent with and in service to the pedagogy).

- The Chair may nominate additional members to be approved by the BoT.

# Endnotes

1. See Appendix A: Five disciplines of a learning organization summarized from *The Fifth Discipline* by Peter Senge (1994).

2. This was given in a lecture at Sunbridge College, in Spring Valley, NY, in 1992, and retrieved from personal notes taken at the time.

3. Steiner wrote and lectured about the threefold spiritual nature of the human being and the three human systems throughout his entire body of work. The sources that provide the most in-depth exploration of the three human systems specifically are the volumes of lectures entitled *Riddles of the Soul: The Case for Anthroposophy* (2009) and *Fundamentals of Anthroposophical Medicine: Four Lectures Given to Doctors* (1986).

4. The list of people who have developed and contributed to the theoretical understanding of social organisms as threefold entities is long. The works of many of them are referenced throughout this book.

5. In the context of this book, the term "natural hierarchy" is used to define a structure that has independent yet interdependent systems where the authority shifts within the structure depending on the specific expertise and particular function needed in a given situation.

6. What Capra means by "power as influence of others" is that rather than investing all authority in a single leader simply by virtue of a position or title, the wisdom and initiative of others is acknowledged as essential to effective decision-making. All people engaged in the work are empowered and invited to influence the outcome of the work.

7. See Figure 1: Threefold Social Order – Threefold Human Being.

8. Original edition published in 1923; fourth edition published in 1977.

9. url:http://www/visembryo.com/baby/index.html

10. Here we see the three principles at work again, this time in the curriculum.

11. Adapted from a drawing from notes taken at a lecture by Gary Lamb at a conference on Waldorf education

12. In Chapter 4 the non-profit society is referenced as an essential constituent group in this organizational rhythmic system. In Canada, a non-profit organization is required to form a society with membership, which becomes the body that is legally and fiscally responsible for the operation of the organization.

13. See note 2 above.

14. In *The Social Mission of Waldorf Education*, Lamb points out that "administration should be an extension and reflection of what takes place and arises out of the classroom rather

than the life of the classroom being shaped by an administration subordinate to [the] political and economic forces [at a macro-society level]." (p.43)

15. Compiled from notes taken at a lecture by Gary Lamb at a conference on Waldorf education

16. See note 15: quote from Lamb's lecture

17. See note 15: quote from Lamb's lecture

18. Drawings by Silvia Formankova, all rights reserved

19. The list is extracted from *Vision in Action: Taking and Shaping Initiatives* (Schaefer et al., 1996, p.42).

20. *Systems Thinking. Personal Mastery, Mental Models, Shared Vision, Team Learning* (Senge, 1994)

21. Drawings by Silvia Formankova, all rights reserved

22. This is also true about the developing embryo and fetus. Note in Figure 3, the difference between the zygote as a collection of cells at the beginning of the first trimester compared to the embryo at the end of the first trimester is remarkable and clearly identifiable. The same kind of identifiable difference can be seen in Figure 4 in the embryo's development at the beginning of the second trimester compared to the fetus at the end of the second trimester. In Figure 5, on the other hand, the differences between the fetus at the beginning of the third trimester and the full-term baby at the end are much more subtle.

23. It is the transition into this phase of development that is often an eye-of-the-needle experience that leads to resistance in a school's leadership groups to give authority to individual leaders. Instead of clearly defining and empowering leadership, Waldorf schools can get stuck in the administrative phase, often trying to return to or recreate its pioneering phase experience where leadership is implicitly carried by and shared within the pioneer initiative group.

24. Drawings by Silvia Formankova, all rights reserved

25. This book is the expanded version of the Gaither Lectures in Systems Science given in May 1979 at the University of California, Berkeley.

26. See Appendix F: Nine Propositions in Search of the Threefold Social Order by Schaefer (n.d.), Proposition 9. ¶1.

27. In Canada, non-profit organizations are governed by laws that require that there be a Non-Profit Society, with a registered Constitution that defines its purpose, and with membership that establishes Bylaws that determine how it governs itself. The membership appoints the Board of Directors (Trustees), who then carries legal and fiscal responsibility for the organization. The establishment of a Non-Profit Society or an equivalent is integral to the forming of a threefold living structure and systems. This action research was conducted in a Canadian Waldorf school, so the need to form a Non-Profit Society as one of the central school bodies was already addressed.

28. A 'vision' is qualitative, descriptive and flexible; a 'model' is preconceived, prescriptive and inflexible.

29. It is important to note that Steiner is NOT referencing the Waldorf school's Board of Directors here but rather trying to indicate the importance of not allowing the political agenda of the government's education department to interfere, through its School Board, in the school's operations.

30. A 'vision' is qualitative, descriptive and flexible; a 'model' is preconceived, prescriptive and inflexible.

31. The threefold form, in the form of three overlapping spheres of influence, must be understood as a living dynamic as well as a static form consisting of these three spheres of activity. The dynamic nature of the threefold form is explored and described throughout this chapter and illustrated using the lemniscate figures.

32. See Appendix B: Summary of old mandate system in existence prior to implementing threefold living systems approach.

33. See Appendix C: Mandate for the Hub Coordinating Committee – Old Mandate System.

34. See Appendix D: Mandate System Review Committee Mandate.

35. See Appendix A: Summary of Five Disciplines of a Learning Organization.

36. See Appendix E: Initial Review Process Findings and Recommendations.

37. Excerpted from a job description for an administrative position called Administrative Team Leader at the Spring Garden Waldorf School.

38. Typically, the pedagogical business and activity of the Pedagogical Realm involve cool and calm, speculative or contemplative activity such as meditative study, dialogue, child study and other spiritual and cognitive activity associated with brain function, i.e., thinking, as opposed to the much more action- and will-focused activity of the organizational 'metabolic system,' the Community & Resource Development Realm, and the heat and energy producing human metabolic system. The organizational 'rhythmic system,' like the human rhythmic system, sits between these two poles and has a mediating, harmonizing quality and a rhythmic, regular, predictable gesture that is neither cognitive nor energizing in nature.

39. Development activities generate financial and human resources, nurture community life and relationships, and improve and develop the physical plant and site. Development activities include site improvements and development, admissions, outreach, advertising and marketing, public relations, community development, parent and volunteer participation, alumni relations, and fundraising and fund development.

40. See note 4.

41. See Appendix E: Initial Review Process Findings and Recommendations.

42. Adapted from Huseman et al., 1982, p.10

43. *dis* – pref. not: disjugate.

    1. Absence of; opposite of: disorientation.

    2. Undo; do the opposite of: dislocate.

    3. Deprive of; remove: dismember

    (*American Heritage Stedman's Medical Dictionary,* n.d.)

    *Ease* – suggests a sense of well-being (Dictionary.com, n.d.)

44. Note that "paralysis of spiritual, creative forces" and "stagnation and decay" are what Karutz claims happen when there is impingement of equality in spiritual life. In this case, the legal-financial realm and the Board of Trustees of the School and the impulse of equality were impinging on the pedagogical realm, the realm of the teachers and the impulse of freedom. The resulting stagnation was evidenced by the lack of stable enrollment and the very high attrition of student enrollment. (See pp.105–106 for the statistics on enrollment and retention at this point before the implementation of the new structure, compared with after.)

45. See Figure 14: Dynamic Human Systems

46. The Venn diagrams of a Waldorf school structure can be seen as expressing this *spatial* form.

47. The leminiscate diagrams of the dynamic relationship between systems in a Waldorf school can express this *temporal* form.

48. In my more than twenty years of working in the Waldorf movement and with Waldorf schools, it is my experience that schools often get stuck in these transitional phases and hence are too often in crisis management mode.

49. See Appendix E: Initial Review Process Findings and Recommendations

50. See Appendix G: Community Forum Envisioning Conference Agenda.

51. See Appendix H: Vision, Values, Mission

52. See Appendix I: Goals

53. See Appendices J and K: Samples that illustrate the evolution over time of a Pedagogical Carrying Group Constitution.

54. See Appendix L: Pedagogical Carrying Group Membership Selection Process.

55. The role of the Pedagogical Administrator became clear as the PCG took up its responsibilities and the position evolved. There was a period of time during which it was not clear what this position would carry. During this transitional time, the three committee chairs carried and shared the work of a Pedagogical Administrator, with the school Administrator filling in the gaps and supporting these teachers in carrying the administrative workload. These three interim Pedagogical Administrators tracked the work and tasks that they carried. The very long list was collated and a job description was created, the position posted and a full-time Pedagogical Administrator hired.

56. The Full Faculty Chair's responsibilities are exclusively in relationship to the Full Faculty Circle. The Pedagogical Administrator provides administrative support for the school's pedagogical business and activities. See Appendix M2, Hypothetical Example of a Full Faculty Meeting Agenda, which includes a list of qualities and skills important for a Full Faculty Chair to possess.

57. See Appendix O: Pedagogical Administrator Job Description.

58. This meeting structure changed recently, with the Full Faculty Circle meeting only once a month, subject to review and adjustment if the new meeting structure is determined to be inadequate.

59. For a sample Pedagogical Committee mandate, see Appendix P: Practical Needs Committee Mandate

60. This system of differentiating the Pedagogical Committees was introduced and guided by Anna Driehuyzen, Vancouver Waldorf School teacher and PCG member. I want to acknowledge her here because this idea was a significant point in the differentiation of the School's systems and one that was clearly driven by a sensibility and capacity for understanding how the principles and impulses at work in the human being translate to a social structure. It resulted in a kind of mini quantum leap in the school's development.

61. As the process of differentiation unfolds, you will see later on how likely confusion about this did happen.

62. See Appendix Q: The Cult of Personality by Walter Daroshin.

63. See Appendix F: *Nine Propositions in Search of the Threefold Social Order* by Christopher Schaefer.

64. See Appendix Q: The Cult of Personality by Walter Daroshin.

65. Ibid.

66. As emphasized in Chapter 1 and earlier in this chapter, Steiner's vision of self-administration was intended to ensure that the school was free of societal economic and political agendas. This was to be safeguarded by establishing a role for the teachers, informed by the curriculum and what happens in the classroom, in determining how the school operated. Transformational servant leadership guiding the formation and form of the administrative structure helps assure that the vision is realized.

67. The organizational 'rhythmic system' contains a sub-system that is specialized in working with the tracking and flow of finances, just as the human rhythmic system encompasses the respiratory system that works in service to the circulatory system by keeping the blood oxygenated and cleaned of the byproduct carbon dioxide.

68. This is again a reference to a natural hierarchy. See note 5.

69. See Appendix I: Goals.

70. The name (and configuration and function) of this group changed over time to Operations Management Group, and now is just called the Management Group.

71. See Appendix H Vision, Values, Mission and Appendix I – Goals.

72. See Appendix R1: Sample Tuition and Fees Agreement, and Appendix R2: Sample Terms & Payment Requirements.

73. See Appendix S: Parent Council Mandate – Example.

74. See Chapter 5 for financial, enrollment and retention statistics.

75. This is an essential point in the success of the arduous process of transforming the Vancouver Waldorf School's organizational structure. Without the participation and collaboration of key staff and community members, the transformation to this point would not have been possible, and while there were many who contributed in various ways, there are a few that I would like to acknowledge as having carried important parts of the process for extended periods of time or provided much needed support from the periphery: Walter Daroshin, Bruce Wilkinson, Sandra Ferens, Anna Driehuyzen, Gerard MacIntosh, Mary-Anne Taylor, Chris McLaughlin, Elaine Mackee, Kyle Morton, Susanne Schonthaler, Geraldine Kline, David Hesketh, Elizabeth Wilby, Keith Schaefer, Anina Formankova and Mary Paradis.

76. This position has been filled for over a decade (up until the writing of this book) by Bruce Wilkinson, who deserves a special mention here because without his dedication, expertise and truly brilliant systems design and management skills, much of the work of building a systems framework to support the transformation would not have been as effective or even possible.

77. The School's external accountant and auditor approval of our new accounting protocol and Chart of Accounts secured for the School the grant that provided the highest level of funding. This was a significant step in securing a source of dependable funding into the future as well as defining the School as more than an educational institution. It also explicitly defined an important aspect of the School's social mission as a community and not only a school.

78. By this point the role of Pedagogical Administrator had been divided and carried by the three Chairs of the pedagogical committees as a transitional step towards clearly defining the role of Pedagogical Administrator. The role was later filled by one person.

79. It was difficult to set an enrollment goal that would achieve this security because the government changes the PSOC ceiling and the grant amounts on a yearly basis, basing them on public school enrollment and spending. However, full enrollment with waiting lists was always the goal, with approximately 25 students in each of the classes in Grades One through Twelve. Early Childhood classes and expenses were excluded in the PSOC calculations.

80. See Appendix F: Nine Propositions in Search of the Threefold Social Order.

81. Ibid.

82. In the Cultural-Spiritual realm, goods and services cannot be purchased like they are in the Economic realm. Therefore tuition paid is actually gift money, not purchase money.

83. The need for and the importance of this highly specialized function, after regular and sometimes desperate requests from existing staff, were eventually acknowledged by the School's trustees, and a dedicated employee was hired, initially on a temporary trial basis, accountable to the Administrator and in service to the whole middle realm. In a mature organization, this Bursar position would exist in addition to a School Administrator position and would be filled by someone with accounting and/or financial expertise that would enable him or her to take up the specific work involved in working with the detailed financial policies, tuition and fees collection, accounting, reporting, budgeting, cash flow planning, and projections. This position would not replace the broader function of the School Administrator.

84. Ibid.

85. While managing the school's finances is the specialized role of the school Bursar, establishing equity via external input and mediation remains an essential function of the School Administrator or Director. In a mature, fully differentiated school, both of these positions will be present.

86. Although, theoretically, the Board of Trustees was not the group responsible for overseeing and managing the Community & Resource Development realm of the school, such a group had not yet been established, so the Board of Trustees was still acting as the Development Carrying Group. A Development Committee was established eventually, although it remained as a sub-management committee of the Board of Trustees until such time as it could function as an independent yet interconnected body, at which time it could be given authority in the Community & Resource Development realm. I understand this committee has since been dissolved. See Appendix T for the mandate that was approved for this committee.

87. See Appendix U: Good Governance Committee Mandate.

88. It is important to remember, as these realms of activity differentiate and specialize that all three realms of activity are born out of the primary impulse of the education. The impulses that lead to specialization are secondary to the pedagogical impulse. See the 'plumbing' diagrams Figures 19, 20 and 21.

89. Transformational leaders and servant leaders are visionaries and generate high levels of trust, serve as role models, show consideration for others, delegate responsibilities, empower followers, teach, communicate, listen, and influence followers. Transformational leadership "occurs when leaders broaden and elevate the interests of [staff and] employees, when they generate awareness and acceptance of the purposes and mission of the group, and when they stir ... [others] to look beyond their own self-interest for the good of the group." (Bass, 1990b, p.21) Bass (1990a) stipulates that this transcending beyond self-interest is for the "group, organization, or society." (p.53) In essence, transformational leadership is a process of building commitment to organizational objectives and then empowering followers to accomplish those objectives.

90. The three-legged stool would have the three administrators in the three respective realms working together to manage and coordinate school operations.

91. A four-legged stool would provide the most stable management group, with the three administrators in the three respective realms working together to manage and coordinate school operations, with the addition of a Bursar to carry the specialized financial work required in a larger, more complex and mature organization.

92. The new management group will now include the Pedagogical Administrator and the Director of Development, plus the new Business and Facilities Manager.

93. Independent Waldorf schools are self-administered and the governance structures often evolve organically or in an ad hoc manner. This was the case at the Vancouver Waldorf School until the restructuring began that was consciously based on the threefold vision/quantum physics paradigm.

94. It is important to note that the number of classes of students in the Early Childhood School, Grade School or High School did not change or increase between the period when the total teacher FTE was 24.5 and when it was increased to 35.4 (with the exception that the configuration of the Early Childhood classes changed, but this had very little impact on the total number of FTEs).

95. See Figure 32: Dynamic of the Pedagogical Realm.

# References

American Heritage® Stedman's Medical Dictionary. Retrieved July 11, 2010, from Dictionary. com website: http://dictionary.reference.com/browse/dis-.

Bass, B.M. (1990a). *Bass and Stogdill's Handbook of Leadership: Theory, Research, & Managerial Applications.* New York: The Free Press.

_____. (1990b). From transactional to transformational leadership: Learning to share the vision. *Organizational Dynamics*, 18 (Winter): 19–31.

Broholm, R. (1990). *The Power and Purpose of Vision: A Study of the Role of Vision in Exemplary Organizations.* Indianapolis: Robert Greenleaf Center.

Brüll, D. (1997). *The Waldorf School and Threefold Structure: The Embarrassing Mandate.* Fair Oaks, CA: Association of Waldorf Schools of North America.

Budd, C. (2003). *The Metamorphosis of Capitalism: Realising Associative Economics.* Canterbury, England: New Economy Publications.

Capra, F. (1996). *The Web of Life.* New York: Anchor Books.

Chalofsky, N. (2005). Reshaping the way we view the world. T+D, 59(11), 54–57. Retrieved from Academic Search Complete database.

Cohen, L. (2006). It's not about management. *Phi Delta Kappan*, 87(6), 45–61. Retrieved from Education Full Text database.

De Geus, A. (1997). *The Living Company.* Boston: Harvard Business School Press.

Dictionary.com Unabridged. Retrieved July 11, 2010, from Dictionary.com website: http://dictionary.reference.com/browse/ease

Donahoe, T. (1993). Finding the way: Structure, time, and culture in school improvement. *Phi Delta Kappan*, 75(4), 298. Retrieved from Academic Search Complete database.

Finser, T. (2007). *Organizational Integrity.* Great Barrington, MA: SteinerBooks.

Finser, S. (2007). *Money Can Heal: Evolving Our Consciousness: The Story of RSF and Its Innovations in Social Finance.* Great Barrington, MA: SteinerBooks.

Gasser, R. (1975). *Atlas of Human Embryos.* New York: HarperCollins.

Greenspan, R. (2007). *An Introduction to Nervous Systems.* Coldspring Harbor, NY: Coldspring Harbor Laboratory Press.

Husemann, F., edited and revised by O. Wolff (1982). *The Anthroposophical Approach to Medicine, Vol. 1.* Hudson, NY: Anthroposophical Press.

Jantsch, E. 1992. *The Self-organizing Universe: Scientific and Human Implications of the Emerging Paradigm of Evolution.* Oxford: Pergamon Press.

Karutz M. (2001). *Forming School Communities*. Fair Oaks, CA: Association of Waldorf Schools of North America.

König, K. (n.d.). Recovered from Karl König Archive at aberdeen@karl-koenig-archive.net.

Lamb G. (2004). *The Social Mission of Waldorf Education*. Fair Oaks, CA: Association of Waldorf Schools of North America.

Levine, D. (1995). The organism metaphor in sociology. *Social Research*, 62(2), 239. Retrieved August 1, 2010, from ABI/INFORM Global. (Document ID: 6840402).

Lewin, R. (1992). *Complexity: Life at the Edge of Chaos*. New York: MacMillan.

Ley, W.C. (1884). Mr. Ruskin's bogies. *Nature: A Weekly Illustrated Journal of Science*, February 14, 1884, p.353. Retrieved August 17, 2010, from http://books.google.ca/books?id=siwVAAAAYAAJ&pg=PA353#v=onepage&q&f=false.

Lievegoed, B. (1991). *Developing Communities*. Stroud, UK: Hawthorne Press.

Molt, E. (1991). *Emil Molt and the Beginnings of the Waldorf School Movement*. Edinburgh: Floris Books.

The National Institute of Child & Human Development and The Carnegie Collection of Human Development (2006). The visible embryo. http://www.visembryo.com/baby.

Parker, S. (2007). *The Human Body Book*. Hudson, NY: DK Publishing.

Patterson, K., R. Russell and G. Stone (2003). Servant Leadership Research Roundtable. Transformational versus servant leadership: A difference in leader focus. Virginia Beach, VA: School of Leadership Studies, Regent University.

Preparata, G. (2006). Perishable money in a threefold commonwealth: Rudolf Steiner and the social economics of an anarchist utopia. *Review of Radical Political Economics*, 38(4), 619–648. doi:10.1177/0486613406293226.

Schaefer, C. and T. Voors (1996). *Vision in Action: Taking and Shaping Initiatives*. Hudson, NY: Lindisfarne Press.

Scharmer, C.O. (2007). Executive summary: Theory U: leading from the future as it emerges (17 pages). Retrieved August 14, 2010 from http://www.presencing.com/docs/publications/execsums/Theory_U_Exec_Summary.pdf.

Schein, E. (2009). Helping: An urgent new role for leaders. *Ivey Business Journal*, 73(5), 5. Retrieved from Regional Business News database.

Senge, P. (1994). *The Fifth Discipline: The Art and Practice of the Learning Organization*. New York: Doubleday.

Senge, P., C.O. Scharmer, J. Jaworski and B.S. Flowers (2004). *Presence: An Exploration of Profound Change in People, Organizations, and Society*. New York: Doubleday.

Spence, M. (1999). *Freeing the Human Spirit: The Threefold Social Order, Money, and the Waldorf School*. Fair Oaks, CA: The Association of Waldorf Schools of North America.

Steiner, R. (1919). Basic issues of the social question. Retrieved from http://wn.rsarchive.org/Books/GA023/English/SCR2001/GA023_c02.html.

_____ (1922). Spiritual ground of education, lecture 7: The organisation of the Waldorf school. Retrieved from http://wn.rsarchive.org/GA/GA0305/19220823p01.html.

_____ (1923). *The Threefold Commonwealth*. London: Anthroposophical Publishing.

_____ (1971). Theosophy. Retrieved from http://wn.rsarchive.org/Books/GA009/English/GA009_index.html.

_____ (1977). *Towards Social Renewal*. London: Rudolf Steiner Press.

_____ (1985). *Renewal of theSocial Organism*. Spring Valley, NY: Anthroposophic Press. Retrieved from http://wn.rsarchive.org/Books/GA024/English/AP1985/GA024_c14.html.

_____ (1986). Fundamentals of anthroposophical medicine: Four lectures given to doctors. Stuttgart, October 26, 27, 28, 1922. GA 314 http://wn.rsarchive.org/Lectures/FundAnthro/FunAnt_index.html.

_____ (1995). *The Spirit of the Waldorf School*. Hudson, NY: Anthroposophic Press.

_____ (1998). *Faculty Meetings with Rudolf Steiner*. Hudson, NY: Anthroposophic Press.

_____ (1996). *The Foundations of Human Experience*. Hudson, NY: Anthroposophic Press.

_____ (2009). *Riddles of the Soul: The Case for Anthroposophy*. Great Barrington, MA: SteinerBooks.

Wheatley, M. (2006). *Leadership and the NewScience*. San Francisco: Berrett KoehlerPublishers.